Palgrave Studies in Risk, Crime and Society

Series Editors
Kieran McCartan
Department of Criminology
University of the West of England
Bristol, UK

Beth Weaver
School of Social Work and Social Policy
University of Strathclyde
Glasgow, Lanarkshire, UK

Risk is a major contemporary issue which has widespread implications for theory, policy, governance, public protection, professional practice and societal understandings of crime and criminal justice. The potential harm associated with risk can lead to uncertainty, fear and conflict as well as disproportionate, ineffective and ill-judged state responses to perceived risk and risky groups. Risk, Crime and Society is a series featuring monographs and edited collections which examine the notion of risk, the risky behaviour of individuals and groups, as well as state responses to risk and its consequences in contemporary society. The series will include critical examinations of the notion of risk and the problematic nature of state responses to perceived risk. While Risk, Crime and Society will consider the problems associated with 'mainstream' risky groups including sex offenders, terrorists and white collar criminals, it welcomes scholarly analysis which broadens our understanding of how risk is defined, interpreted and managed. Risk, Crime and Society examines risk in contemporary society through the multi-disciplinary perspectives of law, criminology and socio-legal studies and will feature work that is theoretical as well as empirical in nature.

More information about this series at
http://www.palgrave.com/gp/series/14593

Shamila Ahmed

The 'War on Terror', State Crime & Radicalization

A Constitutive Theory of Radicalization

palgrave
macmillan

Shamila Ahmed
Department of Criminology
University of Westminster
London, UK

Palgrave Studies in Risk, Crime and Society
ISBN 978-3-030-40137-5 ISBN 978-3-030-40138-2 (eBook)
https://doi.org/10.1007/978-3-030-40138-2

Cover credit: Allkindza

This Palgrave Macmillan imprint is published by the registered company Springer Nature Switzerland AG.
The registered company address is: Gewerbestrasse 11, 6330 Cham, Switzerland

Preface

This book has evolved over the time it has taken to complete it. It started with Palgrave Macmillan inviting me to cover the topic of terrorism, as part of their series on 'Risk and Criminology'. Since the events of September 11th, many social science disciplines have contributed to providing understandings of how risk operates within the 'war on terror'. This has led to the 'war on terror' becoming one of the most vivid and evident examples of our risk saturated world. As I pondered on how to contribute to this area, I couldn't help but think about how risk operates through everyday taken for granted state produced mechanisms and processes. Was it time to start exploring perhaps the biggest instigator of risk in the 'war on terror' states? Would we really stand a chance of reducing terrorism, if the state practices which contribute to radicalization continue? And there it was, the topic of state practices and how they facilitate radicalization—arguably, the biggest area of risk within the 'war on terror'. This standpoint and conceptualization of risk within the 'war on terror' laid bare the reality of just how destructive the 'war on terror' had become.

As this book developed, I wanted it to be one of empowerment, where the narratives I revealed are grounded and legitimized. This aim necessitated the need for these narratives to be deconstructed, their logic to be explained and for me to expose the feelings, perceptions, thoughts and emotions that formed these narratives. It also involved explaining how lived experience, subjectivity and emotions relate to social processes, institutions and those polices which are clearly visible and those that remain invisible. Within this fluidity, where we are impacted by, and impact our social world, values had to form an integral part of understanding these processes. I didn't want these narratives and voices to be misunderstood due to my own failings in representing these voices. Therefore, the processes that assist us in developing our beliefs, values, convictions, autonomy and security in the world, and the reality of having these shattered, had to be exposed. How much could anyone really understand radicalization if they could not comprehend how the social world creates conflict, turmoil, complete helplessness and so on and the impact of these on radicalization? In an attempt to provide these understandings, this book explores what happens when our safety and security are taken away? When the values we believe in and that make us belong to humanity are eroded, and left are feelings of betrayal and worst still, seeing and knowing that these values remain for others?

However, was it enough to say that individuals felt their human right had been broken in the 'war on terror' and therefore felt vulnerable? Or did I need to say, individuals' understandings of human rights are informed by events such as the Holocaust, they understand human rights as their birth rights, and they've been socialized to believe that these form the very rights that bind humanity. I had to clearly articulate how this sense of security, that we will be treated as humans and we are equal was informed by, amongst other things, international human rights law, international humanitarian law, conventions and treaties. Some of these understandings of the 'war on terror' were based on my research with British Muslims and yet, somehow, I had unintentionally removed the humanity from these voices in previous writings.[1]

[1] See Ahmed, S. (2014). Reflections on Conducting Research on the 'War on Terror': Religious Identity, Subjectivity and Emotions. *International Journal of Social Research Methodology*. https://doi.org/10.1080/13645579.2014.976488.

Ahmed, S. (2015). The 'Emotionalization of the War on Terror': Counter Terrorism, Fear, Risk, Insecurity and Helplessness. *An International Journal of Criminology and Criminal Justice, 15*(5), 545–560.

Ahmed, S. (2016). Citizenship, Belonging and Attachment in the 'War on Terror'. *An International Journal of Critical Criminology, 24*(1), 111–125.

The approach I consciously adopted for this book also meant facing other difficult truths. Such an approach meant that as I wrote this book, I easily saw how the 'war on terror', and its inherent state practices divided humanity into two. The 'war on terror' uses one set of individuals, and their right to security, freedom, liberty and life to dehumanize another set of individuals, with identity, nationality and constructed worth constituting the allocation of rights. The thoughts and questions presented in this book are meant to provoke debate and further scrutiny of radicalization, and they are not meant to make for a comfortable read but rather, a realistic read and one where this book leads to as many questions as it attempts to answer. For example, why is it that we are able to recognize the destructive impact of secondary victimization where criminal justice agencies are concerned and, yet, we haven't applied this to the 'war on terror'? After all, those who perceive themselves as possibly being subjected to a reduction of legal rights in the 'war on terror' have also had their trust broken, and they too have lived experiences where institutions impact their experiences of victimization. Further, it could be argued that these institutions don't merely reproduce the processes of disempowerment that impact trust and constitute secondary victimization, but they instigate and create this very process. These institutions are meant to protect us, they exist to rebalance the scales of justice, to maintain social and universal norms and ideals and, yet, the 'war on terror' has undermined this. All these reconfigurations of values, norms and security in the 'war on terror' have had vast implications for our understandings, trust and security in the world. And it was within this context that individuals are suffering from the pain and destruction of realizing that these beliefs are being destroyed and tarnished. I found myself thinking, when the entities that are meant to protect us no longer do and can harm us through treating us differently, what is left to protect us and give us security? Is it fair and just that we are socialized and ask individuals to believe in universal values and then expect them to feel nothing when these values are removed? And I should add that this removal is based on the need to

Ahmed, S. (2019). British Muslims Perceptions of Social Cohesion: From Multiculturalism to Community Cohesion and the 'War on Terror'. *Crime, Law & Social Change, 71*, 581–595.

Ahmed, S. (2019). A Cosmopolitan Response to the 'War on Terror'. *Journal of Theoretical and Philosophical Criminology, 11*, 64–78.

preserve these very values for groups that possess a different identity because, after all, the 'war on terror' frequently stresses the need for measures which preserve 'our values', 'our security' and 'our freedom' and does it really seek to preserve these for all humanity? The questions this book asks are therefore not meant to be comfortable; they are simply the questions that reality forces us to ask.

Aims of This Book

In proposing my 'Constitutive Theory of Radicalization', I have attempted to put the humanity back into my writings on the 'war on terror' and radicalization. An appreciation of the interactions and fluidity of the levels reflects our ability to do what comes naturally and that is to believe, perceive, understand and feel. Each level has a semi-autonomous existence but is also shaped by and impacted by every other level. I do not assume that the theoretical model I have created is perfect, but it has been informed by my previous research with British Muslims and the empirical research discussed in Chap. 2. Collectively this research has highlighted the constitutive nature of the radicalization process and one that interacts with and impacts emotions. In presenting the constitutive theory of radicalization, this book explores the relationships portrayed in the model and details their manifestations, existence and maintenance. This book is therefore about giving narratives agency through demonstrating how the various levels impact emotions. This book concludes through offering ways to deal with this agency and argues that, through working with emotions and agency, there is the potential to divert individuals away from radicalization. This translates into an approach which exists between cognitive radicalization and violent radicalization.

The first aim of this book is to explore how state practices and state crimes have contributed to the existence of Islamist terrorist groups, and more generally terrorism within the 'war on terror'. The second aim of this book is to explore state practices within the 'war on terror' through utilizing literature on state crime to expose the interconnections between state practices, state crime and radicalization. It is hoped that exposure of this nexus will increase awareness of the harms perpetuated by states within the 'war on terror' and how these facilitate radicalization and therefore terrorism. The third aim of this book is to demonstrate how counter-terrorism strategies, which are often based on inflated and manipulated claims of self-defence against the terrorist threat, are allowing states to establish steps towards nationalism, which could in fact lead to nationalism posing a greater threat to human rights than terrorism.

This book follows a chronological format whereby accounts of terrorist attacks and state responses to these attacks are provided. This orthodox discussion is followed by a critical exploration of how states have contributed to the existence of the terrorist organization that carried out the attacks and the contextual factors, including state practices and state crimes which facilitated the attack. Through engaging with literature on state crime and demonstrating the fluidity between state crime, terrorism and radicalization in the 'war on terror', this book provides a different discourse on the 'war on terror', and one which considers the often invisible, and yet perhaps most harmful actions which maintain, facilitate and perpetuate harm within the 'war on terror'.

The first chapter introduces this book and the key terms of state crime and terrorism. It also highlights the problematic construction of the 'war on terror' and how this construction has facilitated a state centric 'war on terror' discourse. This chapter introduces the constitutive theory of radicalization and, in representing this theory, it provides models which demonstrate the interactions between the super macro-universal level, the macro-national level, the meso-societal level, the micro-individual-emotional level and violent radicalization.

Chapter 2 explores the micro-individual-emotional level and therefore the factors which are associated with radicalization and form a theory of radicalization. The space between cognitive radicalization and violent radicalization is explored. It is argued that cognitive radicalization is safe, and the over-criminalization of this perspective is likely to push cognitive radicalization into violent radicalization, and therefore a softer approach is required to counter terrorism. Having explored these variables that form the micro-individual-emotional level, subsequent chapters then assess how state practices and state crimes impact the micro-individual-emotional level, thereby assessing how state crimes have facilitated radicalization and terrorism in the 'war on terror'.

Chapter 3 discusses the terrorist attacks of 9/11, the international and national responses to the attacks and the emergence of the 'war on terror'. The second half of the chapter documents the existence of state crimes in the 'war on terror', through exploring state practices and state crimes in relation to counter-terrorism legislation, Guantánamo Bay and Abu Gharib prisons, and the invasions of Afghanistan and Iraq. It demonstrates how these state practices and state crimes have impacted the micro-individual-emotional level and therefore the variables associated with radicalization.

Chapter 4 explores the relationship between al-Qaeda and the United Kingdom, the United States and Saudi Arabia. It exposes the influence of this relationship on al-Qaeda's perceptions of foreign policy, global injustices and religious interpretation, and how these collectively constituted factors which influenced the emergence of al-Qaeda and the Taliban. This chapter also considers the detrimental impact of state practices and state crimes in the creation of political instability, sectarian violence and humanitarian suffering in Afghanistan, conditions which facilitated the emergence of al-Qaeda.

Chapter 5 contrasts the terrorist attacks in Paris in 2015 with the humanitarian refugee crisis. Following the terrorist attacks in Paris, a state of emergency was declared by the French government. On the international level, there was the further securitization of Europe at the expense of civil liberties and due process. The second half of the chapter documents the power of the securitization discourse to induce fear and promote the dehumanization of those most in need. It demonstrates how the fear of terrorism became synonymous with the fear of refugees, leading countries to abandon their duty towards other human beings. As with the previous chapters, this chapter also explores state practices and state crimes in relation to political instability and terrorism, making evident how wars in Afghanistan, Iraq and Syria led to not only the decay of human life (creating a climate where mass death became collateral damage) but also a reality where individuals had the choice of either joining a terrorist group or potentially dying trying to migrate to a place of safety.

Chapter 6 examines the emergence of ISIS through exploring how state practices and state crimes facilitated the creation of territories that ISIS could exploit to create a terrorist state. It also explores ISIS through considering their interpretation of Islam, their motivation to gain territory to establish a caliphate, and their utilization of 'soft targets', foreign policy and religion to justify terrorism. This chapter demonstrates the similarities between the ideologies used by ISIS to radicalize individuals and the ideologies used by the United Kingdom, United States and Saudi Arabia in radicalizing individuals to fight communism in Afghanistan. This chapter also discusses the roles of the United States, United Kingdom and Saudi Arabia in encouraging and promoting Wahhabism, the similarities between the Sharia law practised by Saudi Arabia and ISIS and how the United States and United Kingdom are complicit in the interstate and intra-state crimes committed by Saudi Arabia.

Chapter 7 examines the future of the 'war on terror'. It makes the case for countering radicalization through a holistic approach, one which includes how state practices and state crime impact the micro-individual-emotional level. This chapter also examines the theoretical, social and political implications of the empirical analysis employed in this book. This chapter brings together all elements of this book to question what they mean for the study of the 'war on terror' and for the dominant 'war on terror' discourses that are prevalent in academic, social and political contexts. This book concludes by encouraging an analysis whereby state crimes are acknowledged, investigated and explored as variables which contribute to radicalization and the existence of Islamist terrorism.

In offering an analysis which combines literature on state crime, terrorism, radicalization and the 'war on terror', this book fills an important gap in knowledge and the way in which the 'war on terror' and, more generally, state crime and terrorism are constructed, investigated and critiqued. It is argued that until state crime is fully explored within the 'war on terror', the 'war on terror' will continue to be partially examined, falsely represented and socially constructed to conceal the actions that maintain terrorism within 'war on terror'.

London, UK Shamila Ahmed

Acknowledgements

This book has journeyed with me for the past three years of my life. During this time, it has been reworked and almost entirely rewritten. This process has involved my perspective and outlook changing. Growing up in the 1990s, I can say that the world I see and experience today is very different to the one I grew up in. It is more polarized, dangerous, divisive, cruel and harsh, words that I am not using through rose-tinted glasses. But today, there is more inequality, forms of racism, oppressive state structures and opposing narratives. Within this contemporary world, I asked myself what my contribution to understanding this world should be? And the answer was simple, to change harmful mechanisms, we must first acknowledge their existence. Of course, that is not enough, but it is a start and we have to start somewhere, right? For me that somewhere was about thinking deeply of the role of academia—was it to produce accounts of what we think is happening to groups of people or to produce accounts based on the voices and narratives of those people? In the last few years, I have frequently found myself in policy and academic environments where self-conferred status, be it a title or societal nepotism, has been used to speak for others. This has been uncomfortable to watch because the reality that unfolds isn't based on the voices that are claimed to be represented: there hasn't even been a dialogue there, but it is based on producing abstract narratives. In this context, these narratives have formed another layer of oppression.

Within my changing experiences of the global world and the local world, I felt unease. Had acts of terrorism and the 'war on terror' not contributed to enough damage that we should try and end these dangerous cycles of violence? And how could we when there is such an unwillingness to understand the causes of terrorism from those that commit these acts? Instead of trying to understand and then prevent, the overwhelming focus is on preserving self-conferred legitimacy. This book is about trying to understand so that we can prevent cycles of violence, harm and suffering. The process of asking hard questions, facing obstructive realities and writing some of the thoughts put forward in this book has been difficult at times, and immensely rewarding at other times.

I would like to thank Stuart Henry and Pippa Catterall for their comments on earlier versions of this book and Denisa Fabokova, David Manlow and Elya Steinberg for their support over the past few years. I would also like to thank Palgrave Macmillan for allowing me the autonomy and freedom to write my response to 'Risk and Terrorism'. I would also like to thank Tasleem Ahmed and Ashfaq Ahmed, for what you've taught me, and Imran Ahmed, Ameer Ahmed and Aneeka Ahmed—siblings are a blessing, I can explore the world and always know that I have you as my base. I also want to thank Lilly and Ayyan. Ayyan—it has been amazing spending time with you, seeing you grow, and making so many happy memories together. I want to dedicate this book to Cookie—I still miss you, your soft temperament and loving nature.

I want to thank Monika Wyszomirska. This book has only been possible because of your support, love and care. With you by my side, I always feel that anything is possible. Living and experiencing life with you is an amazing adventure—I am blessed. Thank you for everything Sweets.

I also wanted to thank all those people, including Dr Stephen Lawrence, Stephanie Austen and Caroline Mungeam who stopped and helped me when I was hit by a car just a few days before submitting this book. Thank you from the bottom of my heart for making one of the worst experiences of my life bearable and for displaying the very humanity and selflessness this book epitomizes.

Contents

1

State Crime, 'Terrorism' and Radicalization

In the first two decades of the twenty-first century, the 'war on terror', a phrase coined in September 2001 by then US President George W. Bush, has included the invasions of Afghanistan, Iraq and Syria, the rise of al-Qaeda (AQ) and the Islamic state in Iraq and Syria (ISIS), and the greatest humanitarian refugee crisis in modern history. In terms of the UK legal system, the 'war on terror' has led to the erosion of civil liberties and human rights. Consequently, the 'rule of law' and due process, principles which formed the basis of the modern liberal state have been reassigned to historic abstract ideals (Maier-Katkin, Mears, & Bernard, 2009; McCulloch & Pickering, 2009; Zedner, 2007). Although centuries have passed since Enlightenment thinkers, such as Cesare Beccaria and Jeremy Bentham, sought to uncover, minimize and banish state discourses and state practices which caused harm in pursuit of a more just, fair and equal society (Walklate, 2003), the 'war on terror' has necessitated the need to expose and critique harmful state practices to limit the exercise of state power and state harm to individuals. In conjunction with the 'war on terror', several political developments including the refugee crisis, US President Trump's travel ban, the growth of the far right in Europe—most notably in Germany, Austria, Hungry, Poland and Italy—and

S. Ahmed, *The 'War on Terror', State Crime & Radicalization*, Palgrave Studies in Risk, Crime and Society, https://doi.org/10.1007/978-3-030-40138-2_1

'Brexit' have demonstrated the return of populist nationalism across the international sphere. The fear of nationalism has been publicly voiced with French President Emmanuel Macron using the 100th anniversary of the First World War armistice to warn of the dangers of nationalism to international harmony (Macron, 2018 cited Chrisafis, 2018). Within this changing socio-political context, the 'war on terror' discourse has become one of the most predominant mechanisms though which states legitimize the introduction of social control mechanisms which facilitate the marginalization and criminalization of those labelled as a threat to nationalism and the nation-state.

Aims of the Book

This book explores how state practices and state crimes have facilitated Islamist terrorism and Islamist terrorist groups, and how the 'war on terror' has contributed to, amongst other harms, the erosion of civil liberties, wars, mass refugees and nationalism. The book seeks to expose and critique harmful state practices and, where possible, ground these practices according to international law, domestic law, conventions and protocols, thereby making it possible to demonstrate how state crimes have facilitated terrorism in the 'war on terror'. When exploring state practices, the book includes law, power, ideology, foreign policy, political crime, human rights issues, and legitimate and illegitimate military, diplomatic and domestic initiatives (Barak, 1991; Friedrichs, 1998) and discourses and policies as forms of state practice. According to Ross (2000: 1), state crime includes

> cover-ups, corruption, disinformation, unaccountability, violations of a domestic and/or international law, as well as those practices, although they fall short of being officially declared illegal, are perceived by the majority of the population as illegal or socially injurious.

As the definition by Ross (2000) demonstrates, populations' perceptions are also important and given the fundamental importance of perceptions in the radicalization process (see Chap. 2), citizens' perceptions are included in the scope of what this book defines as state practices. Through employing a perspective which includes individuals' perceptions, the book takes 'the security of the individual human being—their life, livelihood, dignity, and rights—rather than that of the state as its central point of reference' (Moeckli, 2008: 7). The book therefore adopts a non-state centric perspective which seeks to extend the parameters of state scrutiny within the 'war on terror'.

By conceptualizing state practices as state crime, the book deviates from orthodox perspectives which fail to label state practices as state crime and acknowledge the violation(s) of international law, domestic law, conventions and protocols. The book also diverges from established literature on the 'war on terror' which has predominantly focused on how states have produced discourses and responded to acts of terrorism within the 'war on terror' (Jackson, 2005, 2007, 2008a), the construction of and amplification of global risk in the 'war on terror' (Beck, 2002; Bosworth, Bowling, & Lee, 2008; Spence, 2005; Urry, 2002), counter-terrorism legislation and policing (De Goede, 2008; Grabosky, 2008; Klausen, 2009), human rights and civil liberties (Gearty, 2005; Stohl, 2008a; Tadros, 2007), and the impact of the 'war on terror' on Muslim communities (Ahmed, 2015, 2016; Mythen, Walklate, & Khan, 2009). This literature has been important in revealing the impact of acts of terrorism on state practices, including state policies and legislation and the impact of such policies and legislation on communities. However, this literature has led to the 'war on terror' being conceptualized according to the following linear continuum:

> terrorist attack—state response—impact of state response on state legislation and radicalization

This construction has omitted the role of state practices and state crimes in facilitating radicalization and Islamist terrorist groups because, as Cronin (2006) states, this event-driven focus has failed to adequately explore the emergence of terrorist groups and the mechanisms, motivations, and processes which lead to terrorist attacks.

The first aim of this book is to explore how state practices and state crimes have contributed to the existence of Islamist terrorist groups and radicalization, and therefore terrorism within the 'war on terror'. There is a substantial body of work that can be collectively labelled as forming a 'theory of radicalization' that has focused on the causes of Islamist terrorism. As Chap. 2 demonstrates, this work has explored the social and temporal processes, the education and class background, the influence of religious texts and the psychological processes which influence the radicalization process (Bushman, Ridge, Das, Key, & Busath, 2007; Horgan, 2005; Sageman, 2004; Silke, 2008). There is also a growing volume of work that has explored the rise of Islamist terrorist groups, most notably AQ and ISIS (Braithwaite & Ali, 2013; Cockburn, 2015; Cronin, 2006; Weiss & Hassan, 2015). This book contributes to these areas of literature through exploring how state practices and state crimes intersect with radicalization and should therefore be included as part of a 'theory of radicalization'. Through exploring this fluidity, the book offers an account of how state practices and state crimes are just as important as, if not more important than, other variables in contributing to radicalization and, more specifically, the rise of terrorist organizations, like AQ and ISIS. In examining the intersectionality between Islamist ideologies, state crimes and radicalization, the book asks important questions, such as, how do state practices interact with the radicalization process? Can state crime facilitate the radicalization process? How do factors which have been defined as constituting the state facilitation of terrorism impact established factors which induce vulnerability to radicalization? And, are there state practices and state crimes which facilitate terrorism that have not previously been considered as part of a theory of radicalization? These are questions of great significance because as Habermas (2002) contends, states are actors in the radicalization process and how they respond to threats and the policies they adopt can—for better or worse—make a real difference. In considering the role of state practices and state crimes in creating and maintaining terrorism, the book proposes the following, more accurate, 'war on terror' continuum:

> state practice/+ theory of radicalization—terrorist groups/terrorism—state response/state crime/state crime state practices

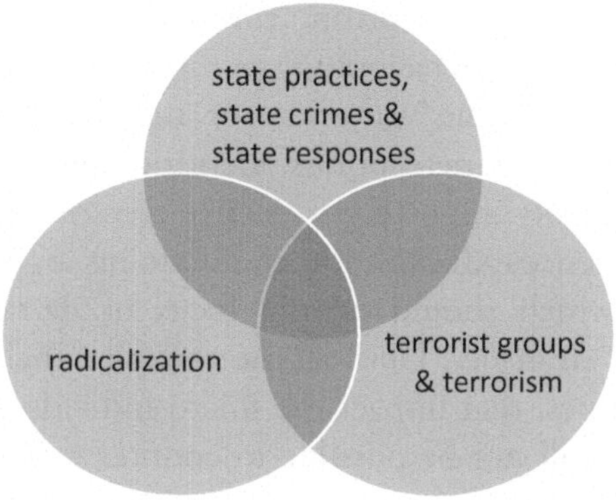

This book proposes a different understanding of the 'war on terror', one whereby the reader is encouraged to explore how state practices violate international human rights law (IHRL) and international humanitarian law (IHL), and the impact of this on radicalization. Therefore, the book includes, as a central focal point, conditions conducive to the spread of terrorism and how state practices and state crimes intersect with these conditions. When discussing conditions pertaining to the growth of terrorism, the following conditions, as identified in the 2006 United Nations (UN) Global Counter-Terrorism strategy, have been included as being conducive to the spread of terrorism:

- prolonged unresolved conflicts,
- dehumanization of victims of terrorism in all its forms and manifestations,
- lack of rule of law and violations of human rights,
- ethnic, national and religious discrimination,
- political exclusion,
- socio-economic marginalization, and
- lack of good governance (UN, 2018).

Although forms of analysis which consider the structural causes of non-terrorism forms of crimes are common, the role of states and structures which create mass suffering, violate human rights and so on is still omitted in explanations of terrorism. Through omitting the role of state practices and state crimes in facilitating terrorism, the orthodox state centric conceptualization of the 'war on terror' neglects the impact of states on individuals' emotions, perceptions, identities, morals and so on. This restrictive and arguably imposed perspective creates a false reality of the factors which influence radicalization and in doing so, it neglects some of the key factors which should be the focus of de-radicalization and counter-terrorism strategies. Until all the variables, including state practices and state crimes, that impact the micro-individual-emotional level are recognized, it will not be possible to counter radicalization because strategies will only address some of the causes of radicalization. Further, the 'war on terror' will continue to be partially examined, represented and understood.

The second aim of the book is to utilize literature on state crime to ground state practices within the 'war on terror'. Although some literature has demonstrated state violations of national laws and international laws in the 'war on terror', most notably the US invasion of Iraq and the treatment of detainees at Guantánamo Bay and Abu Ghraib prison (Hamm, 2007; Kauzlarich, 2007; Kramer & Michalowski, 2005; Kramer, Michalowski, & Rothe, 2005; Smeulers & Niekerk, 2008; Welch, 2008), there is a general absence of literature pertaining to how state actions constitute state crime within the 'war on terror'. This omission is surprising given that state crime literature is perhaps the most developed non-state centric literature within critical criminology. The under-utilization of state crime literature and grounding of state practices according to IHRL and IHL perpetuate the existence of the linear 'war on terror' continuum 'terrorism—state responses' and this conceals state crimes within the 'war on terror'. In doing so, this continuum also maintains terrorism as the core area of focus and threat within the 'war on terror', even though, as Hudson and Walters (2009) state, the 'war on terror' has been a political and humanitarian failure. In offering an analysis of how states facilitate terrorism, the book does not suggest that the state practices and state crimes discussed in the book are the sole causes of terrorism. Rather, it aims to explore another important, but often hidden variable that facilitates the existence of terrorism. It is hoped that such exposure will increase awareness of the harms perpetuated by states within the 'war on terror', and that the labelling of such practices as state crimes ensures that these actions carry the stigma that the label 'crime' implies.

The third aim of the book is to demonstrate how counter-terrorism strategies, which are often based on inflated and manipulated claims of self-defence against the terrorist threat, are allowing states to establish steps towards nationalism, which could in fact lead to nationalism posing a greater threat to human rights than terrorism. Through states introducing controversial counter-terrorism legislation, which deviates from national and international human rights laws, the exploitation of the terrorist threat and subsequent 'war on terror' is contributing to the increasing acceptability of state violations of human rights laws. In such a dangerous climate, individuals and whole populations are increasingly witnessing and experiencing situations where they are denied basic human rights and therefore face a greater risk of harm from nation-states than from terrorist groups.

Definitions of State Crime

Criminology has predominantly focused on crimes committed by the least powerful in society. In contrast, crimes against humanity and crimes such as genocide, which are often perpetrated by the most powerful in society, have been subject to the least amount of criminological attention and scrutiny (Hagan & Rymond-Richmond, 2009; McGurrin, Jarrell, Jahn, & Cochrane, 2013; Michalowski, 2009). This division of interest is shocking because one could assume that the actions that cause the most suffering would receive the most attention, especially given that the core aim of critical criminology is the pursuit of social justice. Although reducing human suffering to numerical figures silences narratives, and the suffering and histories such narratives hold, and is therefore, arguably, a form of dehumanization, the following data reveals the number of deaths committed by states. Governments have been responsible for 170–200 million deaths in the twentieth century alone (Rummel, 1994) and according to Bassiouni (2001), 'state terrorism' is estimated to have caused more than 70 million casualties during the twentieth century, compared to the 100,000 casualties caused by non-state terrorism. Six times as many deaths occurred per war in the twentieth century as in the nineteenth century (Sivard, 1996), with state-sponsored genocide being the leading cause of violent deaths in the twentieth century (Brannigan & Hardwick, 2003). The capacity of state-facilitated violence exceeds that of non-state violence, with state methods including state-instigated mass murder, forcible starvations and genocide against civilians. This capacity increases when one includes the ability of states to 'bring to power and/or keep in power repressive and sometimes brutal governments' (Michalowski, 2009: 306).

Although states have been complicit in creating, maintaining, legitimizing and facilitating violence, criminology has primarily been concerned with exploring the role of the state in administering justice. This perspective has sustained the state as the definer of harm and by virtue, it has maintained the focus of criminology on the socially constructed non-state actions which have been defined as crimes. The murders, mass rapes, forced starvation, displacement, torture of populations based on religion, ethnicity and so on by states has become invisible. Criminology has therefore been complicit in concealing these crimes and through doing so, it has maintained the stratification of humanity, whereby power, status, religion, ethnicity, constructed risk and so on determine one's right to have their suffering acknowledged and labelled through the ideological construction of 'crime'. In this way, death is not about the loss of life, instead it is defined according to the identity of the perpetrator and the identity of the victim. Therefore, identity alone determines how easily mass murder can be labelled as 'collateral damage' (Welch, 2003).

Although critical criminology has made progress in recognizing and documenting state-perpetrated harm and crime, agreement on the criteria to replace state-defined crime has proven difficult. Elements worthy of inclusion have included domestic laws and/or international laws, human rights laws, conventions, protocols and social harm (Barak, 1991; Friedrichs, 2000; Hillyard & Tombs, 2004; Kauzlarich, 2007; Kramer, Michalowski, & Kauzlarich, 2002; Pemberton, 2007). Definitions have also evolved to include omissions as forms of state crime. Kauzlarich, Mullins, and Matthews (2003) argue that state crime is a violation of international or domestic law and it includes omissions, negligence and failures to act that are directly or indirectly related to a state duty. Similarly,

Kramer et al. (2005) have stated that state crime is any action that violates public international law, international criminal law, or domestic law or actions resulting from state failure to exercise due diligence over the actions of its agents. In contrast, human rights definitions prioritize the rights of the individual, and thus crime can be defined as anything that causes social injury or suffering, and/or which violates human rights (Schwendinger & Schwendinger, 1970). Through conceptualizing human suffering beyond the manufacture of the elites that comprise the state, harmful forms of marginalization, oppression, racism, sexism, homophobia and so on become part of our subject matter. There have been calls to widen the definition of state crime to include all forms of violence, oppression and harm by governments (e.g., Barak, 1991; Kauzlarich et al., 2003; Michalowski, 1985; Milovanovic & Henry, 2001; Tifft, 1995; Tifft & Sullivan, 1980). Such a perspective would invariably disrupt the power-knowledge nexus between the state and the discipline (Hillyard & Tombs, 2004), which conceals state harm and limits the focus of criminology.

As previously stated, this book seeks to relate state practices to state crimes and therefore the mechanisms which govern state conduct. This section now grounds definitions of state crime through discussing IHRL and IHL. IHRL consists of treaties, customs and laws which attribute individuals and groups certain rights that must be respected and protected by their states (UN, 2019). IHRL applies both in peacetime and in situations of armed conflict and to all nation-states. However, unlike IHL, some IHRL treaties permit governments to derogate from certain rights in situations of public emergency threatening the life of the nation. For example, Article 4 (1) International Covenant on Civil and Political Rights (ICCPR) reads:

> In time of public emergency which threatens the life of the nation and the existence of which is officially proclaimed, the States Parties to the present Covenant may take measures derogating from their obligations under the present Covenant to the extent strictly required by the exigencies of the situation, provided that such measures are not inconsistent with their other obligations under international law and do not involve discrimination solely on the ground of race, colour, sex, language, religion or social origin. (UNHR, 1966)

Derogation must be necessary and proportional to the crisis; it cannot be introduced on a discriminatory basis and it must not contravene other rules of international law, such as provisions of IHL. There are however certain human rights that can never be derogated from, including the right to life, the prohibition against torture or cruel, inhuman or degrading treatment or punishment, the prohibition against slavery and servitude and the prohibition against retroactive criminal laws (ECHR, 2018).

IHRL has its origins in the Enlightenment and was formalized after the Second World War through the introduction of the Universal Declaration of Human Rights (UDHR) in 1948 and later, the International Covenant on Civil and Political Rights (ICCPR) and the International Covenant on Economic, Social and Cultural Rights, which were both created in 1966 (UN, 2019). The Universal Declaration of Human Rights has been instrumental in the creation of subsequent international treaties, human rights norms, conventions and legal systems (Benhabib, 2007; Foot, 2000; Rothe, 2013). IHRL now exists in several conventions and laws including the Convention on the Prevention and Punishment of the Crime of Genocide (1948); Convention on the Elimination of All Forms of Racial Discrimination (1965); Convention against Torture and Other Cruel, Inhuman or Degrading Treatment or Punishment (1984) and regional conventions including the European Convention on Human Rights (1950). Together these laws and treaties limit the power of the state towards individuals through assigning individual human rights and specifying the obligations of states towards individuals. IHRL is also very clear in specifying the need for states to use force as a last resort and use proportionate means. It covers a wide range of areas regarding individuals' lives, such as the right to assembly, to life, to privacy, to vote and so on. In contrast, IHL is a set of international rules, established by treaty or custom, which are specifically intended to solve the humanitarian problems directly arising from international or non-international armed conflicts.

Although IHRL and IHL are complementary bodies of international law that share some of the same aims, in situations of conflict, IHL prevails since it was conceived specifically to deal with armed conflict (ICRC, 2014). The conventional and customary laws that govern wars constitute the laws of a 'just war' and if a state of armed conflict does exist, IHL provides a complete legal code that defines the circumstances in which a party may lawfully resort to military force, acceptable conduct during armed conflict, and the protection that should be afforded to civilians and combatants during conflict (ICRC, 2014). IHL includes distinctions between civilians and combatants, definitions of civilian objects, what constitutes attacks on civilians, indiscriminate attacks, disproportionate attacks and deliberate acts of war, and the treatment of prisoners, civilians and territories (ICRC, 2014). IHL also includes the four Geneva Conventions of 1949 and the two Additional Protocols adopted in 1977. The fourth Convention pertains to the protection of civilians, including those in occupied territories, the status and treatment of protected persons, obligations of the occupying power vis-à-vis the civilian population and detailed provisions on humanitarian relief for populations in occupied territories; it also specifically prohibits murder, mutilation, torture, cruel, humiliating and degrading treatment, the taking of hostages and an unfair trial (ICRC, 2014).

Under Article 43 of the Hague Regulations 1907,

> [t]he authority of the legitimate power having in fact passed into the hands of the occupant, the latter shall take all the measures in his power to restore, and ensure, as far as possible, public order and safety, while respecting, unless absolutely prevented, the laws in force in the country. (Schwenk, 1945: 393)

However, during the 'war on terror', the United Kingdom and United States have been responsible for violations of this article. Violations have included the failure of the occupying power to secure public safety and protect civilian rights in the wake of widespread looting and violence, along with a host of home demolitions and arbitrary arrests leading to detentions (Amnesty International, 2005). As this book explores, the failure to secure public order and safety in Afghanistan, Iraq and Syria created political instability, which facilitated both sectarian violence and terrorism.

Although there are many laws, conventions and treaties which protect citizens from states, the enforcement of these is problematic. The first problem is the lack of willingness by nations to adhere to these laws. As

Robertson and Merrills (1996) contend, it has been argued that the UDHR was unanimously accepted precisely because it was a forward-looking, non-binding declaration of the UN General Assembly. Similarly, Gareth Pierce, the lawyer for Moazzam Begg, a former detainee of Guantánamo Bay stated,

> there seems to be a new world order, an acceptance of utter illegality. You have all these wonderful treaties after World War Two—the Geneva Conventions, bans on torture—and all of them have been torn up. Effectively you are allowing international law to be re-written. (Gareth Pierce cited Rose, 2004: 39)

The second problem is geo-political power, because as Michalowski (2009: 318) argues, 'the United Nations as a framework for creating and applying international law, is itself an expression of geo-political interests and unequal power relations', and it therefore represents the 'particular interests of powerful members'. This leads one to question how laws created by powerful states can be used when, and if, the harm is committed by those very states (Rothe, 2013). It therefore appears that legalistic definitions and conventions are inherently based on vested interests and thus, susceptible to manipulation, in terms of creation, application and enforcement.

Definitions of Terrorism

This section explores definitions of terrorism and the construction of terrorism as a phenomenon that exists outside state facilitation. The ideological construction of terrorism renders impossible the state facilitation of terrorism and therefore maintains a discourse whereby states exist solely as victims of terrorism. Terrorism remains a contested concept and there are over 200 definitions of terrorism (Jackson, 2008b). Terrorism is also a politically loaded concept that is subject to constant political construction. As Chomsky (1991: 12) argues, one can take a propagandistic approach to studying terrorism, which involves exploring how the concept of terrorism is used 'as a weapon to be exploited in the service of some system of power'. There are three important issues to note from how the construction of terrorism serves the conceptualization of the state in relation to terrorism. This construction, as is discussed below, has determined how both terrorism and state crime have been conceptualized within the 'war on terror'.

The first issue to note is the construction of terrorism as being perpetrated by non-state actors. In the nineteenth century, terrorism was developed as a term to denote violence committed by non-state actors (Boyns & Ballard, 2004; Nacos, 2006). Contemporary orthodox approaches continue to define terrorism as involving the 'deliberate attempt to enact harm… through the use of illegitimate violence with the expressed aim of communicating a political message' (Wight, 2009: 102). The inclusion of 'illegitimate violence' is important. It highlights issues of legitimacy and sovereignty alongside violence, thereby suggesting that perpetrators cannot be state actors, since, as Jackson (2008b) notes, states have a legitimate right to use violence and defend themselves. Similarly, Hoffman (2006) argues that terrorism involves violence committed by non-state entities. This emphasis on non-state actors means that terrorism is constructed to exclude state terrorism, even though most political violence is committed by states (Moeckli, 2008). Through using definitions such as those discussed, academics fail to consider state-perpetrated violence and therefore not only maintain but also reinforce existing power relations that exclude state terrorism (Jackson, 2008b, 2009; Löwenheim & Gazit, 2009; Stohl, 2008b).

This invariably leads to the second issue which emanates from such definitions, the conceptualization of the state as a victim. As the book demonstrates, terrorism is constructed to exist as a binary with non-state actors as the perpetrators and states as the victims. Further, as the above definitions elucidate, terrorism has also been constructed as a form of violence to aide political communication and achieve political change. When one considers this aim critically, then surely sanctions imposed onto countries by the UN are also a form of terrorism, since they inflict suffering onto innocent populations to communicate a political message. It could be argued that such measures constitute a far more dangerous form of terrorism because, as Kapitan (2013) argues, the sanctions imposed by the United States against Iraq led to over a million Iraqis dying. One must therefore note how the construction of terrorism is vital to public perception, with the fear and risk that is so inherently tied to terrorism ensuring that terrorism carries both negative and moral judgement (Hoffman, 2006). And how the construction of sanctions serves to administer public acceptance, and even public support, for the apparent use of non-violent measures.

The third point worthy of discussion is how the construction of terrorism serves to legitimize state measures to counter terrorism, which often portray both war and immense violence as appropriate responses (Jackson, 2005, 2009; Toros, 2018). As Jackson (2008b: 30) contends, the response involves 'counter-terrorism and counter-insurgency operations' morphing 'into terrorism themselves by failing to distinguish between the innocent and the guilty or being highly disproportionate', and military actions which 'go beyond strategic necessity to the use of force for the purpose of intimidating and demoralising civilians'. Academic interest in the 'war on terror' has sustained these concepts because as Stohl (2008b: 5) argues, 'scholars of terrorism have seen state violence and terrorism as outside the bounds of terrorism studies'.

The final issue worthy of consideration is how the power to define terrorism, react to terrorism and prevent terrorism also gives states the ability to misuse their power in the name of terrorism. States are under an international duty to prevent terrorism under United Nations resolution 1373 (which obliged states to criminalize terrorism through their domestic laws and create appropriate punishments) and, as Trapp (2011) contends, this obligation conceptualizes the state as a mechanism to control terrorism and terrorists, rather than treating the state as the cause of terrorism. The state is ignored and represented as a neutral force which exists solely to address acts of terrorism and this problematic construction conceals state actions which help maintain, create and perpetuate terrorism.

The Social Construction of State Crime and 'Terrorism'

The above discussions on state crime and terrorism demonstrate the binary construction of these terms. These constructions dismiss the possible existence of fluidity between state crime and terrorism and terrorism and state crime. This section now explores the relationship between these terms through deconstructing the terms and assessing their similarities and their differences. Interestingly, the very first observation of state violence, state crime and terrorism is that they all involve the use of violence for a political purpose. As Tosini (2007: 666) states, 'war has been accepted as a legitimate means to achieve a political end… During a war, violence deliberately involving civilians can certainly happen'. Similarly, as noted above, terrorism involves violence for political purposes which then challenges the construction of these terms as binaries and, indeed, this leads one to question if there should be a more inclusive definition. The binary construction and differentiation of these terms reflect discussions 'about who is entitled to exercise violence, against whom, and for what purposes' (Saul, 2008: 4). Therefore, the question of legitimacy is core, and legitimacy is another form of social construction. In the construction of legitimacy, the harm and suffering endured, aspects that ought to be the central point of focus, shift to a focus on the perpetrator. The ability of the perpetrator to define not only the severity, but also the visibility of the harm caused reflects ideological construction and manipulation, which provide a lens through which suffering is obscured. The focus on the perpetrator is evident from the following statement by José Lasso Ayala (1996), a former United Nations High Commissioner for Human Rights, who stated, 'a person stands a better chance of being tried and judged for killing one human being than for killing 100,000' humans. The role of power in the ideological construction of state crime has led Green and Ward (2004) to draw on Gramsci's (1971) concept of hegemony. They argue, 'world or global hegemony is a particularly important concept in the study of state crime because it embodies not only universal norms but also the institutions and mechanisms which define how states should behave' (Green & Ward, 2004: 207). The construction of state crime and terrorism rests on the ability of institutions and state actors to infer legitimacy and the attribution of legitimacy on state-perpetrated violence serves to conceal state crimes.

The adoption of another perspective, peace studies, further elucidates the restrictions of such a perpetrator orientated perspective. As a subfield of international relations, peace studies have witnessed a renewed interest in human rights. This focus on human rights has led to some interesting observations on the fluidity between state crime and terrorism. Callaway and Harrelson-Stephens (2006: 680) argue that poor human rights conditions create an atmosphere ripe for terrorism: 'the basis for terrorism is found in deprivation of political, subsistence, and security rights, and therefore any policy designed to decrease terrorism necessarily implies addressing these rights'. Similarly, Case and Sahliyeh (2009: 16) have argued that state limits on freedom and reduced state capacity form the basis for both transnational terrorism and domestic terrorism. They go on to write,

> political grievance, once suppressed, does not simply disappear. Rather, it follows that when the avenue to non-violently express political grievance is closed, the utility in using violent political expression increases. Political violence, and specifically terrorism, becomes a viable alternative for political expression.

There is empirical evidence to suggest that this link is valid. Piazza (2008) explored the relationship between terrorism and failed or failing states. His study found that

> states plagued by chronic failures are statistically most likely to host terrorist groups that commit transnational attacks, have their nationals commit transnational attacks, and are more likely to be targeted by transnational terrorists themselves. (Piazza, 2008: 469)

It therefore appears that reduced state capacity increases the likelihood of terrorism. This approach suggests a very different relationship between state crime and terrorism, indeed demonstrating how state violations of human rights could facilitate terrorism. Such a conceptualization breaks the view of states existing solely as victims of state crime, and instead opens the possibility to explore how the existence of political instability facilitates terrorism. Such a perspective de-privileges the self-proclaimed legitimacy inferred by states onto states and leads one to question, if there should be a more inclusive definition that incorporates the fluidity between state crime and terrorism?

The Reflexive Turn

The reflexive turn denotes the interrogation and questioning of the boundaries of definitions of terrorism and state crime. Terrorism has not always been called terrorism, as Livingston (1994) notes, the Afghan Mujahideen were called 'freedom fighters' before they were reconstructed as Islamist terrorists. This discursive construction, where the labels—terrorist, freedom fighter, human rights activist, liberator and so on—are selectively employed has become increasingly susceptible to political manipulation. The discourses created in the 'war on terror' have been created to validate 'universal ideals' through constructing the enemy as the anti-thesis of these ideals. Jackson (2008a: 379) contends,

> discourses are significant not just for what they say but also for what they do not say... silence can be a deliberate means of distraction.... the suppression or de-legitimisation of alternative forms of knowledge or values, the tacit endorsement of particular kinds of practices, setting the boundaries of legitimate knowledge, or as a kind of disciplining process directed against certain actors—among others.

Questioning these silences is important because just as words and discourses represent vessels of power, so does silence. The silence of criminology in relation to state terrorism can be witnessed from the following statistics. According to Silke (2004: 206) 'only 12, or less than two percent of articles from 1990 to 1999 in the core terrorism studies journals focused on state terrorism'. This book not only questions discourses but also the silences, through maintaining the reflexive turn which involves interrogating the political, cultural and moral values which shape understandings of terrorism and state crime (Drake, 1989). The silence of criminology in addressing the fluidity between state crime and terrorism has started to be addressed through employing a critical approach which assesses the structural level as a level of construction that also requires interrogation. This has led to definitions which incorporate the vast spectrum of possible state involvement in terrorism, including active sponsorship, internal repression, direct control by the state, support for external non-state actors, knowing toleration, unconcern or ignorance, incapacity on the part of the state to prevent domestic actors from providing support and the use of state officials to target dissidents or other political targets outside the state (Byman, 2008; Stohl & Lopez, 1988).

The two dominant definitions that incorporate the fluidity between states and terrorism are state terrorism and state-sponsored terrorism. The term state terrorism was developed to denote the use of terrorism by states. As Grabosky and Stohl (2010) contend, state terror is where states are directly engaged in terrorist activities and the violence is inflicted from above. The emphasis on violence from above, and therefore the structural level, means that institutionalized forms of terrorism can also be considered. Definitions of state terror encompass all variants of state power, and the capabilities and mechanisms that such power grants. In developing and adopting such a perspective, one can also account for the less visible forms of power and harm used by states, such as the power to create and maintain exclusionary and dehumanizing discourses. In this space it is possible to account for and interrogate non-violent state terrorism, that which exists in policies, legislation and institutions. It could be argued that non-violent state terrorism is just as dangerous as violent state terrorism, since it maintains and perpetuates the ideological discourses manufactured to provide legitimacy for state violence and without these discourses, state violence could not be constructed and thus portrayed as being necessary. The following example by Kapitan (2013) reveals the symbiotic relationship between institutionalized violence, ideological discourses and state terrorism. According to Kapitan (2013: 25), state terrorism includes, 'the institutionalized violence exercised against Palestinian civilians throughout Israel's 37-year occupation of the West Bank and Gaza Strip'. He goes on to say,

> the occupation has featured widespread abuses of human rights, including torture, deportation, collective punishment, economic strangulation, destruction of property, confiscation of land, and killing unarmed civilians, actions that are routinely designed to intimidate a civilian population in order to secure political objectives (in this case, control over territory). (Kapitan, 2013: 25)

The increased capacity of states to perpetrate terrorism has also been noted by Wilkinson (1973) when he argues that throughout history, the primary agent of terrorization of civilian populations has been armed military forces. The construction of terrorism, both inside and outside academia, fuels the fallacy of terrorism which not only allows terrorists to be conceptualized as the evil destructors of humanity, in direct contrast to states as the defenders of humanity, but also dismisses state terrorism as the 'main terrorist problem in the world' (Schmid & De Graaf, 1982: 2).

The second term which combines states and terrorism in a way which challenges the orthodox construction of terrorism is state-sponsored terrorism. State-sponsored terrorism considers the immense power of states to control entities which cause harm. As stated previously, legitimacy is a core concept where state violence is concerned, since it can manipulate acts of violence into acts of necessity, which adhere to the principles of proportionality and necessity. Although the monopoly of violence resides with states, state sponsored terror incorporates the purposeful construction of legitimacy. In constructing legitimacy, states actively take measures to conceal what would be considered as illegitimate state actions through using other actors to carry out their desired actions. The use of these actors maintains the appearance of state legitimacy, because in a world where states have the power to define harm and construct the boundaries of what the world should focus on, state involvement becomes invisible. State-sponsored terrorism is where states are indirectly involved by financing, offering intelligence and/or logistical assistance to terrorist organizations (Hoffman, 2006). Similarly, Byman (2005: 10) defines it as 'a government's intentional assistance to a terrorist group to help it use violence, to bolster its political activities, or sustain the organization'. These definitions reveal the key role of states in supporting terrorism and, as Martin (2003) notes, weak and/or totalitarian states are particularly predisposed to sponsoring terrorism. However, for many states the primary motivation for state sponsorship arises from a desire to destabilize or overthrow neighbouring regimes, shape the domestic composition within them, and take advantage of the position this affords the state in intra-regional politics (Byman, 2005; Cline & Alexander, 1986).

In the 'war on terror', one can instantly think of examples of state terrorism such as strategic bombing, the use of drones, imperialism and political oppression. One can also consider the UK sales of arms as a form of state-sponsored terrorism because, as Bantekas and Nash (2007: 219) note, state-sponsored terrorism includes indirect and direct assistance by the state, which could involve 'groups or persons independent from the State, but in receipt of financial aid or weapons, or only logistic support…'. As Chap. 5 demonstrates, the link between the UK sales of arms, state crime and terrorism is a harmonious well-established one, with the sale of arms aiding the existence of both state crime and terrorism. In more recent years, the concept of state-sponsored terrorism has been widened to include cases where states do not support terrorist groups but lack the interest or the capacity to prevent their activities (Byman, 2008; Piazza, 2008). It could be argued that the expansion of the term reflects developments in international policy, because, as Trapp (2011: 9) contends, there are now 13 international conventions and protocols that address 'the state as a potential terrorist actor, and states are subject to an obligation to refrain from participating in, supporting, or acquiescing in acts of international terrorism'.

However, although both state terrorism and state-sponsored terrorism emphasize states as potential facilitators and perpetrators of terrorism, when states do engage in these actions, there is an unwillingness to label such actions as state crimes—even though most of the actions infringe international law, domestic law, conventions and protocols—or to label them as terrorism. The failure to investigate state actions through a neutral lens and the omission of state crime perpetuate the construction of state actions as non-criminal actions. The next section considers how this book provides an analysis of the 'war on terror' which considers the fluidity between states and terrorism, thereby recognizing states as facilitators of terrorism and as having the capacity to commit state crimes through facilitating terrorism.

The Theoretical Framework of the Book

This chapter will now explore how terrorism and state crime will be used in ways which interrogate their meaning, their construction and their power. The use of these terms contributes to the production of knowledge. Although critical criminology has to some extent questioned the political construction of state crime and terrorism, thereby recognizing the active construction and subsequent implications for the usage of these terms, it has constructed itself as a passive entity through failing to critically explore how the academic construction of these terms serves to maintain systems of harm. It could therefore be argued that just as academics are encouraged to make transparent their choices, beliefs, desires, decisions, subjectivities, emotions and so on during the research process, recognizing that these entities impact and shape the production of knowledge that emerges from research, the same transparency should also exist in other forms of scholarly activity, since these too lead to the production of knowledge. Therefore, to provide such transparency, the decisions which informed the perspectives through which the 'war on terror' is analysed in this book will now be discussed.

This book explores how state practices and state crimes have facilitated Islamist terrorism and Islamist terrorist groups in the 'war on terror', and how the 'war on terror' has contributed to, amongst other harms, the erosion of civil liberties, wars, mass refugees and nationalism. The book proposes a new framework within which to understand, analyse, critique and portray the relationship between state crime and terrorism in the 'war on terror'. It does this through examining how states practices and state crimes have facilitated the radicalization process and thus, terrorism. As previously stated, there has been a vast neglect in labelling state actions and state practices as state crimes within the 'war on terror'. Therefore, when assessing state practices in the 'war on terror', and considering the fluidity between state practices and terrorism, the book draws on the concept of state crime and grounds this concept in international law, domestic law, conventions, protocols, social harm and citizens' perceptions. The concepts of state terrorism and state-sponsored terrorism were considered weak because they too exist as separate entities to state crime. The continued use of these terms, state terrorism and state-sponsored terrorism, perpetuates a framework in which the state is privileged through the abandonment of a criteria in which state practices can be acknowledged and labelled as state crimes. As Judith Butler (2006) suggests in *Precarious Life,* the potential for an ethical response to 9/11, to terrorism, and to suffering is curtailed by the monopolization of the legitimate meaning of 9/11 in public discourse. This monopolization constructs the boundaries of the public discourse and what is to be labelled as patriotic and what is to be labelled as criminal. In contrast, the utilization of state crime adopts an ontologically neutral perspective through which it is possible to explore the state as any other entity, and, therefore, it is possible to shift the focus on what should really be the focal point of academic scrutiny—human suffering. In utilizing the label 'crime', the book purposely seeks to accept and indeed reinforce the stigma the label 'crime' carries and ensure that criminal states carry the burden such a label implies (Matthews & Kauzlarich, 2007).

Where the concept of terrorism is concerned, Tilly (2004) contends that the term is politically powerful and analytically elusive. In order to avoid the possibility of being analytically elusive and void of the real world and empirical study, the book employs a grounded analytical perspective. This grounded analytical perspective involves adopting a structural non-state centric perspective through which it is possible to empirically analyse how state crimes have impacted the variables associated with radicalization. Furthermore, in order to assess the role of states and state crime in creating and maintaining terrorism in the 'war on terror', the book explores the 'war on terror' as a whole, as opposed to orthodox approaches which dissect it into discrete events. 'An approach that examines the 'structure' of terrorism has been neglected' (Oliverio & Lauderdale, 2005: 163), even though it is only through exploring all the factors which give rise to terrorism that terrorism can be defeated. Interestingly, through exploring the 'war on terror' as a whole it was possible to assess how some state crimes facilitated radicalization and terrorism decades later, and therefore it was possible to include examples which would have otherwise been omitted due to temporal and spatial limitations.

According to Barak (1991), the study of state crimes must include the law, power, ideology, and foreign and domestic policies. Within the 'war on terror', an assessment of the entities Barak (1991) identifies must involve these entities being examined as fluid entities, and related to active state construction, state manipulation and state use. However, it must also be assumed that they are complex and require deconstruction because as Friedrichs (1998) contends, state crime, human rights, political crime and diplomatic and domestic issues are entangled and complex and must therefore be disentangled. An accurate and holistic study of state crime and terrorism within the 'war on terror' cannot be separated from the entities that Barak (1991) and Friedrichs (1998) identify. This book explores these entities and, where possible, assesses them according to their influence, so that their existence is not taken for granted but instead, they are recognized as facets through which states can possibly facilitate and influence terrorism. In this way the book adopts a critical constructionist and constitutive perspective, one which carves open and recognizes the different avenues through which states exert power and how such vessels of power facilitate radicalization. And one which also recognizes the ability of different avenues and variables to have a degree of autonomy and also to impact and be impacted by other avenues and variables.

When writing about human security, Newman (2016: 1179) states,

> instead of giving up on human security—and indeed the state as a provider of security—a critical academic approach can be pursued that engages with policy but which promotes a greater consideration of the structural dimensions of deprivation and insecurity… The prevalence of these challenges can only be understood—and addressed—in their social, political and economic contexts.

The structural level is considered in relation to terrorism with the book exploring the 'political, social, and economic context' within which terrorism takes place in the 'war on terror'. As Oliverio and Lauderdale (2005) contend, combining an examination of terrorism in its political and historical context with manifestations of terrorism provides a heuristic understanding of the relationship between terrorism and the state.

Although scrutiny of the structural level is one way of adopting a non-state centric approach, another and perhaps more crucial and imperative way is through embracing non-ethnocentric perspectives and more 'socio-political inclusive' perspectives. Gregory (2004) calls for alternative ways of narrating and tracing the turbulent times and spaces in which we live and construct discourses on the 'war on terror', such as the use of stories and perspectives which emanate far from the United States most notably in Iraq, as well as in Afghanistan and Palestine. The absence of a historical and indeed contemporary more 'socio-political inclusive' analysis compounds the existence of terrorism and state crime as two binaries and continues to neglect structural determinants of terrorism. Here, one can draw parallels between mainstream focuses on street crime, which say little about poverty and the role of institutional inequality on crime, and perspectives on terrorism, which say little about how wars and the structural conditions created by states facilitate terrorism.

The importance of adopting perspectives which not only seek to make transparent how state crimes give rise to terrorism but also seek to uncover, critique and interrogate such crimes can be grasped from the following quote. An 'intervention is flawed if it is merely managing human misery or containing the consequences of this or if it serves to directly legitimize or perpetuate the broader structures which give rise to this insecurity' (Newman, 2016: 1180). Therefore, the absence and silence of structural conditions, 'socio-political inclusive' perspectives and evidence can serve to reinforce political-normative perspectives because as Sherman (2009: 6) argues, 'criminology has long been rich in theory, but poor in evidence. And without evidence, liberty has suffered at the hands of theory'. Drawing on the concept of human security,

> a human security intervention would be illegitimate if it diverts attention or resources away from addressing the underlying sources of deprivation. A human security intervention would also be problematic if its operationalization involves concessions to the political authorities which are responsible for the broader situation of deprivation, since this would directly or indirectly endorse those authorities. (Newman, 2016: 1180)

In much the same way, accounts of terrorism which fail to address the underlying causes of terrorism, which include state practices and state crimes, re-affirm the invisibility of the mechanisms of power that give rise to terrorism and directly endorse the authorities which exercise such power.

This book seeks to make the invisible visible through employing a non-statecentric perspective and one which, as Barak (1991) states, involves confronting state criminality through joining the struggle for universal human rights and social justice. The book argues that any criminological scrutiny of state practice must explore the ability of states to condition society and include all variants of state power, such as the power states have to influence the social world, which involves a consideration of foreign policy decisions, the actions of states after wars and so on. As Wilkinson (2001: 41) notes, we need to recognize states' 'overwhelming propensity of coercive power, which have shown the greatest propensity for terror on a mass scale, both as an instrument of internal repression and control, and as a weapon of aggression and subjugation'. It could therefore be argued that rather than exploring state crime and terrorism and perceiving the inclusion of mechanisms of power as a choice, the starting point should be one where it is accepted that the inclusion of state power is a must, as without it academics could be actively legitimizing and maintaining harmful state practices.

To facilitate an approach where power is made visible, this book explores how state practices have maintained the mechanisms, processes and factors which have led to radicalization and rise of Islamist terrorist organizations, like AQ and ISIS. As Post (1998) notes, every terrorist group must be studied in the context of its own culture and history. Through considering AQ and ISIS, the book explores state crimes that have impacted the emergence and existence of each organization. Interestingly, as Moore and Shellman (2008: 4) note, more recent scholarship:

> focuses attention on the escalation and de-escalation processes of political conflict instantiated by actors' strategic behavioural interactions… A common thread running through this new generation of conflict scholarship is a shift from countries as the unit of analysis to the parties to the conflict and their behaviour.

It could also be argued that such an interrogation of parties and their motivation, free-will, agency and actions signify the use of a crime framework to explore terrorist groups, rather than a war framework. The perspective employed in this book prioritizes parties, and in this case, AQ and ISIS. This book will explore how states contributed to the emergence of these groups and how state practices and state crimes sustain the conditions which facilitate radicalization and therefore contribute to the existence of terrorism. In exploring the relationship between state crime and terrorism in the 'war on terror', the book presents an empirically developed conceptual framework. The framework discussed below and presented in the book is the outcome of an analysis of how state crimes have facilitated radicalization and therefore terrorism in the 'war on terror'.

Constitutive Theory of Radicalization

This book explores, investigates and grounds the constitutive relationships portrayed in the constitutive theory of radicalization diagram. It details their manifestations, existence and maintenance. In presenting this theory of radicalization, Chap. 2 discusses the variables which have been associated with facilitating radicalization. These variables collectively form the micro-individual-emotional level which incorporates an individual's identity, perceptions, beliefs, values and feelings. The remaining chapters of the book detail how this level and therefore radicalization is impacted by and impacts the super macro-universal level, the macro-national level and the meso-societal interpersonal level. The analysis demonstrated also explores how state crimes have occurred on these levels within the 'war on terror', and how these state crimes have impacted the micro-individual-emotional level and thereby the variables associated with radicalization. The book proposes that these three levels, individually and collectively, impact the micro-individual-emotional level and therefore have the capacity to impact the variables associated with radicalization.

The purpose of demonstrating the vast role of states in facilitating radicalization through these levels and their inherent variables is, first, to demonstrate that any attempts to counter radicalization must involve efforts to reduce the very state practices and state crimes which maintain the processes of radicalization. Second, assessing the role of states in these processes has vast implications for our understanding of radicalization and terrorism. It demonstrates the dialectic reality of radicalization and through doing so, it challenges the binary construction of 'good' and 'evil' in the 'war on terror'. In drawing out the hybridity of these interactions, questions of blame and responsibility are problematized, and so too are the processes that create those that have been labelled as possessing no humanity and as being against humanity. The deconstruction and problematization of these binaries carve open a space where possible interventions can be discussed and explored. Further, by demonstrating that many of the factors which induce radicalization, and have elsewhere been labelled as 'cognitive radicalization', are natural emotional reactions to the realities manifested in the other levels, it is then possible to work with these emotions. This by extension opens the space between cognitive radicalization and violent radicalization, thereby suggesting that states have the capacity to work with cognitive radicalization and divert it away from manifesting into violent radicalization.

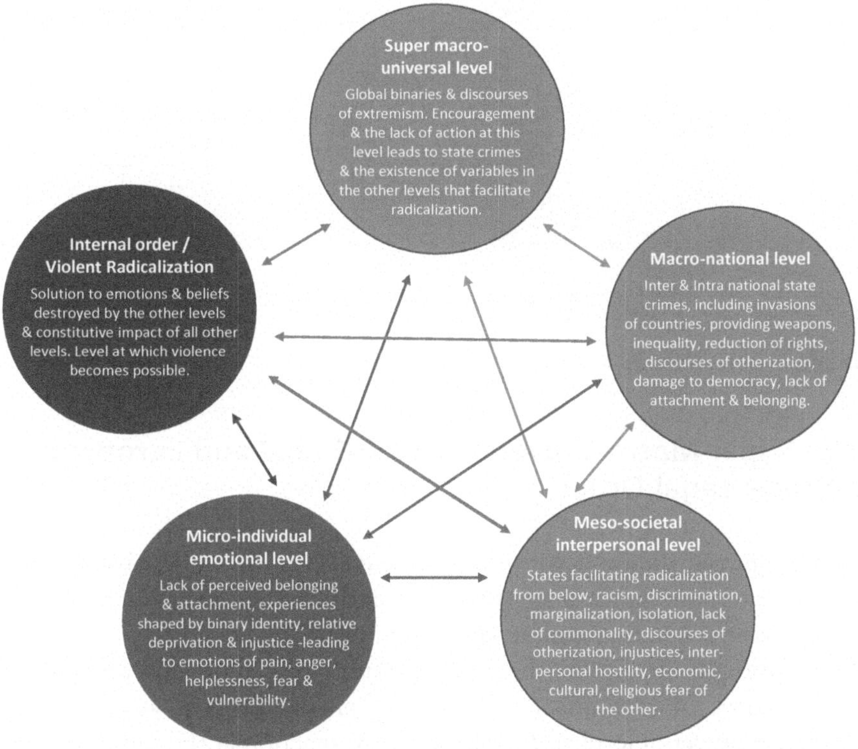

Diagram of levels within radicalization: 'Constitutive theory of radicalization'

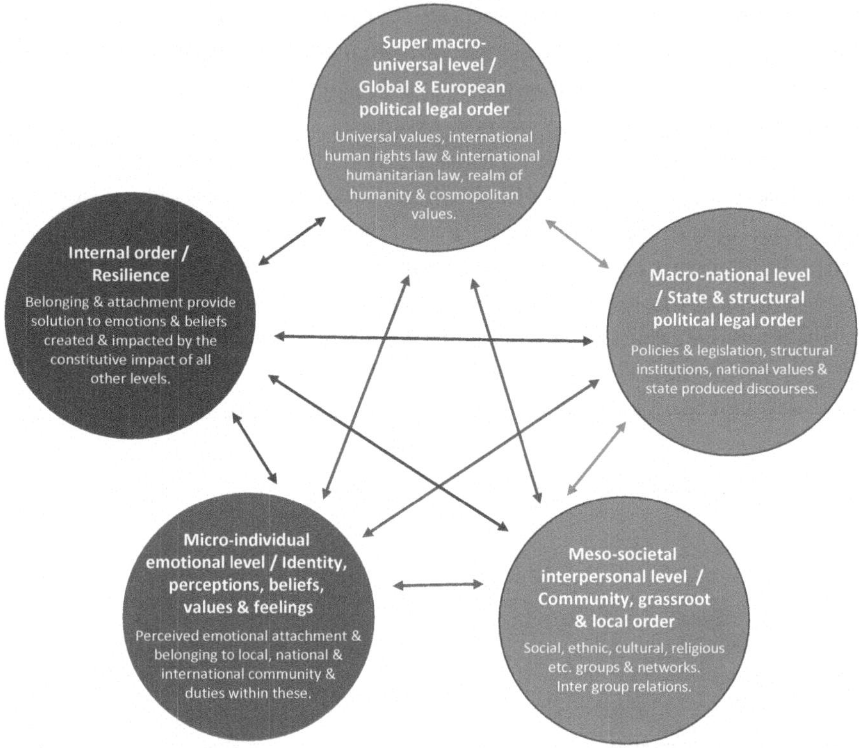

Diagram of levels within 'Constitutive social world'

The Super Macro-Universal Level/Global and European Political Legal Order

Description of the level within constitutive social world: Universal values, international human rights law and international humanitarian law, realm of humanity and cosmopolitan values.

Description of the level in the 'war on terror': Global binaries and global discourses of extremism. Consists of encouragement at the super macro-universal level and where the lack of action at the super macro-universal level leads to state crimes and the existence of variables in the other levels that facilitate radicalization.

The empirical analysis uncovered the super macro-universal level as the first level where state practices and state crimes facilitate radicalization. The super macro-universal level incorporates global institutions such as the United Nations (UN) and the International Criminal Court (ICC). It also incorporates the regulatory mechanisms which exist at this level to regulate state practices, such as international law (IHRL and IHL), conventions and protocols. This level could be conceptualized as 'terrorism from above', since it demonstrates how mechanisms which exist above the state directly facilitate radicalization and terrorism.

In recognizing the super macro-universal level as a level that is meant to shape and influence state actions, this book asks the reader to have an appreciation for the regulatory safeguard mechanisms[1] which exist to govern state practices and the damage that results from a failure to uphold such mechanisms. As the book demonstrates, in the 'war on terror' such deviations lead to macro-national level and meso-societal level inter-state crimes and intra-state crimes which facilitate radicalization. In deconstructing the 'war on terror', the book explores the taken-for-granted state mechanisms of power that feed, maintain, institutionalize and continue to breed the existence of terrorism in the 'war on terror'. The role of the UN and the super macro-universal level in facilitating terrorism has received little coverage and yet it is perhaps one of the most powerful facilitators of radicalization. As this book demonstrates, many of the entities and facets which constitute the macro-national level, meso-societal level and micro-individual-emotional level which facilitate radicalization exist because of UN resolutions such as 1371. UN resolution 1371 encouraged states to extend their mechanisms of social control to prevent terrorism and criminalize terrorism. In this political climate of accelerated state control, the processes which are meant to restrict and ensure that state legislation and state policies adhere to established international regulatory mechanisms have not been exercised. In this way, the super macro-universal level operated as a vessel of power, dictating to states to push the boundaries of their power and control, and yet failed to use this power to restrict violations of human rights and breaches of regulatory mechanisms.

[1] Elsewhere 'safeguards' is used to denote international law, domestic law, conventions and protocols.

The failure to regulate the policies and legislation introduced because of the duty imposed onto states by resolution 1373 is even more surprising (even if one negates the very reality, suffering and horrors which led to the introduction of UDHR and subsequent regulatory mechanisms) given that in 2006, the UN General Assembly adopted the Global Counter-Terrorism Strategy (UN, 2018). This strategy, as stated above, outlined the following conditions as being conducive to the spread of terrorism: prolonged unresolved conflicts, dehumanization of victims of terrorism in all its forms and manifestations, lack of rule of law and violations of human rights, ethnic, national and religious discrimination, political exclusion, socio-economic marginalization and lack of good governance (UN, 2018). However, as the book reveals, all of these conditions have been created by states in the 'war on terror' and these conditions fall into one of the three levels identified (the super macro-universal level, the macro-national level and/or the meso-societal level) and facilitate radicalization. Within this interplay between these structural levels and radicalization, many of the conditions identified by the UN as being conducive to terrorism not only have become a reality in the 'war on terror' but also constitute state crimes. And as this book demonstrates, the existence of such multi-faceted state crimes provides the conditions required for radicalization and directly impacts the variables associated with radicalization, such as perceptions of injustice.

The Macro-National Level/State and Structural Political Legal Order

Description of the level within constitutive social world: Policies and legislation, structural institutions, national values and state-produced discourses.

Description of the level in the 'war on terror': International state crimes and intra-national state crimes, including invasions of countries, providing weapons, inequality, reduction of rights, discourses of otherization, damage to democracy, and lack of attachment and belonging.

The macro-national level was found to incorporate both inter-state crime and intra-state crime. State practices at this level which were found to influence radicalization included the facilitation of dangerous ideologies of otherization and discrimination, and state crimes, such as providing weapons, counter-terrorism legislation and the invasions of Iraq and Afghanistan. Together, these forms of inter-state crime and intra-state crime were found to facilitate radicalization through positively impacting the micro-individual-emotional level, and more specifically perceptions of injustice, suffering, trauma, individuals' sense of belonging and attachment and so on, and UN (2018) identified conditions such as violations of human rights, ethnic, national and religious discrimination, political exclusion, socio-economic marginalization and lack of good governance.

The Meso-Societal Interpersonal Level/Community, Grassroot and Local Order

Description of the level within constitutive social world: Social, ethnic, cultural, religious groups and networks. Inter-group relations.

Description of the level in the 'war on terror': States facilitating terrorism from below through creating the context (political/social/ideological and economic conditions) which facilitate radicalization and terrorism. Also includes racism and discrimination, marginalization, isolation, lack of commonality, discourses of otherization, stigmatization, injustices, interpersonal hostility, and economic, cultural and religious fear of the other.

States were found to facilitate terrorism from below through creating the conditions just specified as existing in the meso-societal interpersonal 'war on terror' level.

The Micro-Individual-Emotional Level/Identity, Perceptions, Beliefs, Values and Feelings

Description of the level within constitutive social world: Perceived emotional attachment and belonging to local, national and international community. Duties within these memberships including ethic of responsibility and empathy.

Description of the level in the 'war on terror': Lack of perceived belonging and attachment to various levels, experiences shaped by binary identity and relative deprivation and injustice, leading to various emotions including pain, anger, helplessness, fear and vulnerability.

As the book demonstrates, all the levels have the capacity to impact the micro-individual-emotional level and therefore identity, perceptions, beliefs, values and feelings. Within the 'war on terror', these levels and the entities within them exacerbate the emotions and perceptions associated with radicalization, such as lack of perceived belonging and attachment, binary identity, relative deprivation, injustice, pain, anger, helplessness, fear, vulnerability and so on. However, as this book reveals, it is also the presence of state crimes within these levels, and their relationships and interactions, that is positively impacting the ability of these factors to facilitate radicalization.

Internal Order

Description of the level within constitutive social world: Resilience, belonging and attachment provide solution to emotions and beliefs created by the constitutive impact of all other levels.

Description of the level in the 'war on terror': Solution to emotions and beliefs destroyed by the other levels and constitutive impact of all other levels. Level at which violence becomes possible.

Traditional frameworks have conceptualized the state and its political legal order as the macro level and the micro-individual level as the lowest level of analysis. This book explores how the super macro-universal level and emotional component of the micro-individual level are relevant to understanding radicalization in the 'war on terror'.

Within the 'war on terror', the super macro-universal level and the global political legal order, via international human rights and institutions such as the UN, have become increasingly relevant. As previously stated, the 'war on terror' has led to the super macro-universal level impacting the macro-national level, the meso-societal interpersonal level and the micro-individual-emotional level. In demonstrating the fluidity between these levels, the book explores how the super-macro level not only impacts the macro-national level and the meso-societal interpersonal level, but also the micro-individual-emotional level and thus identity, perceptions, beliefs, values and feelings. The relationship between these levels is conceptualized as being mutually constitutive. For example, the macro-national level can create autonomous spaces and manipulate the super-macro level and the meso-societal interpersonal level to serve its interests. Such extensions of power lead to the reduction of universal human rights and negatively impact the interpersonal community, and local order. However, acts of terrorism and state reactions to these acts also impact the global and European political legal order and universal values, international human rights law and international humanitarian law, the realm of humanity and cosmopolitan values.

In demonstrating state practices as state crimes and the empirical reality in which they exist, the book reveals not only the vast number of ways in which state crimes have facilitated terrorism within the 'war on terror', but also how discourses of fear, security and nationalism are increasingly eroding human rights. The next chapter provides the context within which to explore these relationships, through discussing the different factors associated with radicalization with subsequent chapters detailing how the super-macro level, the macro-national level and the meso-societal level and their inherent orders have impacted these variables within the 'war on terror'.

References

Ahmed, S. (2015). The Emotionalization of 'War on Terror': Counter-Terrorism, Fear, Risk, Insecurity and Helplessness. *Criminology and Criminal Justice, 15*(5), 545–560.

Ahmed, S. (2016). Citizenship, Belonging and Attachment in the 'War on Terror'. *Critical Criminology, 24*(1), 111–125.

Amnesty International. (2005). *USA: Guantanamo and Beyond: The Continuing Pursuit of Unchecked Executive Power*. Retrieved May 15, 2018, from https://www.amnesty.org/en/documents/AMR51/063/2005/en/

Ayala, J. L. (1996). *Report of the International Tribunal for the Prosecution of Persons Responsible for Serious Violations of International Humanitarian Law*

Committed in the Territory of the Former Yugoslavia Since 1991. Retrieved April 20, 2000, from http://www.un.org/icty/rappannu-e/1996/index.htm

Bantekas, I., & Nash, S. (2007). *International Criminal Law*. Oxon: Routledge.

Barak, G. (1991). Towards a Criminology of State Criminality. In G. Barak (Ed.), *Crimes by the Capitalist State: An Introduction to State Criminality* (pp. 3–18). New York: State University of New York Press.

Bassiouni, M. C. (2001). *International Terrorism: Multilateral Conventions (1937–2001) (International & Comparative Criminal Law)*. New York: Transnational Publishers.

Beck, U. (2002). The Terrorist Threat: World Risk Society Revisited. *Theory, Culture and Society, 19*(4), 39–55.

Benhabib, S. (2007). Twilight of Sovereignty or the Emergence of Cosmopolitan Norms? Rethinking Citizenship in Volatile Times. *Citizenship Studies, 11*(1), 19–36.

Bosworth, M., Bowling, B., & Lee, M. (2008). Globalization, Ethnicity and Racism: An Introduction. *Theoretical Criminology, 12*(3), 263–273.

Boyns, D., & Ballard, J. D. (2004). Developing a Sociological Theory for the Empirical Understanding of Terrorism. *The American Sociologist, 35*(2), 5–25.

Braithwaite, J., & Ali, W. (2013). Crime and War in Afghanistan. Part 1: The Hobbesian Solution. *The British Journal of Criminology, 53*, 179–196.

Brannigan, A., & Hardwick, K. H. (2003). Genocide and General Theory. In C. L. Britt & M. R. Gottfredson (Eds.), *Control Theories of Crime and Delinquency* (pp. 109–131). New Brunswick, NJ: Transaction.

Bushman, B., Ridge, R. D., Das, E., Key, C. W., & Busath, G. L. (2007). When God Sanctions Killing: Effect of Scriptural Violence on Aggression. *Psychological Science, 18*(3), 204–207.

Butler, J. (2006). *Precarious Life: The Powers of Mourning and Violence*. London: Verso.

Byman, D. (2005). *Deadly Connections: States that Sponsor Terrorism*. Cambridge: Cambridge University Press.

Byman, D. (2008). Rogue Operators. *The National Interest*. Retrieved May 15, 2018, from http://nationalinterest.org/article/rogue-operators-2493

Callaway, R., & Harrelson-Stephens, J. (2006). Toward a Theory of Terrorism: Human Security as a Determinant of Terrorism. *Studies in Conflict & Terrorism, 29*(7), 679–702.

Case, E., & Sahliyeh, E. (2009). Origins of Terrorism: An Alternative Way for Political Expression. In S. Ekici, A. Ekici, D. A. McEntire, R. H. Ward, & S. S. Arlikatti (Eds.), *Building Terrorism Resistant Communities: Together Against Terrorism* (pp. 11–23). Retrieved June 10, 2017, from https://epdf.

pub/building-terrorism-resistant-communities-together-against-terrorism-volume-55-na.html
Chomsky, N. (1991). International Terrorism: Image and Reality. In A. George (Ed.), *Western State Terrorism* (pp. 12–38). Oxford: Polity Press.
Chrisafis, A. (2018). Macron Warns of Rising Nationalism as World Leaders Mark Armistice. *The Guardian*. Retrieved March 20, 2019, from https://www.theguardian.com/world/2018/nov/11/trump-joins-macron-and-world-leaders-at-armistice-ceremony
Cline, R. S., & Alexander, Y. (1986). *Terrorism as State-Sponsored Covert Warfare*. Virginia: Hero Books.
Cockburn, P. (2015). *The Rise of Islamic State: ISIS and the New Sunni Revolution*. London: Verso.
Cronin, A. K. (2006). How al-Qaida Ends: The Decline and Demise of Terrorist Groups. *International Security, 31*(1), 7–48.
De Goede, M. (2008). The Politics of Preemption and the War on Terror in Europe. *European Journal of International Relations, 14*(1), 161–185.
Drake, R. (1989). *The Revolutionary Mystique and Terrorism in Contemporary Italy*. New York: John Wiley & Sons.
ECHR. (2018). *Derogation in Time of Emergency*. European Court of Human Rights. Retrieved June 19, 2019, from https://www.echr.coe.int/Documents/FS_Derogation_ENG.pdf
Foot, R. (2000). *Rights Beyond Borders: The Global Community and the Struggle over Human Rights in China*. Oxford: Oxford University Press.
Friedrichs, D. (1998). *State Crime: Volumes I and II*. Aldershot: Ashgate.
Friedrichs, D. O. (2000). The Crime of the Century? The Case for the Holocaust. *Crime, Law and Social Change, 34*(1), 21–41.
Gearty, C. (2005). 11 September 2001, Counter-Terrorism, and the Human Rights Act. *Journal of Law and Society, 32*(1), 18–33.
Grabosky, P. (2008). Community Policing in an Age of Terrorism. *Crime, Law and Social Change, 50*(1–2), 1–5.
Grabosky, P., & Stohl, M. (2010). *Crime and Terrorism*. London: Sage.
Green, P., & Ward, T. (2004). *State Crime: Governments, Violence and Corruption*. Retrieved October 15, 2015, from https://www.dawsonera.com/readonline/9781849641197
Gregory, D. (2004). *The Colonial Present: Afghanistan, Palestine, Iraq*. Oxford: Blackwell.
Habermas, J. (2002). *The Inclusion of the Other: Studies in Political Theory*. Cambridge: Polity Press.

Hagan, J., & Rymond-Richmond, W. (2009). Criminology Confronts Genocide: Whose Side Are You On? *Theoretical Criminology, 13*(4), 503–511.
Hamm, M. S. (2007). High Crimes and Misdemeanors': George W. Bush and the Sins of Abu Ghraib. *Crime, Media, Culture, 3*(*3*), 259–284.
Hillyard, P., & Tombs, S. (2004). Beyond Criminology. In P. Hillyard, C. Pantazis, S. Tombs, & D. Gordon (Eds.), *Beyond Criminology: Taking Harm Seriously* (pp. 10–29). London: Pluto Press.
Hoffman, B. (2006). *INSIDE Terrorism*. New York: Columbia University Press.
Horgan, J. (2005). *The Psychology of Terrorism*. London: Routledge.
Hudson, B., & Walters, R. (2009). Introduction—Criminology and the WAR ON terror. *The British Journal of Criminology, 49*(5), 603–608.
ICRC. (2014). *International Humanitarian Law*. Retrieved June 10, 2018, from https://www.icrc.org/en/doc/assets/files/other/icrc-002-0703.pdf
Jackson, R. (2005). *Writing the War on Terrorism: Language, Politics and Counterterrorism*. Manchester: Manchester University Press.
Jackson, R. (2007). Language, Policy and the Construction of a Torture Culture in the War on Terrorism. *Review of International Studies, 33*(3), 353–371.
Jackson, R. (2008a). The Ghosts of State Terror: Knowledge, Politics and Terrorism Studies. *Critical Studies on Terrorism, 1*(3), 377–392.
Jackson, R. (2008b). An Argument for Terrorism. *Perspectives on Terrorism, 2*(*2*), 25–32.
Jackson, R. (2009). Knowledge, Power and Politics in the Study of Political Terrorism. In R. Jackson, M. Breen Smyth, & J. Gunning (Eds.), *Critical Terrorism Studies: A New Research Agenda* (pp. 66–84). London: Routledge.
Kapitan, T. (2013). 'Terrorism' as a Method of Terrorism. In G. Meggle, A. Kemmerling, & M. Textor (Eds.), *Ethics of Terrorism & Counter-Terrorism* (pp. 21–38). https://www.degruyter.com/viewbooktoc/product/209293
Kauzlarich, D. (2007). Seeing War as Criminal: Peace Activist Views and Critical Criminology. *Contemporary Justice Review, 10*(1), 67–85.
Kauzlarich, D., Mullins, C., & Matthews, R. A. (2003). A Complicity Continuum of State Crime. *Contemporary Justice Review, 6*(3), 241–254.
Klausen, J. (2009). British Counter-Terrorism After 7/7: Adapting Community Policing to the Fight Against Domestic Terrorism. *Journal of Ethnic and Migration Studies, 35*(3), 403–420.
Kramer, R. C., & Michalowski, R. J. (2005). War, Aggression and State Crime: A Criminological Analysis of the Invasion and Occupation of Iraq. *The British Journal of Criminology, 45*(4), 446–469.

Kramer, R. C., Michalowski, R. J., & Kauzlarich, D. (2002). The Origins and Development of the Concept and Theory of State-Corporate Crime. *Crime and Delinquency, 48*(2), 263–282.

Kramer, R. C., Michalowski, R. J., & Rothe, D. (2005). The Supreme International Crime: How the U.S. War in Iraq Threatens the Rule of Law. *Social Justice, 32*, 52–81.

Livingston, S. (1994). *The Terrorism Spectacle*. Boulder, CO: Westview Press.

Löwenheim, O., & Gazit, O. (2009). Power and Examination: A Critique of Citizenship Tests. *Security Dialogue, 40*(2), 145–167.

Maier-Katkin, D., Mears, D. P., & Bernard, T. J. (2009). Towards a Criminology of Crimes Against Humanity. *Theoretical Criminology, 13*(2), 227–255.

Martin, G. (2003). *Understanding Terrorism: Challenges, Perspectives, and Issues*. Thousand Oaks, CA: Sage.

Matthews, R. A., & Kauzlarich, D. (2007). State Crimes and State Harms: A Tale of Two Definitional Frameworks. *Crime, Law and Social Change, 48*(1), 43–55.

McCulloch, J., & Pickering, S. (2009). Pre-Crime and Counter terrorism: Imagining Future Crime in the 'War on Terror'. *The British Journal of Criminology, 49*(5), 628–645.

McGurrin, D., Jarrell, M., Jahn, A., & Cochrane, B. (2013). White Collar Crime Representation in the Criminological Literature Revisited, 2001–2010. *Western Criminology Review, 14*(2), 3–19.

Michalowski, R. J. (1985). *Order, Law and Crime: An Introduction to Criminology*. New York: Random House.

Michalowski, R. J. (2009). Power, Crime and Criminology in the New Imperial Age. *Crime, Law, Social Change, 51*(3), 303–325.

Milovanovic, D., & Henry, S. (2001). Constitutive Definition of Crime: Power as Harm. In S. Henry & M. Lanier (Eds.), *What is Crime? Controversies About the Nature of Crime and What To Do About It* (pp. 165–178). Lanham, MD: Rowman & Littlefield.

Moeckli, D. (2008). *Human Rights and Non-discrimination in the 'War on Terror'*. Published to Oxford Scholarship Online. Retrieved June 10, 2018, from https://doi.org/10.1093/acprof:oso/9780199239801.001.0001

Moore, W. H., & Shellman, S. M. (2008). Conceptualizing a New School of Political Conflict and Terrorism Studies: From Attributes to Behavior and Why Policy Makers will Care. *Perspectives on Terrorism, 11*(12), 3–10.

Mythen, G., Walklate, S., & Khan, F. (2009). 'I'm a Muslim, But I'm Not a Terrorist:' Victimisation, Risky Identities and the Performance of Safety. *The British Journal of Criminology, 49*(6), 736–754.

Nacos, B. L. (2006). *Terrorism and Counterterrorism*. New York: Pearson Longman.

Newman, E. (2016). Human Security: Reconciling Critical Aspirations with Political 'Realities'. *The British Journal of Criminology, 56*(6), 1165–1183.
Oliverio, A., & Lauderdale, P. (2005). Terrorism as Deviance or Social Control: Suggestions for Future Research. *International Journal of Comparative Sociology, 46*(1–2), 153–169.
Pemberton, S. A. (2007). Social Harm Future(s): Exploring the Potential of the Social Harm Approach. *Crime, Law, Social Change, 48*(1–2), 27–41.
Piazza, J. A. (2008). Incubators of Terror: Do Failed and Failing States Promote Transnational Terrorism? *International Studies Quarterly, 52*(3), 469–488.
Post, J. (1998). Terrorist Psycho-Logic: Terrorist Behavior as a Product of Psychological Forces. In W. Reich (Ed.), *Origins of Terrorism: Psychologies, Ideologies, Theologies, States of Mind* (pp. 25–40). Cambridge University Press: Cambridge.
Robertson, A. H., & Merrills, J. G. (1996). *Human Rights in the World: An Introduction to the Study of the International Protection of Human Rights.* Manchester: Manchester University Press.
Rose, D. (2004). *Guantanamo: America's War on Human Rights.* London: Faber and Faber.
Ross, J. I. (2000). Introduction: Protecting Democracy by Controlling State Crime in Advanced Industrialized Countries. In J. I. Ross (Ed.), *Varieties of State Crime and Its Control* (pp. 1–10). Monsey, NY: Criminal Justice Press.
Rothe, D. (2013). A Global Resistance Movement? From Human Rights to International Justice. In E. Stanley & J. McCulloch (Eds.), *State Crime and Resistance* (pp. 199–2019). Oxon: Routledge.
Rummel, R. (1994). *Death by Government.* Somerset, NJ: Transaction Books.
Sageman, M. (2004). *Understanding Terror Networks.* Philadelphia: University of Pennsylvania Press.
Saul, B. (2008). *Defining Terrorism in International Law.* Published to Oxford Scholarship Online. Retrieved June 10, 2018, from https://doi.org/10.1093/acprof:oso/9780199535477.001.0001
Schmid, A. P., & De Graaf, J. (1982). *Violence as Communication: Insurgent Terrorism and the Western News Media.* London: Sage.
Schwendinger, H., & Schwendinger, J. (1970). Defenders of Order or Guardians of Human Rights? *Issues in Criminology, 5*(2), 123–157.
Schwenk, E. H. (1945). Legislative Power of the Military Occupant under Article 43, Hague Regulations. *The Yale Law Journal, 54*(2), 393–416.
Sherman, L. W. (2009). Evidence and Liberty: The Promise of Experimental Criminology. *Criminology and Criminal Justice, 9*(1), 5–28.

Silke, A. (2004). The Road Less Travelled: Recent Trends in Terrorism Research. In A. Silke (Ed.), *Research on Terrorism: Trends, Achievements and Failures* (pp. 186–213). London: Routledge.

Silke, A. (2008). Holy Warriors: Exploring the Psychological Processes of Jihadi Radicalization. *European Journal of Criminology, 5*(1), 99–123.

Sivard, R. L. (1996). *World Military and Social Expenditures*. Washington, DC: World Priorities.

Smeulers, A., & Niekerk, S. (2008). Abu Ghraib and the War on Terror-a Case Against Donald Rumsfeld? *Crime, Law and Social Change, 51*(3–4), 327–349.

Spence, K. (2005). World Risk Society and War Against Terror. *Political Studies, 53*(2), 284–302.

Stohl, M. (2008a). Networks, Terrorists and Criminals: The Implications for Community Policing. *Crime, Law and Social Change, 50*(1), 59–72.

Stohl, M. (2008b). The Global War on Terror and State Terrorism. *Perspectives on Terrorism*. Retrieved June 10, 2018, from http://www.terrorismanalysts.com/pt/index.php/pot/article/view/48/html

Stohl, M., & Lopez, G. A. (1988). Introduction to Terrible Beyond Endurance? The Foreign Policy of State Terrorism. In M. Stohl & G. A. Lopez (Eds.), *Terrible Beyond Endurance? The Foreign Policy of State Terrorism* (pp. 1–13). New York: Greenwood Press.

Tadros, V. (2007). Rethinking the Presumption of Innocence. *Criminal Law and Philosophy, 2*, 139–231.

Tifft, L. (1995). Social Harms Definition of Crime. *The Critical Criminologist, 7*(1), 9–13.

Tifft, L., & Sullivan, D. (1980). *The Struggle to Be Human: Crime, Criminology, and Anarchism*. Orkney: Cienfuegos Press.

Tilly, C. (2004). Terror, Terrorism, Terrorists. *Sociological Theory, 22*(1), 5–13.

Toros, H. (2018). Critical Theories and Terrorism Studies: Ethics and Emancipation. In R. Jackson (Ed.), *Routledge Handbook of Critical Terrorism Studies* (pp. 70–79). London: Routledge.

Tosini, D. (2007). Sociology of Terrorism and Counterterrorism: A Social Science Understanding of Terrorist Threat. *Sociology Compass, 1*(2), 664–681.

Trapp, K. N. (2011). *State Responsibility for International Terrorism*. Published to Oxford Scholarship Online. Retrieved June 10, 2018, from https://doi.org/10.1093/acprof:oso/9780199592999.001.0001

UN. (2018). *UN Global Counter-Terrorism Strategy*. Retrieved June 21, 2019, from https://www.un.org/counterterrorism/ctitf/en/un-global-counter-terrorism-strategy

UN. (2019). *International Human Rights Law*. Retrieved June 21, 2017, from https://www.ohchr.org/en/professionalinterest/pages/internationallaw.aspx

UNHR. (1966). *International Covenant on Civil and Political Rights*. Retrieved June 21, 2017, from https://www.ohchr.org/Documents/ProfessionalInterest/ccpr.pdf

Urry, J. (2002). The Global Complexities of September 11th. *Theory, Culture and Society, 19*(4), 57–69.

Walklate, S. (2003). *Understanding Criminology: Current Theoretical Debates*. Buckingham: Open University Press.

Weiss, M., & Hassan, H. (2015). *ISIS: Inside the Army of Terror*. New York: Regan Arts.

Welch, M. (2003). Trampling Human Rights in the War on Terror: Implications to the Sociology of Denial. *Critical Criminology, 12*(1), 1–20.

Welch, M. (2008). Ordering Iraq: Reflections on Power, Discourse, & Neocolonialism. *Critical Criminology, 16*(4), 257–269.

Wight, C. (2009). Theorising Terrorism: The State, Structure and History. *International Relations, 23*(1), 99–106.

Wilkinson, P. (1973). Three Questions on Terrorism. *Government and Opposition, 8*(3), 290–312.

Wilkinson, P. (2001). *Terrorism vs Democracy: The Liberal State Response*. London: Frank Cass.

Zedner, L. (2007). Pre-crime and Post Criminology? *Theoretical Criminology, 11*(2), 261–281.

2

Revisiting Theories of Radicalization

In presenting the constitutive theory of radicalization, this chapter explores the entities associated with radicalization and that form the micro-individual-emotional level. As the chapter will demonstrate, state interaction, construction, legitimatization and/or any exercise of state power in the existence of the micro-individual-emotional level are generally omitted from theories of radicalization. Having explored these variables, subsequent chapters analyse how state practices and state crimes interact with these factors and the micro-individual-emotional level, and through doing so, the book offers a more holistic theory of radicalization and one that includes the role of state practices and state crimes in facilitating terrorism within the 'war on terror'. The book is also concerned with giving narratives agency through demonstrating how the various levels impact individuals. This concern with agency denotes the belief that if we are to prevent radicalization, then we must understand it from the perspectives of those likely to experience it.

The UK government defines radicalization as 'the process by which a person comes to support terrorism and forms of extremism leading to terrorism' (House of Commons, 2012: 3). Radicalization has become synonymous with adopting extremist beliefs and using violence to achieve

S. Ahmed, *The 'War on Terror', State Crime & Radicalization*, Palgrave Studies in Risk, Crime and Society, https://doi.org/10.1007/978-3-030-40138-2_2

political change (Allen, 2007). Further, as Martin (2014) notes, the conceptualization of radicalization as a gradual process assumes that certain traits and common characteristics can be identified during distinct phases of radicalization. This chapter does not maintain that every terrorist has each characteristic discussed; rather it conceptualizes the factors as having the 'potential' to radicalize individuals, and therefore as factors that must be reduced to successfully prevent radicalization. The differential impact of variables on individuals can be evidenced from biographical studies which revealed that individuals joining the same terrorist organization had different motivations for joining and different personalities, which included a lack of empathy with their victims, dogmatic or an ideological mentality, or a simplistic or utopian worldview (De la Corte, 2007).

It is accepted that radicalization is a process and within this process a distinction has been made between what McCauley and Moskalenko (2012) call 'opinion radicalization', which involves the cognitive commitment to radical ideas, and 'action radicalization', which denotes acting on these radical ideas. This differentiation has also been referred to as 'cognitive radicalization' and 'violent radicalization'. Vidino and Brandon (2012: 9) define cognitive radicalization as the

> process through which an individual adopts ideas that are severely at odds with those of the mainstream, refutes the legitimacy of the existing social order, and seeks to replace it with a new structure based on a completely different belief system.

'Violent radicalization' is defined as occurring 'when an individual takes the additional step of employing violence to further the views derived from cognitive radicalism' (Vidino & Brandon, 2012: 9). This distinction empowers authorities to label individuals as radicalized, even when they are no more likely to commit an act of terrorism than an individual that possesses no cognitive radicalization traits. The power derived from this conceptualization is evident in the vast number of counter-terrorism measures which were introduced after September 11th and, as Chap. 3 demonstrates, these measures had detrimental consequences for the rule of law and suspects' human rights.

According to Prevent (2011: 108), the al-Qaeda Narrative, the Grand Narrative or the Global Extremist Narrative, 'combines fact, fiction, emotion and religion and manipulates discontent about local and international issues' through providing a distorted 'interpretation of religion, history and politics'. The official narrative conceptualizes extremist narratives as being the most significant cause of terrorism, even though there is weak evidence to support this (Kundnani, 2015). The state narrative also constructs perceptions which are facts and true as constituting extremist speech. For example, one perception that has been labelled as dangerous is that the UK response to terrorism has made British Muslims a suspect community, and British Muslims are the most likely to be subjected to the misuse of police power (Sutton, 2015). This perception reflects the reality that British Muslims have been disproportionately subjected to counter-terrorism measures and have therefore accurately been labelled as the new 'suspect community' (Pantazis & Pemberton, 2009; Statewatch, 2007; Walklate & Mythen, 2008). Similarly, those that are critical of and denounce foreign policies have also been labelled as being on the pathway of radicalization (Kundnani, 2015) and yet, as Beck (2006) states, the 2003 march against the UK invasion of Iraq was the largest ever civil demonstration in the United Kingdom and demonstrated that the majority of UK citizens did not support the invasion.

The government narrative and conceptualization of radicalization has many consequences. First, UK counter-terrorism strategies are based on eradicating the very factors which this discourse proposes lead to terrorism. Second, by virtue of the discourse emphasizing some factors which induce radicalization, it also excludes other factors which lead to radicalization. As the following chapters demonstrate, there are a vast number of factors, especially those linked to state practices which positively influence the radicalization process, and yet these are completed omitted from the governmental narrative on the causes of radicalization. And finally, this narrative maintains dangerous binary, exclusionary and harmful practices because, as the book explores, the demonization of some aspects of cognitive radicalization further perpetuates perceptions of criminalization, injustice and isolation, which push individuals towards violent radicalization.

Explanations of radicalization incorporate a multitude of psychological, structural and religious variables which do not exist as distinct entities, rather they are multi-faceted and therefore both impact and are impacted by each other in a myriad of ways. Early psychological theories about terrorists concluded that political violence is caused by fragmented psychosocial identities, with political violence representing a search for identity (Post, 1984). These deterministic individualized perspectives implied that there is a terrorist profile. This was captured with the 'Personal Pathway Model' asserting that terrorist behaviour is the result of unexamined traumatic issues and unresolved narcissistic injuries (Shaw, 1986). Weenink (2015), in his study of 140 subjects who travelled from the Netherlands to Syria, found that behavioural problems and disorders were overrepresented. He wrote,

> [O]ur study offers little room for the *tabula rosa* approach of social psychologists who maintain that radicals are people just like you and me, and the environment is all that explains radicalization. (Weenink, 2015: 29)

However, many studies have found that terrorists are psychologically much healthier and far more stable than other violent criminals and the prevalence of mental illness among samples of incarcerated terrorists is as low as, or lower than in, the general population (Crenshaw, 1992; Ruby, 2002; Silke, 2008).

Although psychological approaches have constructed radicalization and mental illness as a binary, research exploring the role of emotions in the radicalization process has dissected this binary, thus allowing for a greater understanding of how external factors impact individuals. One of the dominant emotions to emerge has been that of powerlessness. Powerlessness denotes the pain, anger, vulnerability and frustration that accompanies an inability to change something, such as having reduced legal rights, having a loved one killed, experiencing marginalization, or racism or criminalization (Boyns & Ballard, 2004; Henderson-King, Henderson-King, Bolea, Koches, & Kauffman, 2004; Lemu, 2016; Speckhard & Akhmedova, 2005). Powerlessness is a strong emotion that can lead to a 'collectivistic shift', whereby one's personal identity becomes fused with that of the group and within this fusion of collective identity, which also incorporates a collective ideology, acts of terrorism help to reduce individuals' sense of powerlessness (Post, Sprinzak, & Denny, 2003). This fusion of identity and ideology demonstrates how individual acts of terrorism are perceived as reducing the powerlessness of the group and therefore as empowering the group. However, it should also be noted that such shifts in identity are also shaped according to cultural, religious and ideological identity and are dependent on historical and cultural contexts.

Speckhard and Akhmedova (2005) carried out an extensive study on Chechen suicide terrorists via interviews with their family members. All interviewees cited traumatic incidents that altered the course of the suicide terrorists' lives. The authors concluded: '[w]hen we looked for the primary motivation in our sample of terrorists we would have to say that it was trauma in every case' (Speckhard & Akhmedova, 2005: 25). Trauma was also found to positively influence the need for religiosity as a form of empowerment. Speckhard and Akhmedova's (2005: 22) study demonstrated that 28 out of 34 suicide terrorists were 'secular Muslims prior to their experiences of trauma', and 27 had no previous relationship to extremist militant groups but sought out radical Wahhabi groups in reaction to the traumas they experienced. Research exploring negative emotional responses to 9/11 revealed that following 9/11 there was an increased use of prayer, with prayer lowering levels of distress, providing spiritual support and increasing optimism about the future (Fischer & Ai, 2008). Therefore, research suggests that powerlessness and trauma, through increasing an individual's need for an ideological system of support, induces vulnerability that can be exploited by terrorist groups that seek to use this vulnerability to radicalize individuals.

However, although trauma might be conceptualized as originating from extraordinary events, within the 'war on terror', the lack of human rights, the pre-crime orientation of counter-terrorism measures and the criminalization of freedom, security and association—which could collective be labelled as marking the institutionalization of the extraordinary into the ordinary—have led British Muslims to experience fear, risk, insecurity, vulnerability and helplessness in the 'war on terror' (Ahmed, 2015). These emotions feed into and interact with what Horgan (2008) identifies as 'emotional vulnerability', which, as Horgan (2008) explains, pre-dispose individuals to terrorism. A study in 2014 also linked vulnerability to radicalization. It surveyed over 600 men and women of Pakistani, Bangladeshi and Muslim heritage in London and Bradford, aged between 18 and 45, and found that depressed and socially isolated individuals are most at risk of radicalization (Bhui, Warfa, & Jones, 2014). It also found that migrants were more resistant to radicalization than those born in the United Kingdom (Bhui et al., 2014). However, research by Post and Sheffer (2007) revealed that 80% of new recruits to the global Salafi jihad came from the diaspora and were the children of Muslim immigrants who instead of experiencing a better life in their new country, experienced hostility which facilitated their radicalization.

Racism, discrimination and otherization have been identified as factors which contribute to the radicalization process through impacting individuals' perceptions of belonging and attachment (Ahmed, 2016). Research also suggests that those with a high degree of religiosity are likely to suffer the most pain from discrimination (Ysseldyk, Matheson, & Anisman, 2011). In the most recent European Union Minorities and Discrimination Survey, one in three Muslim respondents reported experiencing discrimination, with the effect greatest among Muslims aged 16–24 (Blaker, 2015). The discrimination, 'grievance, humiliation, and hatred of Muslims' faced by Muslims is often used by extremists to recruit individuals (Rasool, 2016: 40). Discrimination and hate crime often impact identity. They can heighten Muslims' religious identity (Abdo, 2006; Gould & Esteban, 2016), lead to rejections of this identity (Ahmed, 2016) and positively impact radicalization. Research by Mythen, Walklate, and Khan (2009) found that frustration, stigma and anger were the most frequent sentiments expressed by British Muslims in relation to the 'war on terror'. As this book explores, many of the emotions cited above are linked to political instability, injustice, marginalization, discrimination, pre-crime criminalization, a reduction of legal rights and so on. These are all entities that are created by state exercises of power, either via the creation of discourses, the institutionalization of policies and legislation and/or the failure to act to protect vulnerable groups. Therefore, it follows that if one is to reduce radicalization, the micro-individual-emotional level variables which facilitate radicalization and the role of states in the production and reproduction of these factors must also be addressed.

As previously stated, the 'war on terror' discourse marginalizes certain groups by creating a dichotomy of acceptable beliefs, perceptions and expressions of ideology and identity. This dichotomy is also prevalent in the radicalization process. The idea of 'us and them' is falsely portrayed as part of Islam. Islamists are often seen as 'motivated by a resistance to perceived 'western occupation', they embrace, and indeed perpetuate the dualism of 'western nations' versus Islam and Islamic nations' (Ahmed, 2014: 357). Research by Hoyle, Bradford, and Frenett (2015) revealed how young females, who have joined ISIS and seek to recruit others, promote this binary as justification for planning and engaging in violent attacks against non-Muslims. Islamists politicize religion and portray terrorism as a justified response to perceived national and international injustices. However, there is an overwhelming number of events which do substantiate such claims. As Gerges (2007) states, the Danish cartoons, US support of Israel and the invasion of Iraq create the perception that there is a crusade against the Muslim world. One can also note the prevalence of states as the core instigators in these events. The idea of 'fighting occupation' is a powerful one, and one that bin Laden exploited when the United States had its military bases in Saudi Arabia (where the two most holy Islamic sites, Mecca and Medina, are located) (Milne, 2009). Pape (2003) emphasizes that every single suicide attack campaign between 1980 and 2001 was aimed at regaining its community's sovereignty by trying to force the withdrawal of foreign military intervention. Academics have also explored how the word 'war' sustains the binary with Islamists highlighting how such measures constitute a crusade and a 'war' that must be defeated through acts of terrorism (Bergen, 2006; Wright, 2015). As Silke (2010: 4) argues, 'successful terrorist campaigns' enter 'a blame phase where all parties attempt to place the responsibility for *all* atrocities at the feet of the other'.

In the 'war on terror' states use, and arguably exploit, universal principles of freedom, justice, democracy and human rights to legitimize the introduction of counter-terrorism measures to preserve these principles. The introduction of these measures, measures which erode these very principles, creates a self-defeating 'war on terror' because it perpetuates and institutionalizes, as a form of state control, all the variables, such as injustice and powerlessness, which are known to facilitate terrorism. Such state interventions fuel terrorism because, as Cronin (2009) notes, terrorism is a weapon of the weak and powerless; by oppressing individuals and giving them no chance to correct the perceived injustices, states force considerable weakness onto them which leads to asymmetric acts of revenge or self-help justice. This stark imbalance of power fuels perceptions of injustice, with terrorist groups radicalizing vulnerable individuals into believing that acts of terrorism are the only way to restore some form of equality and gain even a bit of power. Injustice combines personal life experiences with historical, political and/or religious events, and these induce not only moral outrage but also a sense of personal outrage (Meloy, Roshdi, Glaz-Ocik, & Hoffmann, 2015). As an interviewee said during research conducted by Post et al. (2003: 179), with 35 Middle Eastern terrorists incarcerated in Israeli and Palestinian prisons, 'you have to understand that armed attacks are an integral part of the organization's struggle against the Zionist occupier. There is no other way to redeem the land of Palestine and expel the occupier'. Acts of terrorism are therefore used to redress grievances and injustices.

The 'war on terror' has evolved in its ability to cause human suffering. The threat of terrorism now intersects with the catastrophic humanitarian crisis in Syria, intra-state conflict in Iraq, Afghanistan and Syria, and the growing ability of the ISIS to inflict harm. The UK government has argued that visits to countries including Pakistan, Palestine and Afghanistan have contributed to the radicalization of British Muslims (HM Government, 2014; House of Commons, 2012; Security Service, 2014). However, as Harding (2014) points out, many individuals visited these countries on humanitarian grounds. Within the 'war on terror' states have engaged in invasions and they have not only violated their responsibility in IHRL and IHL in invading these states but also left these countries suffering immense humanitarian crisis and in a state of political instability.

The 'war on terror' is real; it impacts emotions and perceptions and fuels human suffering in invaded countries. The various mechanisms of control and prevention introduced and sustained by states as part of the 'war on terror' have had implications for understandings of identity, with the demonization of Islamic identity being prevalent at both the national level and the international level. The transitional nature of such marginalization, criminalization and otherization has impacted British Muslims belonging to the Ummah, with research finding that prior to joining extremist groups, recruits 'had a very strong connection to other Muslims across the globe' (Silke, 2008: 110). As previously stated, personal and political grievances have an enormous capacity to fuel powerlessness, which can positively facilitate radicalization and the fusion of one's identity with that of the collective group identity (Post et al., 2003; Speckhard & Akhmedova, 2005). Similarly, research by Hamm and Spaaij (2015) on 98 US lone-wolf terrorists found that the subjects began with a personal and political grievance, which then led to an affinity with an extremist group. These findings mirror those of the study by Speckhard and Akhmedova (2005), where an affiliation with an extremist group followed experiences of trauma. Trauma and grievances therefore impact identity and although religious identity is a powerful social identity, anchored within a sacred and eternal worldview, thus offering unity and empowerment, in some cases the search for this sacred empowering identity can lead individuals to groups that advocate violent expressions of religious identity (Beit-Hallahmi, 2015; Ysseldyk, Matheson, & Anisman, 2010). This sense of responsibility and strong identification is exploited by extremists, who, as Lemu (2016: 46) suggests, place the burden of alleviating suffering onto Muslims through incorporating two questions into their narrative,

> 1. can a true Muslim choose to do nothing after witnessing all the injustice taking place against Islam and Muslims—discrimination, Islamophobia, violence, misery, humiliation, suffering, human rights abuses, etc.? 2. What will your response be to the suffering of innocent Muslims and the attack on Islam—if indeed you have faith—especially when no peaceful solutions are practical or realistic.

These questions are very powerful and challenge individuals' sense of responsibility and their faith. Within this context and considering how trauma, injustice, powerlessness, suffering, human rights abuse and so on impact radicalization, one must ask the extent to which states have impacted these realities and processes within the 'war on terror'?

Of particular interest is how in the 'war on terror' states appeal to individuals' sense of morality in wanting to introduce measures which protect and keep sacred our universalistic principles of freedom, justice, democracy, human rights and so on. Yet, when this morality impacts individuals' sense of obligation and duty to ease the trauma and grievances which arise through a destruction of the values of freedom, justice, democracy, human rights and so on, there is an ignorance of how powerful this impact can be and, indeed, the strong motivations to take actions to preserve these values. It could then be argued that not only discourses of identity, perceptions and beliefs but also concepts of morality, duty and obligation have been restricted in the 'war on terror'. Whereas individuals are encouraged to exercise these values against otherized groups, the very expression of these concepts, when the instigator is the state, as already stated in relation to the official narrative, has been constructed as symbolizing radicalization.

Morality can also be infused with religious doctrines forming a comprehensive guide which covers, amongst other things, the purpose of one's life, and the very meaning attached to one's existence (Bhatia, 2000). As Colvard (2002: 2) argues when writing about terrorists,

> people who are willing to use violence in the service of a political idea are usually rather ordinary human beings … not devils or psychopaths but people who may base their actions on morality, commitment, and group loyalty, which in other circumstances we would consider admirable.

It is possible to argue that where individuals witness the suffering of others, it impacts their beliefs in a just world (Correia, Vala, & Aguiar, 2001). In the presence of a reality where fundamental values are being eroded, violated and diminished, individuals may feel compelled to commit acts of violence in a bid to restore their belief in a just world.

From the perspective of those that resort to violence, violence is about acting according to their humanity, a humanity whereby acts of self-sacrifice and violence are far less destructive than the violence being inflicted by states. Research by Holt (2010a, 2010b, 2015) on Palestinian women that have committed failed terrorist attacks and the families of those that have successfully committed suicide terrorist attacks revealed that the perpetrators of these attacks conceptualized the violence as acts of sacrifice, and acts of empowerment to counter living under oppressive conditions. Similarly, the parochial altruism hypothesis, which stipulates that religious terrorists engage in violence out of moral obligations to the in-group rather than cost-benefit analysis, has empirical support (Sheikh et al., 2014). Concepts of sacrifice and moral obligation are very powerful and intersect with values. As previously explained, terrorist groups are very creative in formulating and manipulating ideologies, perceptions, beliefs and religion to promote violence and terrorism. They are also able to exploit both individuals' morality and the very characteristics of the 'war on terror', such as the 'war on terror' as being a war on Islam, the death of children and the infliction of a total loss of life onto whole populations. It could therefore be argued that by simply recognizing the conditions that give rise to terrorism, the destruction of universal values and the consequences of harmful state practices in the 'war on terror', they adopt a realist perspective of the 'war on terror' and one which allows them to remain successful in continuing to recruit individuals and carry out acts of terrorism.

The implications of the 'war on terror' on duty, morality, humanity and so on have made political Islam increasingly relevant. However, one can differentiate between different interpretations of Islam and their understandings of these concepts. For example, Alexiev (2004) compares Sufism and Wahhabism stating that Sufism is striving for personal spiritual purification, while Wahhabism represents the struggle for the worldwide victory of Islam. Therefore, Wahhabism is more outward looking, thereby making it possible for Wahhabism to have relevance to the geopolitical landscape, whereas Sufism is more inward looking. In a world where injustices and suffering exist, Wahhabism is more likely to be portrayed as the only viable solution by Islamists. Wahhabis adhere to takfiri, which 'refers to radicalized Muslims who feel that it is a religious and moral obligation to wage jihad against kafir or non-believers' (Githens-Mazer, 2010: 5). In a project by the Singapore Religious Rehabilitation Project (RRP), which involved 500 interviews with jihadist detainees and their families, the researchers noted that researchers noted that several terms had two major interpretations that of al-Qaeda and/or its followers and a more classical, mainstream interpretation of the concept. The themes of jihad[1]—Bayat, Darul Islam, Ummah, Takfir, Shaheed[2] and Al-Wala Wal Bara[3]—demonstrate the different interpretations within Islam and how terrorist groups manipulate Islam to justify violence and terrorism.

Islamist terrorists often advocate a return to an earlier version of Islam. As Ashour (2009) states, Salafism comes from the word salaf (predecessors or ancestors) and is based on the ideology of the Sahaba (companions of Muhammad), the first three generations of Muslims who are constructed as practicing pure Islam. The construction of Salafism as the authentic form of Islam has meant that different understandings of Islam, like mystical Islam (Sufism) or Shi'ite Islam, have been portrayed as being illegitimate. Salafism insists on the individual's right to interpret religious texts, like the Qur'an and the hadith for himself or herself through the practice of ijtihad (independent reasoning) (Roy, 1994), and this has contributed to the text being misinterpreted and manipulated for personal gain. However, although Salafism, as with other ideologies, is not monolithic, there are some core features which exist across most interpretations of Salafism. First, as already mentioned, Salafism advocates the restoration of the 'true' Islam. Second, all interpretations demonstrate the

---

[1] Jihad or Struggle (al-Qaeda's view) was war according to al-Qaeda's perspective, with armed jihad being the highest form of jihad, in contrast to Islamic scholars who saw the concept as meaning the 'striving for excellence', which included the jihad for goodness (al khair), human development, prosperity, education, family, friendship and nation-building' and the jihad 'against evil (asy-syarr), one's inner self, and intrusions upon one's laziness, stupidity, hatred and arrogance' (Quiggin, 2009: 21).

[2] Shaheed or Istishhad, according to al-Qaeda's view, advocates becoming 'a shaheed or 'martyr' by the act of suicide bombing. They believe that they will be rewarded in heaven for this action'. In contrast, Islamic scholars' view is that 'Suicide is an act that is strongly forbidden in the Qur'an and the Haddith. Allah has granted you a body. Only Allah can decide when the body will be taken back' (Quiggin, 2009: 22).

[3] Al-Wala' Wal Bara (al-Qaeda's view) 'fosters an atmosphere of "us versus them". Al-Wala means "those to whom they are loyal" or simply, "their friends". *Al-Bara* refers to those whom they hate or their enemies'. According to Islamic Scholars' view, 'there is not, nor should there be, an "us versus them" mentality in either Islam or in humanity. All human beings are creatures of God and we therefore must show respect to each other. This implies a multi-racial, multi-religious society. Islam must be seen as a *Rahmah* (Blessing) to the Universe' (Quiggin, 2009: 22).

importance of the hadith as demonstrating how true Islam should inform individuals' lives (Wiktorowicz, 2006). By virtue of religion being held as the only legitimate source of power and governance, other forms of governance, such as democracy, are dismissed. Therefore, the perceived export of democracy to Islamic countries is viewed as promoting ideologies that run contrary to Islam and therefore threaten Islam. This gives way to the third common feature, the justification of engaging in a jihad against perceived and constructed aggressors, with Salafis believing that loyalty should only be demonstrated to Muslims, and there should be minimal contact and interaction with non-Muslims (Husain, 2011). According to Wiktorowicz's (2006) work on post-9/11 Salafism, the Saudi regime consists of Salafi purists who not only advocate a very narrow and restrictive interpretation of Islam but also globally disperse these ideas. It is therefore possible to comprehend how, given the aim of the regime to spread Islam and the resources and finances dedicated to this, a Salafi purist version has increasingly become the most dominant version of Islam. Salafism is therefore a politicized version of Islam, with Chap. 6 demonstrating how the status of Saudi Arabia as a state allows it to ensure the growth of Salafism through exporting Salafism and criminalizing more moderate schools of Islamic thought.

One can note how geo-politics and religion inform different forms of terrorism. Anders Breivik killed 77 individuals in Norway in 2011. Breivik saw himself as a crusader fighting for Christendom against the growing Islamization of Europe and the 'cultural Marxism' that allowed Islam to expand over Europe (Pantucci, 2011). The use of violence therefore continues to transcend religions and as Rehman (2007: 836) notes,

> religious intolerance and terrorism have been the great predisposing factors of history. Within the texts of religious scriptures, various forms of torture and genocide are sanctioned. In that sense, Islam, as an instrument of exploitation is no different from other religions and philosophies.

Empirical research on religious interpretation and terrorism revealed that people who believe God sanctions violence are more likely to behave aggressively and use violence (Bushman, Ridge, Das, Key, & Busath, 2007). ISIS also demonstrate this through manipulating religious text to legitimize violence and this has positively facilitated the ability of ISIS to recruit members (Hassan, 2015). Although Chap. 6 demonstrates the direct use of religion by Saudi Arabia to commit violence and human rights abuses, it could be argued that the ideology of universalism, humanity and liberalism is similarly exploited by states to legitimize the suffering of innocent individuals, and to influence political action. Therefore, within the 'war on terror', just as terrorists exploit religious ideology to influence political action via violence, states use religion and ideologies of universalism, humanity and liberalism to legitimize the use of violence to influence the geo-political landscape. The purpose of abandoning power relations is that it carves open a space where actions, ideologies and impacts are assessed based on what they represent and not what we are taught and socialized to believe they represent. There is no difference between states using universalism to justify state crime and violence and terrorists exploiting religion to justify terrorism and violence.

This chapter has discussed the micro-individual-emotional level and the variables within this level that facilitate radicalization. Many of these variables exist and permeate through forms of mechanisms which involve state power. The following chapters explore state practices and state crimes within the 'war on terror' and relate these practices to the factors discussed above. And through exploring how state practices and state crimes can facilitate terrorism, the book uncovers a range of state-produced factors which positively impact radicalization. A perspective which considers the constitutive relationship between state harms and terrorism, as this book does, opens the possibility of considering how these state harms could be decreased and how individuals could be guided towards responding to them, and the other factors associated with radicalization in non-violent ways. The orthodox conceptualization of the 'war on terror' 'terrorism–state response' nexus has huge implications for not only omitting understandings of how state behaviours facilitate terrorism, but also through neglecting this, the impact of state practices and state crimes on individuals' emotions, perceptions, identities, morals and so on is also dismissed. Such an imposed and reductionist perspective creates a false reality of the factors which influence radicalization, and through doing so it neglects some of the key factors which should also be the focus of counter-terrorism strategies and academic scrutiny of the 'war on terror'. Until all factors which influence radicalization are recognized, it will not be possible to redirect individuals away from this process. And until academics include how state power permeates with these factors and/or contributes to the existence of new factors, it could be argued that academia constitutes yet another vessel through which state harm is made invisible and the voices of those that are radicalized is silenced.

References

Abdo, G. (2006). *Mecca and Main Street: Muslim Life in America After 9/11*. Oxford: Oxford University Press.

Ahmed, S. (2014). Constitutive Criminology and the 'War on Terror'. *Critical Criminology, 22*(3), 357–371.

Ahmed, S. (2015). The Emotionalization of 'War on Terror': Counter-Terrorism, Fear, Risk, Insecurity and Helplessness. *Criminology and Criminal Justice, 15*(5), 545–560.

Ahmed, S. (2016). Citizenship, Belonging and Attachment in the 'War on Terror'. *Critical Criminology, 24*(1), 111–125.

Alexiev, A. (2004, March). *Understanding Sufism and Its Potential Role in US Policy*. Nixon Centre Conference Report. Retrieved from http://www.islamawareness.net/Sufism/sufism_us_policy.pdf

Allen, C. E. (2007). *Threat of Islamic Radicalization to the Homeland*. Testimony before the U.S. Senate Committee on Homeland Security and Government Affairs. Retrieved March 14, 2018, from http://www.investigativeproject.org/documents/testimony/270.pdf

Ashour, O. (2009). *The De-Radicalization of Jihadists: Transforming Armed Islamist Movements*. New York: Routledge.

Beck, U. (2006). *The Cosmopolitan Vision*. Cambridge: Polity Press.

Beit-Hallahmi, B. (2015). *Psychological Perspectives on Religion and Religiosity*. East Sussex: Routledge.

Bergen, P. L. (2006). *The Osama bin Laden I know: An Oral History of Al Qaeda's Leader*. New York: Free Press.

Bhatia, S. (2000). Can We Return to the Concept of Duty in a Culture of Rights? Implications for Morality and Identity. *Culture & Psychology, 6*(3), 303–316.

Bhui, K., Warfa, N., & Jones, E. (2014). Is Violent Radicalisation Associated with Poverty, Migration, Poor Self-Reported Health and Common Mental Disorders? *PLoS ONE, 9*(3), e90718. https://doi.org/10.1371/journal.pone.0090718

Blaker, L. (2015). The Islamic State's Use of Online Social Media. *Military Cyber Affairs, 1*(*1*), 1–9.

Boyns, D., & Ballard, J. D. (2004). Developing a Sociological Theory for the Empirical Understanding of Terrorism. *The American Sociologist, 35*(2), 5–25.

Bushman, B., Ridge, R. D., Das, E., Key, C. W., & Busath, G. L. (2007). When God Sanctions Killing: Effect of Scriptural Violence on Aggression. *Psychological Science, 18*(3), 204–207.

Colvard, K. (2002). What We Already Know About Terrorism: Violent Challenges to the State and State Response. *Harry Frank Guggenheim Review, 1*(*1*), 1–5.

Correia, I., Vala, J., & Aguiar, P. (2001). The Effects of Belief in a Just World and Victim's Innocence on Secondary Victimization, Judgements of Justice and Deservingness. *Social Justice Research, 14*(3), 327–342.

Crenshaw, M. (1992). How Terrorists Think: What Psychology Can Contribute To Understanding Terrorism. In L. Howard (Ed.), *Terrorism: Roots, Impact, Responses* (pp. 71–80). London: Praeger.

Cronin, A. (2009). *How Terrorism Ends: Understanding the Decline and Demise of Terrorist Campaigns*. Princeton, NJ: Princeton University Press.

De la Corte, L. (2007). Explaining Terrorism: A Psychosocial Approach. *Perspectives on Terrorism*. Retrieved March 14, 2018, from http://www.terrorismanalysts.com/pt/index.php/pot/article/view/8/html

Fischer, P., & Ai, A. L. (2008). International Terrorism and Mental Health: Recent Research and Future Directions. *Journal of Interpersonal Violence, 23*(3), 339–361.

Gerges, F. A. (2007). *Journey of the Jihadist: Inside Muslim Militancy*. London: Harcourt.

Githens-Mazer. (2010). *Rethinking the Causal Concept of Islamic Radicalisation* (Working Paper). The Committee on Concepts and Methods. Retrieved October 21, 2016, from http://www.concepts-methods.org/Files/WorkingPaper/PC%2042%20Githens-Mazer.pdf

Gould, E., & Esteban, F. K. (2016). The Long-Run Effect of 9/11: Terrorism, Backlash, and the Assimilation of Muslim Immigrants in the West. *The Economic Journal, 126*(597), 2064–2114.

Hamm, M., & Spaaij, R. (2015). *Lone Wolf Terrorism in America: Using Knowledge of Radicalization Pathways to Forge Prevention Strategies*. Washington, DC: National Institute of Justice.

Harding, N. (2014). British Jihadis in Iraq and Syria: How Should We Deal with Them When They Come Home. *The Independent*. Retrieved May 10, 2018, from http://www.independent.co.uk/news/uk/home-news/british-jihadi-fighters-in-iraq-and-syria-how-should-we-deal-with-them-when-they-come-home-9771290.html

Hassan, H. (2015). The Secret World of Isis Training Camps: Ruled by Sacred Texts and the Sword. *The Guardian*. Retrieved May 10, 2018, from http://www.theguardian.com/world/2015/jan/25/inside-isis-training-camps

Henderson-King, D., Henderson-King, E., Bolea, B., Koches, K., & Kauffman, A. (2004). Seeking Understanding or Sending Bombs: Beliefs as Predictors of Responses to Terrorism. *Peace and Conflict: Journal of Peace Psychology, 10*(1), 67–84.

HM Government. (2014). *CONTEST: The United Kingdom's Strategy for Counter Terrorism*. Annual Report. Retrieved May 10, 2018, from https://www.gov.uk/government/uploads/system/uploads/attachment_data/file/302155/CONTESTannualreport2013.pdf

Holt, M. C. (2010a). The Unlikely Terrorist: Women and Islamic Resistance in Lebanon and the Palestinian Territories. *Critical Studies on Terrorism, 3*(3), 365–382.

Holt, M. C. (2010b). Agents of Defiance and Despair: The Impact of Islamic Resistance on Palestinian Women in the West Bank and Gaza Strip. *Totalitarian Movements and Political Religions, 11*(3–4), 397–415.

Holt, M. C. (2015). Resistance Narratives: Palestinian Women, Islam and Insecurity. In A. A. El-Affendi (Ed.), *Genocidal Nightmares: Narratives of Insecurity and the Logic of Mass Atrocities* (pp. 153–170). London: Bloomsbury Academic.

Horgan, J. (2008). From Profiles to *Pathways* and Roots to Routes: Perspectives from Psychology on Radicalization into Terrorism. *The Annals of the American Academy of Political and Social Science, 618*(1), 80–94.

House of Commons. (2012). *Roots of Violent Radicalisation Nineteenth Report of Session 2010–12*. London: The Stationery Office Limited.

Hoyle, C., Bradford, A., & Frenett, R. (2015). *Becoming Mulan? Female Western Migrants to ISIS*. Institute for Strategic Dialogue. Retrieved October 21, 2016, from http://www.strategicdialogue.org/ISDJ296

Husain, E. (2011). Should Egypt Fear the Rise of Salafis? *The Atlantic*. Retrieved March 22, 2018, from https://www.theatlantic.com/international/archive/2011/12/should-egypt-fear-the-rise-of-the-salafis/249377/
Kundnani, A. (2015). *A Decade Lost: Rethinking Radicalisation and Extremism*. London: Claystone.
Lemu, M. N. (2016). Notes on Religion and Countering Violent Extremism. In H. Abadi (Ed.), *Countering Daesh Propaganda: Action-Oriented Research for Practical Policy Outcomes* (pp. 43–50). Atlanta: The Carter Center.
Martin, T. (2014). Governing an Unknowable Future: The Politics of Britain's Prevent Policy. *Critical Studies on Terrorism, 7*(1), 62–78.
McCauley, C., & Moskalenko, S. (2012). Recent US Thinking About Terrorism and Counterterrorism. *Terrorism and Political Violence, 22*(4), 224–245.
Meloy, J. R., Roshdi, K., Glaz-Ocik, J., & Hoffmann, J. (2015). Investigating the Individual Terrorist in Europe. *Journal of Threat Assessment and Management, 2*(3–4), 140–152.
Milne, S. (2009). *Terrorism and Counter-Terrorism: Ethics and Liberal Democracy*. Oxford: Blackwell Publishers.
Mythen, G., Walklate, S., & Khan, F. (2009). 'I'm a Muslim, But I'm Not a Terrorist': Victimisation, Risky Identities and the Performance of Safety. *The British Journal of Criminology, 49*(6), 736–754.
Pantazis, S., & Pemberton, S. (2009). From the 'Old' to the 'New' Suspect Community: Examining the Impacts of Recent UK Counter-Terrorism Legislation. *The British Journal of Criminology, 49*(5), 646–666.
Pantucci, R. (2011). What Have We Learned About Lone Wolves from Anders Behring Breivik? *Perspectives on Terrorism, 5*(5–6), 27–42.
Pape, R. (2003). The Strategic Logic of Suicide Terrorism. *American Political Science Review, 97*(3), 343–361.
Post, J. M. (1984). Notes on a Psychodynamic Theory of Terrorist Behavior. *Terrorism, 7*(2), 241–256.
Post, J. M., & Sheffer, G. (2007). The Risk of Radicalization and Terrorism in U.S. Muslim Communities. *The Brown Journal of World Affairs, 13*(2), 101–112.
Post, J. M., Sprinzak, E., & Denny, L. (2003). The Terrorists in Their Own Words: Interviews with 35 Incarcerated Middle Eastern Terrorists. *Terrorism and Political Violence, 15*(1), 171–184.
Prevent Strategy. (2011). *Prevent Strategy*. London: The Stationery Office Limited.
Quiggin, T. (2009). Understanding al-Qaeda's Ideology for Counter Narrative Work. *Perspectives on Terrorism, 3*(2), 18–24.

Rasool, E. (2016). Preventing the Synapse: Transmission of Daesh Religious Signals in Search of Receivers. In H. Abadi (Ed.), *Countering Daesh Propaganda: Action-Oriented Research for Practical Policy Outcomes* (pp. 38–42). Atlanta: The Carter Center.

Rehman, J. (2007). Islam, "War on Terror" and the Future of Muslim Minorities in the United Kingdom: Dilemmas of Multiculturalism in the Aftermath of the London Bombings. *Human Rights Quarterly, 29*, 831–878.

Roy, O. (1994). *The Failure of Political Islam*. Cambridge: Harvard University Press.

Ruby, C. L. (2002). Are Terrorists Mentally Deranged? *Analyses of Social Issues and Public Policy, 2*(1), 15–26.

Security Service. (2014). *Foreign Fighters*. Retrieved May 1, 2018, from https://www.mi5.gov.uk/home/the-threats/terrorism/international-terrorism/international-terrorism-and-the-uk/foreign-fighters.html

Shaw, E. D. (1986). Political Terrorists: Dangers of Diagnosis and an Alternative to the Psychopathology Model. *International Journal of Law and Psychiatry, 8*(3), 359–368.

Sheikh, H., Atran, S., Ginges, J., Wilson, L., Obeid, N., & Davis, R. (2014). The Devoted Actor as Parochial Altruist: Sectarian Morality, Identity Fusion, and Support for Costly Sacrifices. *Cliodynamics, 5*, 23–40.

Silke, A. (2008). Holy Warriors: Exploring the Psychological Process of Jihadi Radicalization. *European Journal of Criminology, 5*(1), 99–123.

Silke, A. (2010). The Psychology of Counter-Terrorism: Critical Issues and Challenges. In A. Silke (Ed.), *The Psychology of Counter Terrorism* (pp. 1–18). Routledge. Retrieved from https://www.dawsonera.com/readonline/9780203840269

Speckhard, A., & Akhmedova, K. (2005). Talking to Terrorists. *The Journal of Psychohistory, 33*(2), 125–156.

Statewatch. (2007). *The UK Police Terrorism Arrest Statistics (Excluding Northern Ireland) from 11 September 2001–31 March 2007*. Retrieved May 1, 2018, from http://www.statewatch.org/news/2007/jul/05uk-terr-arrests.htm

Sutton, R. (2015). *Preventing Prevent? Challenges to Counter-Radicalisation Policy on Campus*. London: The Henry Jackson Society. Retrieved May 1, 2018, from http://henryjacksonsociety.org/wp-content/uploads/2015/10/Preventing-Prevent_webversion3.pdf

Vidino, L., & Brandon, J. (2012). *Countering Radicalization in Europe*. London: The International Centre for the Study of Radicalization and Political Violence (ICSR). Retrieved May 1, 2018, from http://icsr.info/wp-content/uploads/2012/12/ICSR-Report-Countering-Radicalization-in-Europe.pdf

Walklate, S., & Mythen, G. (2008). How Scared Are We? *The British Journal of Criminology, 48*, 209–225.

Weenink, A. (2015). Behavioral Problems and Disorders Among Radicals in Police Files. *Perspectives on Terrorism, 9*(2), 17–33.

Wiktorowicz, Q. (2006). Anatomy of the Salafi Movement. *Studies in Conflict and Terrorism, 29*, 207–239.

Wright, J. D. (2015). A Social Identity and Social Power Perspective on Terrorism. *Contemporary Voices: St Andrews Journal of International Relations, 6*(3), 76–83.

Ysseldyk, R., Matheson, K., & Anisman, H. (2010). Religiosity as Identity: Toward an Understanding of Religion from a Social Identity Perspective. *Personality and Social Psychology Review, 14*(1), 60–71.

Ysseldyk, R., Matheson, K., & Anisman, H. (2011). Coping with Identity Threat: The Role of Religious Orientation and Implications for Emotions and Action Intentions. *Psychology of Religion and Spirituality, 3*(2), 132–148.

3

The Emergence of the 'War on Terror'

This chapter introduces the 'war on terror' and discusses the ways in which the terms 'terrorism' and 'state crime' have been conceptualized and manufactured in the 'war on terror'. This chapter explores the construction of the 'war on terror' discourse, and how language was used to legitimize the introduction of new counter-terrorism legislation and the invasions of Afghanistan and Iraq.

As the heritage of social constructionism demonstrates, human agents use language to construct reality; language shapes everything we know, believe and understand (Berger & Luckmann, 1966; Schutz, 1967). It can lead to the expression of our humanity, love and compassion, and it can also form the motivation that provides the impetus for mass murder and denies others even a modicum of humanity. History has demonstrated how the discourses associated with identities have led some groups to be constructed as mere commodities, born to assist others in their quest for wealth and assumed 'superiority', thereby justifying the shackling of their physical shell and their inner spirit and psyche. Words, language and discourses create and maintain power, and in doing so, they represent an ideological construction that leads to normative discourses which render invisible the purposeful manipulation of reality in

S. Ahmed, *The 'War on Terror', State Crime & Radicalization*, Palgrave Studies in Risk, Crime and Society, https://doi.org/10.1007/978-3-030-40138-2_3

producing those very discourses. It therefore follows that one must consider the construction, and thus, the ontological reality which influenced and shaped the normative and populist understandings of terrorism and the 'war on terror'. Although the act of terrorism is a social construction, so too is the application of this label to an act and form of behaviour. An act becomes an 'act of terrorism' through being labelled an 'act of terrorism', and the greatest power for the attribution of this label resides with states. Acts of terrorism and state responses to these acts are the product of careful self-fulfilling ideological construction and manipulation. State responses to terrorism are also dependent on securing credibility and legitimacy for counter-terrorism responses (Anderson, 2003; Gambari, 2006; Leffler, 2004; Nye, 2002; Rees & Aldrich, 2005).

The terrorist attacks of 9/11 were unique in the political response they provoked. This response has received much attention; academics have discussed the nature of this response in relation to civil liberties, the construction of terrorism, international wars and so on (Ahmed, 2015, 2016; De Goede, 2008; Gearty, 2005; Grabosky, 2008; Klausen, 2009; Stohl, 2008). However, there has been a scarcity in exploring this response through the lens of state crime and therefore a perspective which permits an analysis of state responses according to international law, domestic law, conventions, protocols, social harm and citizens' perceptions. The first section of this chapter considers how the ideological construction of 9/11 and the political and legal response to 9/11 facilitated the existence of state crime in the 'war on terror'. The second half of this chapter critically explores the binary construction of terrorism and state crime in the 'war on terror', the various forms of state crime that have taken place in the 'war on terror' and how these have facilitated radicalization and therefore terrorism.

The date 9/11 must be understood in relation to the end of the Cold War, the rise of religious and political Islam (Crockatt, 2003), as well as, amongst other things, the construction of fear, weapons of mass destruction, arms deals, oil and foreign policy and geo-political bias. The events of September 11th had a profound impact on the world and its understanding of threat, risk, violence and safety. As Oliverio and Lauderdale (2005: 160) state,

> the extraordinary drama of watching two of the most prominent pillars of the global economy be destroyed in the blink of an eye and with the 'simplest' of methods'… 'left many people horrified and resolute that 'terrorism' must cease to exist.

The global response to the attacks was vital in constructing the boundaries which framed interpretations and understandings of the terrorist attacks. The United States and the United Kingdom, amongst other states, conceptualized the response to the terrorist attacks as a war. In a television interview on 16 September 2001, British Prime Minister Tony Blair stated: 'the fact is that we are at war with terrorism … it is a war, if you like, between the civilised world and fanaticism' (Blair, 2001 cited McInnes, 2003). War became synonymous with terrorism in a discourse which proclaimed that fanatics could be stopped only through military warfare. However, as Ruggiero (2007: 214) states, this warfare approach involved a 'coalition of governments attacking a coalition of peoples'. It gave 'those who want to invade and destroy "carte blanche" to do as they wish' (Ruggiero, 2007: 212). The emerging 'war on terror' discourse articulated an enemy identifiable by their (racial) appearance and, through doing so, it produced a racist global discourse (Mutimer, 2007). The 'war on terror' discourse, with its emphasis on military warfare, was important not only in defining the terrorist attacks but also in contouring the boundaries of acceptable state responses.

However, although states manufacture legitimacy in relation to expanding social control and justifying the actions that are most likely to be perceived as unwanted, unnecessary and draconian by the civilian population, there is another level that can serve to carve open the space of creating legitimacy, and that is the super macro-universal level. It was the super macro-universal level that sketched the territory of state responses to 9/11. As stated in the introduction, this book seeks to examine the 'war on terror' through a grounded perspective, and this necessitates that the super macro-universal level should also be considered. It could be argued that the super macro-universal level has predominantly been conceptualized as responding to humanitarian events. This conceptualization has rendered invisible the power of institutions such as the UN, in relation to facilitating state actions that violate the mechanisms—IHRL and IHR, conventions, and protocols—which govern state practices. By virtue of such an omission, the histories, dangers and mass sufferings which led to these very safeguards are also neglected, as are the consequences of violations of these regulatory mechanisms. These mechanisms were created and exist to protect civilians from the most devastating and dehumanizing forms of state practice. Therefore, their exercise and use can either saves millions of individuals or their lack of enforcement can lead to the death of millions (as Chap. 5 discusses in relation to Somalia, Kosovo, Rwanda and Bosnia). The failure of action at this level has been acknowledged, both politically and academically as leading to millions of individuals dying, it has even been demonstrated how states have avoided interventions through choosing not to use words such as 'genocide' (Stanton, 2007). This reality is not merely based on the construction of legitimacy to do nothing through denying the existence of genocide, but also on dismissing the suffering that influenced the creation of IHRL and IHR, conventions, and protocols. In dismissing these safeguards, in an instance the words and events which led to the creation of the UDHR and subsequent IHRL, IHR, conventions and protocols lose their meaning. Yet these words denote and symbolize individuals' common humanity, the rights of all women and men, notions which over time have formed part of individuals' innate understanding of justice, so that justice can be a force that provides commonality and unites humanity. One only needs to read the UDHR to remember the vast suffering which led to its creation, and the safety, compassion and humanity present in the words. Thus, in recognizing the super macro-universal level and its universal standard of human rights as a level that shapes and influences state actions, this book maintains an acute awareness of the vast harms and dangers which occur when these safeguards are ignored. Deviations for these safeguards lead to what this book defines as macro-national-level inter- and intra-state crime facilitated terrorism and meso-societal level facilitated terrorism, as this chapter now explores.

The UN facilitated the existence of state crimes within the 'war on terror' through providing the geo-political conditions in which these state crimes could take place. On 28 September 2001, the Security Council of the United Nations adopted resolution 1373. The resolution called on states to work together to suppress terrorist attacks, fully implement the conventions relating to terrorism, and criminalize terrorism through creating domestic laws and punishments (Happold, 2003; Moeckli, 2008; Turner, 2016). The extent to which the UN, via resolution 1373, could be conceptualized as being the sole facilitator of state crime in the 'war on terror' is questionable, especially since the resolution merely put a duty onto states and states exercised their own autonomy and discretion in introducing mechanisms to counter terrorism. However, although the autonomy of states cannot be denied (and this book does not seek to suggest the UN as being the sole instigator of state crime within the 'war on terror'), the book does seek to account for the role of resolution 1373 in opening, influencing and shaping the domain for state responses to the 9/11 terrorist attacks. Resolution 1373 constructed the framework and parameters of necessary state responses, and as De Goede (2008) notes, the obligation created by resolution 1373 meant that states were unable to produce responses to terrorism that were based on non-violence. The resolution therefore instantly made it possible for states to deviate from non-violent responses which prioritized human rights and, through doing so, it encouraged and accelerated the existence of counter-terrorism measures which prioritized security, at the expense of human rights.

Resolution 1373 also led to the establishment of the UN's Counter-Terrorism Committee (CTC). The role of the CTC was to monitor the obligations imposed on member states by the Security Council in resolution 1373. Although the CTC could have constituted a mechanism through which potentially dangerous and harmful policies were challenged, instead it represented an avenue through which powerful states could pursue their own interests. As Byrnes (2008: 131) notes, this 'legislative' function by the Council was 'largely driven by the efforts of the US to use the authority of the Council to advance an energetic agenda against terrorism', which included 'pushing a predominantly US/Western agenda and endeavouring to impose it on the rest of the world'. The introduction of the CTC perpetuated the existence of the UN as an expression of geo-political interests that creates and maintains unequal power relations. As Michalowski (2009: 318) states, 'the United Nations as a framework for creating and applying international law, is itself an expression of geo-political interests and unequal power relations'. It represents the 'particular interests of powerful members'.

One can note how the factors which facilitate radicalization at both the individual level and the geo-political Ummah level, as the previous chapter explored, are exacerbated through the existence of differential geo-political power. As this book goes on to explore, the invasions, counter-terrorism measures and discourses produced in the 'war on terror'—the very entities which constitute state crime—are an expression of geo-political power and facilitate the very factors which induce radicalization. Therefore, it is possible to comprehend how via state actions, the super macro-universal level of the international rule of law and universal standard of human rights leads to powerlessness, injustice, grievances and inequality, all factors which positively impact radicalization (Hamm & Spaaij, 2015; Post, Sprinzak, & Denny, 2003; Speckhard & Akhmedova, 2005). It could also be argued that the power vested at the super macro-universal level is inherently based on global inequality because IHRL, IHR, conventions and protocols are not equally enforced and this selective exercise of power means that some states are able to engage in forms of inter-state crime and intra-state crime without consequences and condemnation. As this book demonstrates, although the safeguards that exist on the super macro-universal level should, in theory, protect citizens against self-interest and inequality, in reality the universal level is a sphere which has extended state power in the 'war on terror'. Therefore, rather than accepting and indeed taking for granted the existence of this power at the super macro-universal level, questioning this power and the use of this power helps to demonstrate how the super macro-universal level can exist as a mechanism which facilitates state crimes in the 'war on terror'. It also helps one to question the reality in which state crimes emerged in the 'war on terror' and to recognize how factors, such as geo-political power and inequality, influenced the emergence of these crimes. Therefore, the super macro-universal level can exist as a mechanism which facilitates state crimes in the 'war on terror', and through positively influencing the creation of these state crimes, it impacts and indeed feeds into the radicalization process and, thus, the micro-individual-emotional level.

In terms of deconstructing and exploring the impact of resolution 1373, Scheinin (2005) analysed approximately 640 reports which had been submitted to the CTC by member states under resolution 1373, to consider the role of human rights in the counter-terrorism policies and measures introduced by states. Scheinin (2005) concluded that, when countering terrorism, the CTC had not been clear in its duty to respect human rights. Indeed, some states saw the CTC as encouraging the introduction of counter-terrorism measures, regardless of their implications for human rights. The duty placed on states under resolution 1373 and the lack of oversight provided what Judith Butler (2002) calls the 'frames of terror'. These are constructions of reality which provide moral justification for retaliation. Within this context of what could be conceptualized as 'elite encouragement', the UN utilized its power to place a legal duty onto states to create measures to counter terrorism and punish terrorists. However, it failed to equally and adequately distribute power to restrain and curtail the policies which deviated from established human rights laws. It could therefore be argued that within this context, the US government felt able to invade Afghanistan and Iraq without UN approval. After all, the 'frames of terror' present at the super macro-universal level worked to construct non-human rights complicit state reactions as acceptable. Although these invasions overstepped legal and moral boundaries (Saurette, 2005), no action was taken by the UN which led to the continuation of these invasions. Here a direct link can be made to how the super macro-universal level leads to macro-national level inter-state crime facilitated terrorism, and the consequences of this on meso-societal level state crime facilitated terrorism. As this book demonstrates, the lack of enforcement led to a series of measures being introduced to counter terrorism, including the invasion of Iraq. And within Iraq, state crimes not only occurred, but following the invasion, even though under Article 43 of the Hague Regulations 1907, an occupying power must restore and maintain public order and civil life (Schwenk, 1945), the post-Iraq invasion context included unresolved conflicts, a lack of rule of law and violations of human rights, ethnic, national and religious discrimination, political exclusion, socio-economic marginalization and lack of good governance. These were all factors which, as previously specified, have been recognized by the UN (2018) as being conducive to the spread of terrorism. And these factors also constitute meso-societal level state crimes that facilitate terrorism.

In conjunction with resolution 1373, the UN Security Council also created resolution 1624 (UN, 2005). Resolution 1624 extended the duty of states to prosecute suspected terrorists in their domestic courts and required states to introduce legislation to prevent the incitement and glorification of terrorism (UN, 2005). It is possible to connect the super macro-universal level and the macro-national level because, as is evident later in the chapter, this resolution set the basis for the introduction of various forms of counter-terrorism regulations and laws which constitute intra-state crime. These measures deviated from established human rights laws and due process, and positively impacted the micro-individual-emotional level and, thus, the factors which facilitate radicalization such as perceptions of discrimination, inequality and a lack of human rights.

In 2006 the UN General Assembly adopted the Global Counter-Terrorism Strategy which further institutionalized counter-terrorism within nation-states (UN, 2018). The Global Counter-Terrorism Strategy outlined four pillars to counter terrorism, which included:

1. Addressing the conditions conducive to the spread of terrorism. These conditions were identified as including, but not limited to, prolonged unresolved conflicts, dehumanization of victims of all forms of terrorism, lack of rule of law and violations of human rights, ethnic, national and religious discrimination, political exclusion, socio-economic marginalization, and lack of good governance.
2. Measures to prevent and combat terrorism.
3. Measures to build states' capacity to prevent and combat terrorism and to strengthen the role of the United Nations system in that regard.
4. Measures to ensure respect for human rights for all and the rule of law as the fundamental basis for the fight against terrorism. (UN, 2018)

However, as this book demonstrates, within the 'war on terror' states have contributed to the existence of the conditions which contribute to terrorism and through doing so, they have not only facilitated terrorism but also maintained it. When one thinks of the variables that have been discussed in the previous chapter, and the relationship between these and the state, it starts to become increasingly clear that states have introduced the very mechanisms which impact the micro-individual-emotional level. For example, invasions and domestic counter-terrorism measures have impacted perceptions of inequality, human rights, a lack of belonging and so on. And furthermore, these collectively induce the very conditions identified by the UN as being conducive to terrorism.

The European Union also created a European Counter Terror Policy, which expanded the criminalization of activities related to terrorism such as 'criminalising terrorist support, and asset freezing' (De Goede, 2008: 161). Therefore, on the international level and the European level, international security and national security were given prominence at the expense of human rights. Terrorism was also constructed according to a US/western agenda which amplified the global risk of terrorism to western countries (Lyon, 2007; Mathew, 2008). Through the exercise of power via the UN and the EU, the super macro-universal level of international law and universal human rights became an active agent in the construction of terrorism. It contoured the boundaries of the 'war on terror' and outlined what was deemed necessary for global security. The two UN resolutions (1373 and 1624) placed duties onto states to create new legislation and the lack of oversight into the measures introduced provided the conditions within which state crimes could become a more plausible reality. In assessing the cumulative impact of these resolutions, one must remember the unique power of the UN as an international organization. In design and existence, it is above any nation-state and, through acting as a forum for the global community, it has the consent and the authority of its members to place duties onto states and uphold international laws, treaties, protocols and conventions (McGrew & Held, 2002). By considering the 'war on terror' as opposed to single acts of terrorism, this book reveals the relationship between the super macro-universal level, via the introduction of resolutions and the lack of oversight, and the macro-national level and meso-societal level and radicalization.

Following 9/11 and the introduction of resolution 1373 and resolution 1624, the United Kingdom introduced CONTEST and the four counter-terrorism principles of Prevent, Pursue, Prepare and Protect. The United Kingdom also introduced the Channel programme, which was aimed at disrupting the processes which led individuals to become radicalized. The programme dispersed the duties of preventing and countering terrorism to several institutions, including social workers, schools, colleges and universities, health services, housing officers, and the prison and probation service. These services now had a legal duty to refer vulnerable individuals to the Channel coordinator. Following an assessment by the coordinator, if a person is judged to be at risk of becoming radicalized an intervention may be initiated; or, if they are judged to be already too deeply involved in violent extremism, the police and/or the security services will become directly involved. Although the Channel programme was meant to signify a softer approach to countering terrorism, thereby deviating from the first phase of Prevent, which was acknowledged as leading to religious profiling and radicalizing British Muslims (House of Commons, 2012), it in fact increased institutions' ability to profile and criminalize those 'deemed' to be radicalized and thus increased the possibility of ethnic and religious discrimination (Bonino, 2013; Halliday, 2016; Mythen, Walklate, & Peatfield, 2016; Ragazzi, 2017; Thomas, 2016).

Resolutions 1373 and 1624 and the subsequent introduction of counter-terrorism legislation had vast implications for human rights, with claims of threats, risk and the protection of national security pushing the boundaries of established IHRL and IHL. There is a plethora of legislation which governs state treatment of its citizens, with the super macro-universal level of international law and universal human rights governing against the arbitrary use of state power against individuals, especially where this power takes a discriminatory form. Given the presence of identities in the most grotesque forms of genocide in history, a central focus of IHRL and IHL is the protection from discrimination. More specifically, within the counter-terrorism context this translates into states having an obligation to combat terrorism, whilst respecting existing human rights laws, including the right to non-discrimination under international law (Moeckli, 2008). However, when one considers the measures introduced to prevent and counter terrorism, it becomes evident that these measures increased the likelihood of religious discrimination and ethnic discrimination. They did so on both an individual level and a group level, and as the previous chapter demonstrated, such forms of discrimination positively feed into the radicalization process. And it is the existence of such discrimination that leads individuals to seek out groups who share the discriminated identity, even when these groups have extremist views (Beit-Hallahmi, 2014; Ysseldyk, Matheson, &

Anisman, 2010). It is also through the absence of action when violations of human rights laws occur that the international human rights framework becomes eroded and damaged. This failure to act has the capacity to impact individuals' perceptions of justice and belief in a just world, (again factors which induce radicalization) (Correia, Vala, & Aguiar, 2001; Post et al., 2003) and to create the context whereby extremists can ask Muslims, what they are willing to do in the face of such injustices (Lemu, 2016)?

It could be argued that UN resolutions constructed international security and national security as overriding human rights and due process, and the existence of this hierarchical construction served to legitimize the introduction of mechanisms that prioritized security at the expense of human rights. The counter-terrorism measures introduced were unique in their capacity to quash due process. As Zulaika (2009) points out, the exceptional practices contributed to a self-fulfilling prophecy for the need for extraordinary counter-terrorism measures to counter extraordinary levels of insecurity. The exceptional discourse of the 'war on terror', with its innate manufacture of state vulnerability and insecurity, as a fundamental feature of the 'war on terror' permitted the institutionalization of practices designed to provide security. However, the institutionalization of the 'war on terror' discourse also represented a tremendous step towards aiding state capacities to violate human rights. Various pieces of legislation were introduced and, as this chapter demonstrates, these measures pushed human rights and due process back to the era of pre-legality (Gearty, 2005).

The first piece of legislation, the Anti-Terrorism, Crime and Security Act 2001 (ATCSA), was introduced a few weeks after the 9/11 attacks in the United States. The legislation introduced the indefinite detention of international terrorist suspects. The focus of this legislation on non-UK nationals raised questions regarding the discriminatory nature of this legislation. In particular, it violates Article 14 of the European Convention of Human Rights (ECHR), which includes

> the enjoyment of the rights and freedoms without discrimination on any ground such as sex, race, colour, language, religion, political or other opinion, national or social origin, association with a national minority, property, birth or other status. (ECHR, 1998: 13)

The ATCSA also introduced indefinite detention for suspects which, it could be argued, contravenes Article 3 of the ECHR, 'the prohibition on torture' which states that no one shall be subjected to 'inhumane and degrading treatment and punishment' (ECHR, 1998: 7). Due to the absence of a specified sentence, suspects are left without the security of knowing when they are likely to be released, which could be interpreted as constituting 'inhumane and degrading treatment' (ECHR, 1998: 7). The standard of proof utilized in the legislation is that of 'reasonable suspicion', with this standard determining the use of detention and punishment. The use of reasonable suspicion, as opposed to a fair trial, violates an individual's human right to a fair trial, thus violating Article 6 of the ECHR. The right to a fair trial is the universal standard through which a suspect's innocence or guilt should be established, as stated in Article 10 of the UDHR (Weissbrodt & Hallendorff, 1999). The right to a fair trial is such an absolute right that, under the Fourth Geneva Convention, military personnel have the right to a fair trial; this also includes the right to see the evidence on which the accusation and prosecution are based (Orakhelashvili, 2008).

In December 2004, a special committee of Law Lords concluded that holding foreign nationals without trial breached the European Convention of Human Rights and the Human Rights Act 1998 (The Guardian, 2009). In light of the Law Lords ruling, the United Kingdom derogated from Article 5(1) of the ECHR. In 2004, in *A. v. Secretary of State*, the use of derogation was considered by the House of Lords. The House of Lords concluded that the state's detention provisions were not proportionate to this public emergency, with Lord Hoffman stating, 'the real threat to the life of the nation, in the sense of a people living in accordance with its traditional laws and political values, comes not from terrorism but from laws such as these' (Hoffman, 2004 cited Dyer, White, & Travis, 2004). Although the judgment by Lord Hoffman was an attempt to redress the balance between national security and human rights, the 'war on terror' discourse continued to be exploited to introduce controversial counter-terrorism legislation. One can instantly note how one piece of legislation impacts so many of the variables associated with facilitating radicalization, in inducing injustice, grievances and marginalization. It also impacts UN (2018) identified factors, such as a lack of rule of law, violations of human rights and discrimination. And it clearly goes against the fourth pillar of the UN Global Counter-Terrorism Strategy, which is to guarantee that all measures introduced respect human rights and the rule of law, as the fundamental basis for the fight against terrorism (UN, 2018).

The Prevention of Terrorism Act 2005 (PTA) introduced control orders for UK and non-UK citizens. Under this legislation, suspects were electronically tagged, relocated from their homes, only allowed visitors with the permission of the Home Office and had limited access to means of technology and communication, such as the telephone and internet. These orders are an infringement of Article 5 of the ECHR, an 'individual's right to liberty and security' (ECHR, 1998: 8). A review of the Act by the British Parliamentary Joint Committee on Human Rights (JCHR) concluded that the combination of obligations and restrictions imposed on a suspect could themselves constitute an unlawful deprivation of liberty (JCHR, 2005). Although the orders were issued for 12 months, they could be renewed every 12 months and therefore exist for an indefinite period. The legislation also directly interfered with Article 8(1) of the ECHR, 'an individual's right to a private and family life' (ECHR, 1998: 11). The Act also contravened Article 3 of the ECHR, 'the prohibition on torture' (ECHR, 1998: 7). In 2005, the European Committee for the Prevention of Torture (CPT) interviewed individuals subject to control orders in the United Kingdom. The interviews by the CPT revealed that being subject to a control order left suspects severely depressed, anxious, and experiencing considerable distress with symptoms of post-traumatic stress disorder (CPT, 2005). Amnesty International (2010) noted how, because suspects of control orders have not been charged with an offence, they were not entitled to any of the safeguards afforded to those suspected of a crime. Control orders were therefore found to violate the following ECHR articles:

1. Articles 6(2) under which 'everyone charged with a criminal offence shall be presumed innocent until proved guilty according to law',
2. Article 6(3) everyone charged with a criminal offence has the following minimum rights:

(a) to be informed promptly, in a language which he understands and in detail, of the nature and cause of the accusation against him;
(b) to have adequate time and facilities for the preparation of his defence;
(c) to defend himself in person or through legal assistance of his own choosing or, if he has not sufficient means to pay for legal assistance, to be given it free when the interests of justice so require;
(d) to examine or have examined witnesses against him and to obtain the attendance and examination of witnesses on his behalf under the same conditions as witnesses against him;
(e) to have the free assistance of an interpreter if he cannot understand or speak the language used in court'. (ECHR, 1998: 9–10)

The right to a fair trial, as already stated, is as an absolute right that has existed since the UDHR. It has become one of the fundamental pillars of international law and human rights (Ahmed & Butler, 2006). In doing so, it informs our understanding of justice and a recognition that we are equal to every human and therefore part of the same humanity.

Although the UN asked states to reduce the conditions conducive to terrorism, in the name of security, safety and protection of humanity and universal values, the United Kingdom introduced counter-terrorism measures which violated human rights and the rule of law, conditions specified by the UN as being conducive to terrorism. An interesting interaction between the super macro-universal level and the macro-national level becomes apparent and one can note how, within the 'war on terror' the super macro-universal level of international law and universal human rights exists as a facilitator of IHRL violations. One can also note the conflicting roles of the UN. On the one hand it places a duty on states to create laws and legislation to counter terrorism, but it also positively influences the existence of the very entities that give rise to terrorism. When states facilitate these factors, there is a lack of action. In such a dialectic exchange and use of power, states are increasingly breaking IHRL laws, whilst also creating the conditions which facilitate terrorism, leading to circumstances that make security appear a necessity in the first instance. One can therefore argue that the 'war on terror' has become a self-defeating war. As already noted, it is a war that states portray as being needed to preserve and maintain universal values of human rights, freedom and democracy, and yet states introduce measures which violate these very values. It is such conditions and contradictions that, as Chap. 2 revealed, facilitate radicalization and give validity and a sense of legitimacy to the kind of questions that Lemu (2016) stated, extremists ask. Here one must think that if 'discrimination, Islamophobia, violence, misery, humiliation, suffering, human rights abuses' did not exist, then what possible power could extremists have in asking these questions (Lemu, 2016: 46)? The power and legitimacy for these questions have been formed through the existence of a reality where these entities permeate into an individual's daily lives. As research by Ahmed (2015, 2016) demonstrated, British Muslims believe that counter-terrorism measures are something that they are likely to experience.

The Terrorism Prevention and Investigation Measures Act 2011 abolished control orders and replaced them with Terrorism Prevention and Investigation Measures (TPIMs) (Statutory Instruments, 2011). Under this legislation, suspects can be 'relocated' to another part of the country without their consent, be restricted from entering an area or specific types of places, or from associating with other people and using mobile phones (TPIMA, 2011). However, relocating an individual raises concerns about their 'right to a private and family life', as per Article 8 of the ECHR (ECHR, 1998: 11). Their marginalization could also increase the risk that they will engage or re-engage in terrorism (Liberty, 2011) with social isolation facilitating radicalization (Bhui, Warfa, & Jones, 2014).

In 2014, David Anderson QC, the United Kingdom's Independent Reviewer of anti-terror legislation stated in his report on the TPIM (Terrorism Prevention and Investigation Measures) scheme that there were ten TPIM subjects, of which nine had been transferred from control orders in 2012 (Anderson, 2015). Anderson (2015) concluded that TPIMs should continue, but they should only be used as a last resort, and the standard of proof for involvement in terror activity should be changed from 'reasonable suspicion' to a 'balance of probabilities'. Although TPIMs were meant to be less unlawful than control orders, it has been argued by the Public Bill Committee that

> 'the TPIM regime essentially mirrors the control order system in all of its most offensive elements including:—abrogation of the constitutional

> safeguards which protect the right to a fair trial…' and 'imposition of punitive and potentially unending restrictions on individuals in the absence of criminal due process'. (Liberty, 2011: 3)

The revised TPIMs replaced 'curfews' with an 'overnight residency' and 'relocation' was abolished (Turner, 2016). In 2012, the Protection of Freedom Act was introduced, and it reduced the maximum period of pre-charge detention from 28 to 14 days. However, it also contained a provision whereby the maximum period could be increased to 28 days in response to an unspecified 'urgent' situation that could arise in the future (Legislation.gov.uk, 2012).

The main expansion of state control has occurred via the introduction of counter-terrorism legislation following terrorist attacks. However, in 2015, the growth of ISIS and the construction of the refugee crisis, as providing an avenue through which terrorists could enter the United Kingdom, led to the reform of TPIMs in the Counter Terrorism and Security Act 2015. The Counter Terrorism and Security Act 2015 (CTSA) reintroduced the forced relocation of individuals subject to a TPIM. The Equality and Human Rights Commission and Liberty gave the following assessments of the TPIM regime:

> the proposed TPIMs regime may still fail to comply with Convention rights, in particular the right to liberty and security (Article 5), the right to a fair trial (Article 6), the right to respect for private and family life (Article 8), freedom of expression (Article 10) and prohibition of discrimination (Article 14). (Liberty, 2011)

Therefore, the new legislation carried many of the ECHR violations identified in earlier pieces of counter-terrorism legislation. The standard of proof in TPIMs was also changed to a 'balance of probabilities'. Interestingly, the use of the civil law standard of proof is part of a larger construction legitimizing the lack of rights afforded to suspects under this legislation, such as those guaranteed in Articles 6(2) and 6(3) of the ECHR for suspects in criminal law. The legislation also introduced temporary exclusion orders. A temporary exclusion order can be imposed if the Secretary of State reasonably suspects that an individual is or has been involved in terrorism-related activity. The legislation allows the state to seize an individual's passport and deny them entry into the United Kingdom. These measures contravene the right to freedom of movement and the right to return to one's own country (Joint Committee on Human Rights, 2015). Given the lack of oversight and retribution in infringing established safeguards, it is not surprising that national laws have been introduced which could be labelled as draconian, and actually violate UN General Assembly resolution 60/158 the Protection of Human Rights and Fundamental Freedoms While Countering Terrorism, 2005 (General Assembly, 2006).

In 2016, the Investigatory Powers Act was introduced. The Act contains some of the most sweeping surveillance powers in the EU and threatens to have devastating consequences for privacy and other human rights in the United Kingdom (Amnesty International, 2016). It has also been referred to as the 'Snoopers Charter' because it institutionalizes intrusive surveillance powers, including powers for bulk interception, bulk acquisition, access to bulk personal data sets and bulk equipment interference (hacking) (Burgess, 2017). The Act received criticism from the UN's privacy chief, who warned that the bill violated the right to privacy and ran contrary to the Europe Court of Human Rights jurisprudence (Cannataci, 2018). The final piece of legislation is the Immigration Act 2014, and it is perhaps one of the most controversial pieces of legislation introduced. Under the Act, the Home Secretary can deprive a foreign-born, naturalized British citizen of their sole nationality, even if it renders them stateless. This Act violates the right to life: as present in Article 3 in the UDHR, Article 6 in the International Covenant on Civil and Political Rights (ICCPR) and Article 2(1) of the ECHR, which imposes a 'positive' or 'substantive' obligation on states to protect life (ECHR, 1998).

During the 'war on terror' counter-terrorism legislation has been introduced, which violates many of the laws that exist to protect human rights and even the very foundations of universal human rights, the UDHR. In this respect, a UN Report stated that each limiting measure must pass the test of legality, necessity and proportionality for it to be lawful under IHRL (UN, 2008). Many of the measures discussed above fail this test and when they have been subject to internal scrutiny, they have been judged to be illegitimate and disproportionate (Hoffman, 2004; Liberty, 2011). One must therefore ask, how are British Muslims to perceive these measures and with which evidence, and therefore legitimacy, are they able to counter questions such as those posed by Lemu (2016)? One can therefore observe how the super macro-universal level and its resolutions and lack of action, and the macro-national level and its state crimes, facilitate radicalization, and therefore the variables that form the micro-individual-emotional level.

The role of the UN in the 'war on terror' has been a contradictory one and a dangerous one. For example, UN resolution 1624 placed a duty on member states to adopt measures to prohibit incitement to commit a terrorist act or acts (Ruperez, 2006). The Terrorism Act 2006 introduced into the UK law the offence of encouraging terrorism, which criminalized statements which are likely to be understood as a direct or indirect encouragement of terrorist acts. One clause in the Act was particularly controversial. It provided that among the statements likely to be understood as indirectly encouraging an act of terrorism are those glorifying such acts, at least where members of the public would reasonably infer that they should emulate them (Hare & Weinstein, 2009). Here, one can again witness the transition of power from the super macro-universal level of international law and universal human rights to the state level and trace the link between the duty placed on member states by the UN and the subsequent introduction of new legislation. It then seems surprising that with the UN setting the tone for the geo-political landscape of the 'war on terror' and specifying what exercises of power via legislation this should include, it then reveals the damaging impact of such measures. The United Nations (2008) Protection of Human Rights and Fundamental Freedoms While Countering Terrorism report concluded that although states may prohibit 'incitement' to criminal acts, the line between this and the criminalization of other forms of expression is crossed all too often. UN Secretary-General Ban Ki-Moon considered that 'laws should only allow for the criminal prosecution of direct incitement to terrorism, that is, speech that directly encourages the commission of a crime, is intended to result in criminal action and is likely to result in criminal action' (UN, 2008). On UNESCO World Press Freedom Day in May 2015, four UN experts on freedom of expression stated that '[c]riminal responsibility for expressions relating to terrorism should be limited to those who incite others to terrorism; vague concepts such as "glorifying", "justifying" or "encouraging" terrorism should not be used' (Shepherd, 2017). However, these vague concepts were revealed as being important components of resolution 1624, because as Amnesty International (2017) argues, it was the UN that first highlighted the need for states to criminalize the glorification of terrorism. The duty placed on member states by the UN to create laws clearly specified the need for states to introduce legislation to criminalize, as opposed to being encouraged to introduce policies orientated at reducing incitement without criminalizing. It then follows that the use of a law and order framework makes human rights law violations a greater possibility. This example further demonstrates the interaction between the super macro-universal level encouraging states to introduce legislation, and this legislation impacting the macro-national level, the meso-societal level and facilitating terrorism, because as stated above, even in relation to legislation to criminalize the incitement of terrorism, the UN recognizes that this legislation positively facilitates terrorism (UN, 2008). This could also therefore be conceptualized as a further example of how the 'war on terror' is a self-defeating war, through facilitating the very factors which give rise to terrorism.

As stated earlier, the exercise of state control and the violation of international safeguards must be understood in terms of state power. State power includes the ability to disperse discourses and create and shape those discourses. It also includes the ability to institutionalize discourses, through creating policies and laws which then govern society. In contrast, the scope of harm identified by the UN is governed by its ability to impose duties onto member states, which then contour the terrain within which counter-terrorism legislation emerges and dictates the criteria of what constitutes acceptable measures and unacceptable measures. The void of international safeguards leads to states increasing in power via the institutionalization of social control mechanisms. The growth of state power is worrying, especially when one considers the crimes and suffering such safeguards were designed to eliminate. The manipulation of realities also assists states in introducing controversial counter-terrorism measures, and derogation represents one of the ways in which states can possibly manipulate events and their associated risk and threat to deviate from their legal obligations to citizens. There are situations which allow for derogation from the rights as set out in ECHR and the ICCPR. Article 15(1) of the ECHR reads:

> In time of war or other public emergency threatening the life of the nation any High Contracting Party may take measures derogating from its obligations under this Convention to the extent strictly required by the exigencies of the situation, provided that such measures are not inconsistent with its other obligations under international law. (ECHR, 1998: 13)

Similarly, Article 4(1) ICCPR reads:

> In time of public emergency which threatens the life of the nation and the existence of which is officially proclaimed, the States Parties to the present Covenant may take measures derogating from their obligations under the present Covenant to the extent strictly required by the exigencies of the situation, provided that such measures are not inconsistent with their other obligations under international law and do not involve discrimination solely on the ground of race, colour, sex, language, religion or social origin. (UNHR, 1966: 3)

Both articles cite the need for measures conceptualized as 'emergency measures' to still conform to IHRL and IHL, and the need for measures to be necessary because as the UN (2008) has highlighted, measures that do not meet the test of necessity challenge the international rule of law and universal human rights.

Terrorism has been, as this book explores, constructed as constituting an emergency, thereby justifying the introduction and use of 'enhanced' emergency powers (Amnesty International, 2017). The Civil Contingencies Act 2004 reflects what the state constructs as an emergency and therefore the circumstances under which it deems it legitimate to abandon human rights. The Act defines an emergency as:

> (a) an event or situation which threatens serious damage to human welfare in a place in the United Kingdom, (b) an event or situation which threatens serious damage to the environment of a place in the United Kingdom, or (c) war, or terrorism, which threatens serious damage to the security of the United Kingdom. (Legislation.gov.uk, 2004)

The two key points to note from this legislation are the inclusion of a situation which, first, threatens serious damage to human welfare and, second, threatens serious damage to the security of the United Kingdom. Counter-terrorism legislation not only damages values of due process, equality and justice but also positively influences the radicalization process through impacting these very factors (Ahmed, 2015, 2016; Post et al., 2003). And although, the UN (2018) specifically states that counter-terrorism measures should not involve discrimination, counter-terrorism policies marginalize individuals to create 'them' and 'us' binaries, and through doing so, they negatively impact the concept of universal human rights (Ahmed, 2015). Therefore, the existence of these measures positively impacts many of the variables associated with the radicalization process (such as discrimination, racism, injustice, lack of human rights) and thus the micro-individual-emotional level.

One can also take the fact that an emergency is conceptualized as existing when there is a situation which threatens serious damage to human welfare and the security of the United Kingdom, and ask the following questions, do measures which infringe so many universal values (such as equality, justice, rule of law and due process) not also constitute a threat to welfare? Do they not also constitute a threat to security through positively impacting radicalization?

Through creating the very reality discussed above, the 'war on terror' encourages the separation of humanity into those that are perceived as deserving human rights, and those that are constructed as less deserving of human rights. One can note the purposeful manipulation of discourses and the state misuse of value-laden concepts of 'peace, justice, progress, and civilization' (Schmitt, 1996: 54). In the first instance, the introduction of counter-terrorism measures is constructed as being an absolute necessity to preserve these concepts, but then the counter-terrorism measures introduced infringe and create a parody of these very concepts. This is the irony of the state centric 'war on terror' narrative, and it is a narrative shrouded in hypocrisy that terrorists exploit to radicalize young Muslims. The belief in natural rights, which according to Locke (2014 cited Hunt 2016), would include the right to life, liberty and property and, according to Rawls (1971), the right to freedom and individual autonomy are rights that individuals believe in, with research by Ahmed

(2016) demonstrating how the curtailment of these rights in the 'war on terror' has negatively impacted British Muslims' perceptions of justice and belonging. The presence of measures which are perceived as constituting injustice gives rise to radicalization and perpetuates and validates the Islamist ideology of western measures as religiously profiling Muslims. In this way, the UK counter-terrorism legislation discussed above not only violates IHRL and IHL but also facilitates terrorism by positively impacting the micro-individual-emotional level.

The 'war on terror' needs to be understood through the mechanisms of power that feed it, maintain it, institutionalize it and essentially continue to breed its existence. The role of the UN and the super macro-universal level in facilitating terrorism has received no coverage. Yet it is perhaps the most powerful facilitator because, as this book explores, many of the state crimes which exist in the macro-national level and the meso-societal level were influenced by the UN resolutions. In this way the super macro-universal level has operated as a vessel of power, influencing states to push the boundaries of their control and use the law and order framework to introduce new legislation. This chapter has thus far considered how the 'war on terror' impacted state practices towards their own citizens via the introduction of new legislation, and therefore how the super macro-universal level impacted macro-national-level intra-state crimes and how these have positively impacted radicalization. This chapter now explores the wider impact of the 'war on terror' on state interactions with other states and non-UK citizens, and therefore the impact of the super macro-universal level on macro-national level inter-state crimes.

The Impact of the 'War on Terror' on Other States

The 'war on terror' influenced not only state practices towards their own citizens but also state practices with other states. The engagement between different states is governed by both IHRL and IHL. These collectively challenge state power and dictate what constitutes acceptable and unacceptable state actions during wartime and peacetime (Ignatieff, 2002;

Stigall, Blakesley, & Jenks, 2009). However, although on the abstract level, IHRL and IHL have evolved to minimize state harms, for example, following the World Conference on Human Rights in 1993, state avoidance of human rights commitments via appeals to cultural relativity became increasingly judged as illegitimate (Dunne, 2007). In reality, state actions which violate human rights are increasingly common. As this book reveals, this reality is a product of geo-political power and ideological discourses manufactured to make the prevalence of controversial expansions of state power appear necessary.

As already argued, IHRL is relevant to terrorism, and most notably through the UDHR and the ICCPR. Both documents contain references to the right to life: Article 3 in the UDHR and Article 6 in the ICCPR (UN, 1948; UNHR, 1966).

> IHRL is composed of both conventional treaties and customary law which operate to limit the power and the behaviour of states. Whereas the United Nations governs its members and some treaties govern only those states that have formally adopted the treaty, IHRL requires all states, regardless of whether a state has adopted a human rights treaty, to respect and ensure certain human rights, such as the right to life. (ICRC, 2003)

There are also some provisions that states must always afford citizens, such as the respect for life, which is an IHRL provision that cannot be derogated and must continue to exist, even during armed conflict (General Assembly, 1970). Whereas IHRL applies at all times, IHL applies during armed conflict and exists as a set of international rules, established by treaty or custom, which are specifically intended to solve the humanitarian problems directly arising from international or non-international armed conflict (ICRC, 2003). The conventional and customary laws that govern wars constitute the laws of a just war, and if a state of armed conflict does exist, IHL provides a complete legal code that defines areas of warfare including, when a party may lawfully resort to military force, acceptable conduct during armed conflict, the use of force, and rules for protecting civilians (ICRC, 2003).

Within the 'war on terror', the United States has argued that IHL is the only legal system applicable and therefore the only system governing the use of force against military targets (Evangelista, 2008). Through failing to acknowledge and indeed follow IHRL, the United States has sought to evade the rules and regulations present on IHRL. Acknowledging the existence of IHRL within the 'war on terror' would mean that the United States would have to abide by rules based on prioritizing 'a harmonious relationship between the state and individuals under its jurisdiction' whereas, being governed solely by IHL means that state interactions with enemy combatant are dictated by the laws governing combat and thus less stringent laws (Provost, 2002: 8). The US government has argued that IHRL and more specifically, the right to life, which as just stated is protected in both UDHR and ICCPR were not applicable in its armed conflict with international terrorist organizations like AQ. And it has similarly claimed that detainees at Guantánamo and the other prisons used in the 'war on terror' (detaining at least 70,000 individuals) have no legal status because they fall into no recognizable legal category, and are therefore not protected under international law (Corn et al., 2015; Forsythe, 2006).

The United States has argued that the 'new paradigm' of counterterrorism 'renders obsolete the Geneva conventions and therefore the rights attributed to prisoners through these conventions' (Gonzales, 2002). The 'war on terror' therefore represents active attempts by the US to construct the parameters of the 'war on terror' as not incorporating established IHRL, IHL, treaties and customs. According to Donald Gregg, a former national security advisor to the US government, the denial of safeguards, such as those in the Geneva Conventions, 'cleared the way for the horrors that have been revealed in Iraq, Afghanistan and Guantanamo' Bay and made 'a mockery of the administration's assertions that a few misguided enlisted personnel perpetuated the vile abuse of prisoners' (Lewis, 2005: xvi). Therefore, within the 'war on terror' there are also examples of how state failures to uphold established IHRL and IHL have contributed to wider forms of human rights abuse.

As noted above, the decision to deny safeguards and thus the applicability of IHRL and IHL leads to a lack of rule of law and human rights violations which can facilitate terrorism (UN, 2018). These conditions constitute the meso-societal level because they lead to the political, social, ideological and economic conditions which facilitate terrorism and terrorist groups from below. One can also note the prevalence of geo-political power and inequality in shaping state conduct, because it could be claimed that not all nations are able to exert such influence and power that they are able to deny the existence of IHRL. Thus, the ability to circumvent condemnation and the application of state crime is dependent on which country is making such denials. It is the existence of such geo-political inequality which feeds into the grievances, the dualism of 'western nations' versus 'Islam and Islamic nations' and moral outrage which all directly facilitate radicalization and thus terrorism (Ahmed, 2014).

The Geneva Conventions also inform the laws of war. The Conventions describe the conditions which constitute an armed conflict and would therefore activate the rules and customs of IHL. The Geneva Convention was influenced by the post-Second World War socio-political context in which it was created. It therefore contains articles pertaining to the protection of populations against certain consequences of war, the status and treatment of protected persons, obligations of the occupying power vis-à-vis the civilian population and provisions on humanitarian relief for populations in occupied territory (ICRC, 2014). The first Convention protects wounded soldiers during war. The second Convention pertains to the protection of wounded, sick and shipwrecked military personal at sea during war. The third applies to prisoners of war and replaces the Prisoners of War Convention of 1929 (ICRC, 2014). The Convention also protects civilians and other non-military targets from direct or indiscriminate attack in non-international armed conflicts and outlines guidelines relating to prisoners of war, their treatment, the use of judicial proceedings and the necessity for prisoners to be released without delay after active conflicts (ICRC, 2014). The fourth Convention protects civilians, including those in occupied territory, and covers situations of non-international armed conflicts, including traditional civil wars, internal armed conflicts that spill over into other states, or internal conflicts in which third states or a multinational force intervenes alongside the government (ICRC, 2014). It requires humane treatment for all persons in enemy hands, without any adverse distinction, and prohibits murder, mutilation, torture, cruel, humiliating and degrading treatment, the taking of hostages and unfair trial (ICRC, 2014).

According to the Geneva Conventions and the Protocols of 1977, a state of armed conflict between states and international terrorist groups cannot exist, and therefore the use of force in the 'war on terror' must be governed by the rules and customs of IHRL and the right to life (Evangelista, 2008; Hoffman, 2004). However, within the 'war on terror', the United States has refused to declare prisoners as prisoners of war and clarify their legal status, as required under the Third Geneva Convention (Engin & Rygiel, 2007). These decisions have been ideological, serving the intention to deny suspects their basic human rights. In making this case to 'bypass the Geneva Convention, the US administration said that detainees at Guantánamo were not 'prisoners of war' and were 'unlawful enemy combatants' because they had not worn uniforms or carried weapons openly and had chosen to disregard international law prohibiting the targeting of civilian populations' (Holloway, 2013: 48). The classification of detainees as 'unlawful enemy combatants' meant that they were not afforded the conditions of imprisonment prescribed by the 1949 Geneva Conventions for 'prisoners of war'. The fourth Convention requires detainees to be tried by a constituted court and afforded all the 'customary international legal requirements for a fair trial, including the right of accused persons both to be present at their trial and to see the evidence against them' (Mathew, 2008: 161). The issue of classification is essential here, and of interest is how a state is able to manufacture discourses and, in this case, use its power to construct detainees as 'unlawful enemy combatants'. As Dunér (2005) states, by refusing to clarify their status in a tribunal, detainees had neither access to the US judicial system nor the safeguards which are attributed to prisoners of war under the Geneva Convention. This construction and use of power, as Cohen (2001: 107) suggests, serve to 'mask, sanitize, and confer respectability', which all act to conceal and deny state crimes. The discourses created by states are just as powerful and dangerous as acts of state crime, because these discourses legitimize acts of state crime and therefore construct the context within which IHRL and IHL are breached. It could therefore be argued that there is a need to widen the scope of state crime to incorporate the state manufacture of discourses, because any treatment and analysis of state harm must include their power to manipulate knowledge and construct self-serving truths.

The 'war on terror' discourse was constructed as preserving freedoms, democracy and universal values against the terrorist threat. However, when one considers how the United States has used its power to deny the existence and applicability of the Geneva Conventions, it is possible to comprehend how the manipulation of these values served to create the socio-political conditions (lack of good governance, rule of law and violations of human rights) conducive to terrorism. These conditions form the grass root-level conditions which facilitate terrorism, and through doing so, they positively impact the micro-individual-emotional level. In this way, state actions can be conceptualized as being multi-faceted because, in the first instance, they deviate from established legal safeguards and, in the second instance, they lead to the creation of the socio-political and ideological conditions that impact the micro-individual-emotional level and facilitate terrorism. And perhaps more importantly, the destruction of these universal values undermines the moral basis of the 'war on terror' through creating a reality in which the self-defeating nature of the 'war on terror' can be evidenced, legitimized and exploited by terrorists. As research by Speckhard and Akhmedova (2005) demonstrated, the 'war on terror' negatively impacts individuals' beliefs in universal values, and the breakdown in perceptions of such values facilitates the radicalization process. Similarly, research by Ahmed (2015) demonstrated that the erosion of these values leads to negative emotions, such as pain, anger, and helplessness.

As is becoming increasingly clear, since 9/11 the US commitment to international and domestic human rights laws and treaties has been severely undermined (Harrelson-Stephens & Callaway, 2009). Within this context, public anxieties reflect the magnitude of western constructions of the 'war on terror', with a CNN poll revealing that 45% of the American public would not object to torturing someone if it would provide information about terrorism (Williams, 2001). This poll evidences the extent to which inhumane activities have gained public support in the 'war on terror'. Torture constitutes the inhumane treatment of another human being, inflicting suffering and punishment onto them for the purpose of eliciting information. The grotesque nature of torture has made it one of the most legislated acts in IHRL and IHL, with torture also constituting a war crime.

The European Convention for the Protection of Human Rights and Fundamental Freedoms covers torture. Article 3 is the prohibition of torture and states, 'no one shall be subjected to torture or to inhuman or degrading treatment or punishment' (ECHR, 1998: 7). Article 3 of the ECHR also includes the right not to be sent to a territory where individuals face the risk of torture, inhuman or degrading treatment (ECHR, 1998). The rights afforded by Article 3 are absolute, with no exceptions, not even in cases of public emergency threatening the life of the nation. Similarly, the ICCPR prohibits torture, cruel, inhuman or degrading treatment, as does the Geneva Convention (UNHR, 1966). Article 1 of the Convention against Torture and Other Cruel, Inhumane or Degrading Treatment or Punishment (CAT) defines 'torture' as an act that inflicts

> severe pain or suffering, whether physical or mental, is intentionally inflicted on a person for such purposes as obtaining from him or a third person information or a confession, punishing him for an act he or a third person has committed or is suspected of having committed, or intimidating or coercing him or a third person, or for any reason based on discrimination of any kind, when such pain or suffering is inflicted by or at the instigation of or with the consent or acquiescence of a public official or other person acting in an official capacity. (OHCHR, 1987)

It also requires participation or acquiescence of a public official and the pain has to be inflicted for particular purposes, such as gaining a confession from a person (OHCHR, 1987). Torture is unique in the level of sanctions it has received. As Manderson (2008: 38) states,

> legal systems throughout the world outlawed torture long, long before capital punishment. In the US, torture has always been contrary to the 8th Amendment; it is the paradigmatic example of 'cruel and unusual punishment'.

Manderson (2008) raises some interesting points about torture and how it is constructed as being far worse than capital punishment. From reading the definitions above, there are several points worthy of attention. The first is the emphasis on pain, and thus taking a mental and a physical form. This infliction of pain deviates from most western systems of punishment where the deprivation of liberty constitutes punishment. And the second point worthy of mention is the emphasis on public officials, which demonstrates the connection of the individual to some official capacity and this capacity is linked to the state and the agent acting on behalf of the state.

In the 'war on terror', torture has been institutionalized. Guantánamo Bay is placed in a unique territory which has special and jurisdictional status in American law (De Londras, 2014). It has been claimed that Guantánamo Bay is both a place of exceptional measures and a legal black hole (Wilson, 2003). It is estimated that between the years 2002 and 2004, more than 660 captives (including a number of British nationals) have been sent to Guantánamo bay (Steyn, 2004) and by 2005, 'only 4 out of 549 prisoners held for two to three years at the Guantánamo Bay detention camp had been charged with a specific offence' (Ericson, 2008: 63). Individuals held in the prison include those from Gambia, Bosnia, Mauritania, Pakistan, Egypt, Indonesia, Thailand, United Arab Emirates, United Kingdom and Afghanistan (Amnesty International, 2006). According to Human Rights First (2018), by October 2018 the total number of individuals held at the prison was 780, 9 detainees have died at the facility and there are currently 26 detainees who are being held for indefinite detention without charge or trial.

Within the 'war on terror' the transfer of suspects to prisons such as Guantánamo Bay and other countries is extremely common. Article 3.1 of CAT contains an absolute prohibition on refoulement:

> no State Party shall expel, return ("refouler") or extradite a person to another State where there are substantial grounds for believing that he would be in danger of being subjected to torture. For the purpose of determining whether there are such grounds, the competent authorities shall take into account all relevant considerations including, where applicable, the existence in the State concerned of a consistent pattern of gross, flagrant or mass violations of human rights. (OHCHR, 1987)

Extradition arrangements between the United States and the United Kingdom are governed by parts 2 and 3 of the United Kingdom's Extradition Act 2003. Prior to 9/11, as Fitzpatrick (2003: 459) contends, 'counterterrorism was located in the realm of international criminal law, in which extradition treaties, refugee law, and human rights norms imposed significant legal constraints'. However, as previously stated, 9/11 changed the legal status of terrorism by constructing terrorism as an act of warfare. And therefore after 9/11 captives had been transferred to 'detention centers chosen increasingly for their invulnerability to scrutiny by national courts, human rights bodies, and agencies responsible for the application of humanitarian law' (Fitzpatrick, 2003: 460). 'Between 2004 and 2013, the US made 106 extradition requests to England, Wales and Northern Ireland compared with 48 made in the other direction' (Liberty, 2014: 21). Included in the extradition to the United States were Babar Ahmad and Syed Talha Ahsan. Prior to 9/11, they created a website which had the service provider in Connecticut, and after 9/11 this website came to be perceived by US authorities as supporting the Taliban (Peirce, 2010).

There have been many accusations of torture amongst coalition forces. Rashid Rauf, a Birmingham resident AQ suspect, was captured by Pakistan's Inter-Services Intelligence (ISI) agency. According to his cellmate, he was tortured by the ISI, an organization that frequently kidnaps suspects and tortures them (The Guardian, 2009). According to Human Rights Watch (2009: 2), 'although there is no evidence of UK officials directly participating in torture, they are complicit in his torture because it is inconceivable that the UK government was unaware of the systematic use of torture in Pakistan', given the close relationship between the two countries. 'Second, UK officials engaged in acts that virtually required that they knew about the use of torture in specific cases', because they met four men 'shortly after sessions in which the individuals had been tortured, when it was likely that clear and visible signs of torture were present' (Human Rights Watch, 2009: 2). Human Rights Watch (2009: 6) demonstrates how the Committee Against Torture 'has indicated that an individual is complicit in torture if he or she has given "tacit consent" or "acquiesced" to the torture and knew or should have known that it was taking place'. As Human Rights Watch (2009) states, complicity in torture should and does amount to torture and therefore constitutes a state crime. And as previously stated, it is one of the most criminalized forms of state crime. Research by Ahmed (2015) found that British Muslims perceive counter-terrorism measures as something that they are likely to be subjected to and how the perception of these measures as a group experience exacerbates emotions of vulnerability. The existence of torture therefore impacts vulnerability, powerlessness and individuals' perceptions that they could be subjected to inhuman measures, which are all factors which facilitate radicalization (Ahmed, 2015; Boyns & Ballard, 2004; Henderson-King, Henderson-King, Bolea, Koches, & Kauffman, 2004; Post et al., 2003; Speckhard & Akhmedova, 2005). One can therefore conclude that the existence of torture constitutes the existence of macro-national-level state crime facilitation of radicalization.

It appears that civil liberties, due process and human rights are not maintained with state culpability regarding torture receiving no sanctions because officials who choose to ignore torture are not reprimanded. In contrast, security is prioritized with individuals criminalized for failing to disclose their suspicions of another individual's intentions to commit an act of terrorism under the Terrorism Act 2000. Such differences in the use of power and punishment are utilized by extremists who cite such examples as evidence of injustice, discrimination and differential treatment (Lemu, 2016). When these two examples are deconstructed, it seems unjust that individuals can face a custodial sentence for not disclosing someone that 'might' commit an act of terrorism and yet, an individual who knows of torture, an act that has been outlawed prior to capital punishment can deviate from their responsibility to disclose the act. Therefore, it could be argued that the 'war on terror' is a war which possesses pockets of power which encroach civil liberties and human rights through the securitization agenda, and these vessels of power form a powerful mechanism which is setting a precedent for the violation of international safeguards. The whole construction of the 'war on terror' sets the boundaries of necessity and within this reality, torture, as with any other violation of law does not just happen. Rather, there is the active mechanism of construction to contour the boundaries of the discourse to legitimize its use, and instructions are conveyed to individuals to carry out the torture.

In October 2006, George W. Bush signed the 2006 Military Commissions Act, which classified detainees who were non-US citizens as 'unlawful enemy combatants', thereby denying them habeas corpus rights even though they had not been charged with any offence (Roberts,

2007). The Act signified the further institutionalization of security through denying suspects the protection afforded to prisoners of war and thus placed the suspects outside the laws of war. In 2002, a CIA analyst visiting Guantánamo to investigate the poor quality of intelligence gathered during interrogations concluded that war crimes were occurring at the prison (Holloway, 2013). As Mathew (2008: 166) states, a report by the UN Commission on Human Rights found that the

> conditions of detention, in particular, the uncertainty about the length of detention and prolonged solitary confinement, amount to inhumane treatment and to a violation of the right to health as well as a violation of the right of detainees under Article 10(1) of the ICCPR to be treated with humanity and with respect for the inherent dignity of the human person.

Amnesty International (2005) estimated that 70,000 people had been detained outside the United States in the context of the 'war on terror' and reported on evidence of the use of stress positions, isolation, hooding, sensory deprivation, the use of dogs, cruel and prolonged use of shackles, the use of loud music and strobe lights at Guantánamo Bay. Amnesty International has also denounced the interrogation techniques used by the United States in Guantánamo as torture (Amnesty International, 2006).

There have been attempts in court to challenge the construction and placement of suspects as 'non-enemy combatants'. In *Rasul v. Bush*, contrary to the US administration, the court ruled that federal judges have jurisdiction in habeas cases filed from Guantánamo Bay leading the administration to create legislation to deny habeas rights to detainees (Rasul et al. v. Bush, et al., 2004). On 29th June 2006, in *Hamdan v. Rumsfeld*, the Court found that detainees had the right to challenge their classification as an enemy combatant before a neutral decision maker, which led to the establishment of the Combatant Status Review Tribunals (Rehman, 2007). In *Benchellali et al. v United States of America*, individuals detained in Guantánamo Bay who had been captured or arrested in Afghanistan or Pakistan stated that they had been held without charge or access to legal assistance, and had not been brought before a court (Byrnes, 2008). The UN Working Group on arbitrary detention concluded that the detention was arbitrary, and in violation of Article 9 of the UDHR, which states that 'no one shall be subjected to arbitrary arrest, detention or exile' (UDHR, 1948) and Article 9 of the ICCPR[1] (Byrnes, 2008: 145). The treatment and classification of detainees therefore constitute state crime according to a multitude of IHRL and IHL.

The torture of suspects at Abu Gharib prison has also been well documented. In 2004, the abuse at the prison was exposed by journalist Seymour M. Hersh after he gained access to an army report which described the sadistic criminal abuse at the prison, which involved prisoners being hooded, humiliated, beaten, naked and made to perform sexual acts (Hersh, 2004). As Perezalonso (2010: 153) states, the graphic evidence was a 'reminder of the power of the sovereign to dispose of human life at will, to render bare life and to create exceptional spaces of indistinction between law and violence'. However, the power of the sovereign state wasn't just demonstrated through its ability to use torture, but also in its lack of accountability when the abuse was publicized. On 7 May 2004, US Secretary of Defense Donald Rumsfeld apologized to Congress for the 'fundamentally unAmerican' scenes at Abu Ghraib (Holloway, 2013: 47). Interestingly, these un-American acts were seen as being the result of a few 'rotten apples'. However, as Holloway (2013: 47) argues, 'those put on trial alleged that they had been encouraged to soften up detainees for questioning by military interrogators' and that 'direct responsibility for the scandal went up the chain of command at least as far as Rumsfeld, and possibly higher'.

[1] (1) Everyone has the right to liberty and security of person. No one shall be subjected to arbitrary arrest or detention. No one shall be deprived of his liberty except on such grounds and in accordance with such procedure as are established by law. (2) Anyone who is arrested shall be informed, at the time of arrest, of the reasons for his arrest and shall be promptly informed of any charges against him. (3) Anyone arrested or detained on a criminal charge shall be brought promptly before a judge or other officer authorized by law to exercise judicial power and shall be entitled to trial within a reasonable time or to release. It shall not be the general rule that persons awaiting trial shall be detained in custody, but release may be subject to guarantees to appear for trial, at any other stage of the judicial proceedings, and, should occasion arise, for execution of the judgement. (4) Anyone who is deprived of his liberty by arrest or detention shall be entitled to take proceedings before a court, in order that that court may decide without delay on the lawfulness of his detention and order his release if the detention is not lawful. (5) Anyone who has been the victim of unlawful arrest or detention shall have an enforceable right to compensation (UNHR, 1966).

A US Senate Report led by Dianne Feinstein on CIA torture was released in December 2014. This report demonstrated that CIA investigation techniques (harsh interrogations, inhumane treatments and torture) had proved ineffective in the production of useful intelligence and in fighting terrorism (Scherrer & Bigo, 2015). The desire to humiliate and use rendition to torture and dehumanize suspects (Hirsh & Isikoff, 2004; Saurette, 2005) represents the creation of mechanisms designed to achieve self-legitimacy through denying the humanity of suspects, and thus the need and requirement for IHRL and IHL. Here the presence of macro-national-level state crimes directly erodes the rule of law, thus predisposing the ideology of 'us' and 'them', an ideology that is also utilized by terrorists to justify the otherization and violence against groups classified as 'them' (Ahmed, 2014; Hoyle, Bradford, & Frenett, 2015). Torture also directly feeds into many of the conditions highlighted by the UN (2018) as facilitating terrorism. Torture combines the abandonment of universal values with discrimination and involves the use of inhumane practices. It was also recognized in the United Kingdom that these measures could radicalize individuals with former Law Lord, Steyn, stating 'the type of Justice meted out at Guantanamo Bay is likely to make martyrs of the prisoners' (Steyn, 2004). The existence of torture therefore feeds into the micro-individual-emotional level through impacting discrimination, injustice, trauma, powerlessness, vulnerability, a lack of belonging, victimization, and suffering which are relevant to the radicalization process.

Thus, the 'war on terror' marked the globalization of a new security agenda, designed to interpret the perceived terrorist threat through the abandonment of human rights and due process and, in such a climate, the need for measures consistent with IHRL and IHL obligations was abandoned. Within the 'war on terror', 'politically cultivated fear' as Green and Ward (2004) call it, was used as a lens through which to construct the actions created as being necessary to defeat terrorists. Macro-national-level inter-state crimes, notably the invasion of Afghanistan and Iraq, took place, and as this book explores, these state crimes facilitated the existence of terrorism through impacting the meso-societal interpersonal level and the micro-individual-emotional level.

The first invasion was the invasion of Afghanistan. On 7 October 2001, an international coalition led by the United States launched a war against the Taliban regime in Afghanistan. One can note the immediacy with which this war was initiated, commencing less than a month after the 9/11 terrorist attacks. The invasion was constructed as a necessity to counter the terrorist threat of Osama Bin-Laden and the Taliban in Afghanistan. The attack on the base of the Taliban and the al-Qaeda organization in Afghanistan was called 'Enduring freedom' and constituted the first stage in the 'war on terror' (Crockatt, 2003). One could argue that it is rather hypocritical to name the operation 'Enduring freedom' when war uses security measures which restrict the very civil liberties and human rights associated with freedom, with research revealing how the suffering and trauma associated with war and political repression facilitate radicalization (Lemu, 2016; Speckhard & Akhmedova, 2005). Therefore to, first, engage in a war and, second, name this war 'Enduring freedom' demonstrates the extent of ethnocentric construction within the 'war on terror', and how ethnocentrism in the 'war on terror' works to obscure the existence of actions that positively influence the growth of terrorism. Although the choice to describe these actions as ethnocentric may not be obvious, when one considers the number of Afghan civilians who died, or indeed the imposition of a pro-coalition government in the country following the invasion, it really does demonstrate the power of the coalition to define what they believe is freedom from their perspective. There is a complete neglect of how the citizens from Afghanistan might perceive a war that destroys their infrastructure and imposes a government. As the following chapters reveal, such an imposition, as in Iraq, led to anything but freedom for the groups that became oppressed by the pro-coalition government and this facilitated the rise of ISIS. Here one can also observe how, as previously stated, the vulnerability and powerlessness experienced by those living under politically oppressive regimes facilitate acts of terrorism (Cronin, 2009; Post et al., 2003).

An estimated 3400 Afghan civilians were killed by US military action between the start of the Afghanistan attack in October 2001 and end of March 2002 (Herold, 2017). By 2016, 'approximately 111,000 people had been killed and more than 116,000 people had been injured in the war in Afghanistan' (Crawford, 2016: 1). In terms of the reconstruction of Afghanistan, between March and September 2002, 1.7 million refugees are estimated to have returned to Afghanistan, but the lack of funding for reconstruction meant that many were finding it difficult or impossible to survive (Turton & Marsden, 2002). As Green (2002) states, the foreign policy used by the United States inflicted a far larger magnitude of death, suffering and destruction than bin Laden could have ever hoped to achieve. The immediate devastation of war is evident through the number of individuals killed and injured. One can also note how the 'war on terror' is a self-defeating war because the very suffering and fear it aims to counter and eliminate, it breeds itself. It renders invisible those very principles of freedom, liberty and respect for human rights that it claims it is trying to preserve through creating mechanisms of power, and more importantly, institutional practices which abandon these very principles. However, through doing so, it also creates a dichotomy of the world and humanity, which, as previously stated, is exploited by extremists and directly feeds into radicalization. Here one can ask the obvious question:

If the 'war on terror' is meant to eliminate the suffering and fear that terrorism creates, but in doing so, it creates wars, prisons and other mechanisms of social control which not only cause suffering, but also violate the very safeguards that are meant to protect humanity and further, are disproportionately used against individuals who possess certain identities within humanity, then does the 'war on terror' not cause the very suffering and damage that it is meant to prevent?

The power to create a narrative, especially one of self-legitimization, is dangerous and evident in both discourses of radicalization and discourses of counter-terrorism and the 'war on terror'. However, what also becomes evident in both discourses is how they dissect humanity into two. The 'war on terror' discourse advocates the destruction and dehumanization of one group, defined by its identity to preserve the rights, freedoms, values and humanity of another group. Within this context the humanity of one group is prioritized to such an extent that it is used to legitimize the denial of basic human rights and humanity of another group. One can draw the comparisons between such elevations of rights for one group, and the denial of rights of another group in the 'war on terror', and genocide. Genocide also possesses these very characteristics and the slicing of humanity into two, with identity being the definer of rights and constructed humanity. Islamists also use these very processes to legitimize acts of violence and terrorism. They afford no humanity and rights to those who are killed. However, it could be argued that whereas genocide, terrorism and the 'war on terror' all lead to, and indeed, invoke the same processes to claim legitimacy for their violence, where the perpetrators are the state, then far more damage is inflicted. The damage in the first instance is to the loss of life and in the second instance, it is the corrosive impact of these actions on universal values and human rights. Here a differentiation must also be afforded to actions by states and actions by non-state actors. States are meant to protect citizens and, in doing so, they provide a sense of security to citizens in fulfilling the role of maintaining justice and punishing those that undermine justice and the values of society. However, when states are the perpetrators of such injustice, then there is no sense of security left. Research by Ahmed (2015) demonstrated that since the 'war on terror' British Muslims' perceptions of injustice have caused much more damage because it is the state and state institutions which are responsible. The damage to participants' sense of security led to emotions of pain, and a sense of insecurity and loss. The lack of avenues through which participants could voice experiences of injustice and discrimination further excerbated perceptions of loss. As many participants in the study explained, if you believe that the police will protect you and then this security goes, there is nothing left to protect you. This sense of loss and insecurity impacted participants' sense of humanity and belief in a just world, which are powerful mechanisms of radicalization.

In March 2003, the United States launched 'Operation Iraqi Freedom', which involved the invasion of Iraq (Stohl, 2008). There is a certain irony when one looks at Iraq and weapons of mass destruction because as Pliger (2002: 63) notes, 'securing arms and "dual purpose" equipment deals' were not influenced by the 'gassing of 5,000 Kurds in Halabja' following Saddam Hussein's invasion of Kuwait. Pliger (2002) is demonstrating how the construction of war as a necessity is an ideological construction. Necessity is a concept that is fashioned and constructed and, thus, it has no independent ontology. However, within the 'war on terror', the decision not to intervene when crimes against humanity were taking place in

Iraq, and the decision to intervene based on the suspicion of Iraq possessing weapons of mass destruction is portrayed as an independent reality that is dispersed through the populist media. However, in 2005, a *BBC Newsnight* report claimed to have uncovered documents showing the Bush administration made plans to secure Iraqi oil even before 11 September 2001 (Thornton, 2005). Oil was believed to be the main reason for the invasion of Iraq, leading some to re-label the 'war on terror' as the 'war for oil' (Rashid, 2008). The invasion of Iraq for oil further fuels claims of western occupation, and the exploitation of Islamic/Muslim territories that help validate the extremist narrative of western imperialism, that is so vital in the radicalization process (Milne, 2009; Rasool, 2016). The 'war on terror' not only leads to two foreign interventions, one in Afghanistan and one in Iraq, but these interventions were also illegal, therefore increasing their capacity to radicalize individuals. These invasions therefore constitute macro-national-level inter-state crime facilitated terrorism.

The invasion of Iraq was a violation of international law, as designated by the UN and the Nuremburg charter (Kramer & Michalowski, 2005). The United Nations' Charter specifies:

> all members shall refrain from the threat or use of force against the territorial integrity or political independence of any state, or in any state in which the United Nations is taking preventive or enforcement action. (United Nations, 2006, Article 2, Chapter 1:4)

The only exception to Article 2(4) is found in Article 51 of the Charter:

> nothing in the present Charter shall impair the inherent right of individual or collective self-defense if an armed attack occurs against a Member of the United Nations, until the Security Council has taken measures necessary to maintain international peace and security. (UN, 2006)

The intention of this article is to allow a state under direct attack to defend itself. However, a state can only exercise this right when an international plan of action has been authorized by the UN Security Council (Kauzlarich, 2007). The United States and the United Kingdom failed to secure a United Nations Security Council resolution authorizing the use of force leading Kofi Annan, the United Nations Secretary-General, to declare the 'intervention as unlawful' and many international lawyers to condemn the invasion as a substantial breach of law (BBC News, 2004).

The invasions created a three-tier system of facilitating radicalization. First, there were the immediate consequences of the invasions, which had the potential to radicalize individuals through demonstrating inequality and injustice because the invasions were unlawful. Second, there was the potential of witnessing the murder, suffering and injustice that civilian populations endured because of the war, which also facilitates radicalization. And finally, the long-term consequences of war can radicalize individuals in a plethora of ways, and these include the UN-defined factors of prolonged unresolved conflicts, the lack of rule of law and the lack of global governance (UN, 2018). As already mentioned, political instability facilitates terrorism with research by Piazza (2008), concluding that terrorists are more likely to reside in weak states plagued with failures. The duty to rebuild states is specified in Article 43 of the Hague Regulations 1907 (Schwenk, 1945).

According to IHRL and IHL and conventions, the United States and the United Kingdom have been responsible for substantial violations of IHRL and IHL. Violations of IHL have included the failure to rebuild a state, secure public safety and protect civilian rights (Amnesty International, 2005). Breach of IHL also pertains to the 'illegal transformation of the Iraqi economy since the Fourth Geneva Convention (1949) clearly bans occupying powers from restructuring the economy in their own vision' (Welch, 2008: 261). This demonstrates the relationship between all three levels. The United States and the United Kingdom were able to violate IHRL and IHL because they knew that there would be a lack of regulation and sanctions at the super macro-universal level. The immunity granted to countries is subject to geo-political power, which in turn results in actions being constructed and perceived according to the identity of the perpetrators, as opposed to a focus on the actions and consequences of these actions. This geo-political power and the resultant global inequality feed into the narrative terrorists use to demonstrate the existence of global inequality, global injustice, and therefore a global binary. These binaries and their actions work to maintain power and privilege in the west. Such geo-political power also served to legitimize macro-national-level inter-state crime in the form of the invasion of Iraq and Afghanistan, which facilitates the variables which increase radicalization at the meso-societal level. During the meso-societal level, states facilitate terrorism from below through creating the context, and therefore the political, social, ideological and economic conditions that promote radicalization and terrorism. As Chap. 6 explores, the US and UK coalition left Iraq in a state of political, social and economic instability which contributed to sectarian violence, anarchy and destruction, and these conditions facilitated the emergence of ISIS. Theories of radicalization often omit state-facilitated terrorism and yet, as Chap. 6 explores, these state-produced conditions create the meso-societal grassroot level conditions in which terrorist groups emerge and are sustained.

However, as part of a contextual analysis of the conditions which facilitated political instability in Iraq, one must consider the role of UN sanctions. The purpose of this book is to be ontologically neutral, to suspend prior assumptions of social construction, as much as possible, and to assess the less obvious and often-hidden aspects of social, political, economic and humanitarian life that fuel terrorism. Sanctions represent ideological construction at its most powerful. They are constructed as alternatives to military action, and therefore as powerful nations kindly pursuing humane alternatives to military action. However, in order to be ontologically neutral, one must ask the question: What do sanctions mean in reality? In populist constructions, 'economic sanctions' are used to mask the denial of basic amenities and the reader, or the observer, is not taught to question what sanctions involve.

The 'Oil for Food Program' was a programme imposed on Iraq by the United Nations and under this programme Iraq exported oil for food, medicine and other necessary items. This programme banned items including electrical equipment, ambulances, baby food, bandages, blankets, cannulas for intravenous drips, infant catheters, chlorine and other water purification chemicals, cleaning agents, dialysis equipment, angina and epilepsy medication, incubators, medical swabs, medical journals, medical syringes, nasogastric tubes, flour, oxygen tents, paper, pencils, pencil sharpeners, school books, soap, shampoo, steel plate stethoscopes, surgical instruments, toilet paper, toothpaste and brushes (Simons, 1998,

2002). The list of items is truly shocking, with the banning of some of these items clearly contributing to the death of civilians. These sanctions created mass suffering and death.

- One of the first reports on the sanctions in Iraq was written in 1991 and stated 'nothing that we had seen or read had quite prepared us for the particular form of devastation which has now befallen the country. The recent conflict has wrought near-apocalyptic results upon the economic infrastructure of what had been, until January 1991, a rather highly urbanized and mechanized society' (Ahtisaari, 1991: 5).
- The Aga Khan report (Khan, 1991) stated that the government ration system was meeting only one-third of the country's needs. Malnutrition was climbing among children and families were engaging in famine-coping strategies such as selling possessions to purchase food.
- More than 500,000 children are estimated to have died as a direct result of sanctions by 1997, and UNICEF estimated that around a million children under five were chronically malnourished, even though malnutrition was not a problem prior to the sanctions (UNICEF, 1998).
- And the Situation of Children and Woman in South and Central Iraq report and the Situation of Children and Women in Northern Iraq report stated that if the substantial reduction in under-five mortality during the 1980s had continued through the 1990s, there would have been half a million fewer deaths of children under-five in the country as a whole during the eight year period 1991–1998 (UNICEF, 1999a, 1999b).

In an interview, Madeleine Albright (1996), the US Ambassador to the United Nations at the time, was asked if the half a million children who had died were worth the price? Albright replied: 'I think this is a very hard choice, but the price—we think the price is worth it'. Such a statement directly fed into perceptions of inequality and the perception that humanity has been separated into those that deserve human rights and those that do not—with religious identity being the definer of this differentiation. As Green and Ward (2004) contend, sanctions violate the human rights the UN are meant to uphold, and such violations of human rights could be considered as criminal. The other point worthy of consideration is how poverty and instability lead to sectarian violence and facilitate the emergence of terrorism. If one compares economic sanctions and terrorism, it appears that both are used to influence politics and achieve political change. Even if one considers the impact of both policies, sanctions are arguably more dangerous in terms of the scope and extent of their destruction of life and infrastructure than acts of terrorism. Yet, one is completely legitimized, even though it doesn't just produce instant direct victims; it also debilitates an entire generation and population leading to the existence of suffering that lasts generations. Here, the need to explore state crimes as part of theories of radicalization becomes clear, because one is unable to explain the political, social, ideological and economic climate in Iraq, Syria and Afghanistan—three countries from which terrorist groups have emerged, without exploring the role of states in creating the conditions which allowed these groups to flourish in such environments. And as this book demonstrates, in most cases it is the existence of state crimes which have led to the existence of the very conditions which facilitate terrorism. This, in itself, reconceptualizes the understanding and placement of states in theories of radicalization and in academic conceptualizations of the 'war on terror'. Indeed, it demonstrates that the event-focused approaches to terrorism omit entire processes of how states have facilitated terrorism.

This chapter has discussed the emergence of the 'war on terror'. In exploring the construction of the 'war on terror', it has demonstrated how principles of universalism were instinctively tied to the legitimization of the 'war on terror'. However, this construction not only led to the binary division of humanity within the 'war on terror', but it would also constitute the mechanisms through which radicalization could be maintained. This construction led to the suffering and questioning of morality and one's place within humanity, for not only direct victims of terrorist attacks but also whole populations that have been constructed as potential terrorists. In this way the 'war on terror' became a self-defeating war and one which incites, perpetuates and facilitates radicalization. Equally as importantly, it became a discourse which threatens emotional security in the world through disrupting and disturbing the mechanisms designed to protect humanity and therefore one's sense of attachment and belonging to humanity. Through such a conceptualization of the 'war on terror' and grounding of the 'war on terror' via human rights safeguards, it is possible to comprehend the vast damage of the 'war on terror' and situate this damage alongside increasingly more prevalent concepts such as institutional betrayal and victimization. Such an understanding offers the opportunity to engage in the reality of the 'war on terror' from the perspective of those that are impacted by the 'war on terror' and through an understanding of this reality, it is then possible to reduce the evidence-based factors which facilitate radicalization.

References

Ahmed, S. (2014). Constitutive Criminology and the 'War on Terror'. *Critical Criminology, 22*(3), 357–371.

Ahmed, S. (2015). The Emotionalization of 'War on Terror': Counter-Terrorism, Fear, Risk, Insecurity and Helplessness. *Criminology and Criminal Justice, 15*(5), 545–560.

Ahmed, S. (2016). Citizenship, Belonging and Attachment in the 'War on Terror'. *Critical Criminology, 24*(1), 111–125.

Ahmed, T., & Butler, I. J. (2006). The European Union and Human Rights: An International Law Perspective. *European Journal of International Law, 17*(4), 771–801.

Ahtisaari, M. (1991). Report on Humanitarian Needs in Iraq in the Immediate Post-Crisis Environment by a Mission to the Area Led by the Under-Secretary-General for Administration and Management, 10–17 Mar 1991. Retrieved May 1, 2019, from http://www.casi.org.uk/info/undocs/s22366.html

Albright, M. (1996). Punishing Saddam. *60 Minutes*, CBS television. Retrieved May 1, 2018, from https://www.youtube.com/watch?v=UYagQuqK31s

Amnesty International. (2005). *Guantánamo and Beyond: The Continuing Pursuit of Unchecked Executive Power.* Retrieved May 1, 2018, from https://www.amnesty.org/download/Documents/84000/amr510632005en.pdf

Amnesty International. (2006). *United States of America: Military Commissions Act of 2006—Turning bad policy into Bad Law.* Retrieved May 1, 2018, from http://web.amnesty.org/library/Index/ENGAMR511542006

Amnesty International. (2010). *United Kingdom: Five Years On: Time to End the Control Orders Regime*. Retrieved May 1, 2018, from http://www.amnesty.org.uk/uploads/documents/doc_20571.pdf

Amnesty International. (2016). *Investigatory Powers Act Legalises Sweeping Surveillance Powers for UK Government*. Retrieved May 1, 2018, from https://www.amnesty.org.uk/press-releases/investigatory-powers-act-legalises-sweeping-surveillance-powers-uk

Amnesty International. (2017). *Dangerously Disproportionate: The Ever-Expanding Security State in Europe*. Retrieved May 1, 2018, from https://www.amnesty.org/en/latest/campaigns/2017/01/dangerously-disproportionate/

Anderson, D. (2015). *Terrorism Prevention and Investigation Measures in 2014: Third Report of the Independent Reviewer on the Operation of the Terrorism Prevention and Investigation Measures Act 2011*. Retrieved May 1, 2018, from https://assets.publishing.service.gov.uk/government/uploads/system/uploads/attachment_data/file/411824/IRTL_TPIMs_2014_final_report__web_.pdf

Anderson, J. (2003). American Hegemony After 11 September: Allies, Rivals and Contradictions. *Geopolitics, 8*(3), 35–60.

BBC News. (2004). Iraq War Illegal, Says Annan: The United Nations Secretary-General Kofi Annan has told the BBC the US-led invasion of Iraq was an Illegal Act that Contravened the UN Charter. Retrieved May 1, 2018, from http://news.bbc.co.uk/1/hi/world/middle-east3661134.stm

Beit-Hallahmi, B. (2014). *Psychological Perspectives on Religion and Religiosity*. London: Routledge.

Berger, P., & Luckmann, T. (1966). *The Social Construction of Reality*. New York: Penguin Putnam.

Bhui, K., Warfa, N., & Jones, E. (2014). Is Violent Radicalisation Associated with Poverty, Migration, Poor Self-Reported Health and Common Mental Disorders? *PLoS One*. https://doi.org/10.1371/journal.pone.0090718

Bonino, S. (2013). Preventing Muslimness in Britain: The Normalisation of Exceptional Measures to Combat Terrorism. *Journal of Muslim Minority Affairs, 33*(3), 385–400.

Boyns, D., & Ballard, J. D. (2004). Developing a Sociological Theory for the Empirical Understanding of Terrorism. *The American Sociologist, 35*(2), 5–25.

Burgess, M. (2017). What is the IP Act and How Will It Affect You? *Wired*. Retrieved May 1, 2018, from http://www.wired.co.uk/article/ip-bill-law-details-passed

Butler, J. (2002). Explanation and Exoneration, or What We Can Hear. *Grey Room., 7*, 56–67.

Byrnes, A. (2008). More Law or Less Law? The Resilience of Human Rights Law and Institutions in the 'War on Terror'. In M. Gani & P. Mathew (Eds.), *Fresh Perspectives on the War on Terror* (pp. 127–158). ANU E Press. Retrieved from https://www.jstor.org/stable/j.ctt24hf7j

Cannataci, J. (2018). *Statement by Mr. Joseph Cannataci, Special rapporteur on the Right to Privacy*. United Nations Human Rights Office of the High Commissioner. Retrieved May 10, 2019, from https://www.ohchr.org/EN/NewsEvents/Pages/DisplayNews.aspx?NewsID=22858&LangID=E

Cohen, S. (2001). *States of Denial: Knowing about Atrocities and Suffering*. Cambridge: Polity.

Corn, G. S., Schoettler Jr., J. A., Brenner-Beck, D., Hansen, V. M., Jackson, R. B., Jensen, E. T., et al. (2015). *The War on Terror and the Laws of War: A Military Perspective*. Oxford: Oxford University Press.

Correia, I., Vala, J., & Aguiar, P. (2001). The Effects of Belief in a Just World and Victim's Innocence on Secondary Victimization, Judgements of Justice and Deservingness. *Social Justice Research, 14*(3), 327–342.

CPT. (2005). Report to the Government of the United Kingdom on the Visit to the United Kingdom Carried out by the European Committee for the Prevention of Torture and Inhuman or Degrading Treatment or Punishment (CPT) from 20 to 25 November 2005. Retrieved May 10, 2019, from http://www.cpt.coe.int/documents/gbr/2006-28-inf-eng.pdf

Crawford, N. C. (2016). *Update on the Human Costs of War for Afghanistan and Pakistan, 2001 to mid-2016*. Retrieved May 10, 2019, from https://watson.brown.edu/costsofwar/files/cow/imce/papers/2015/War%20in%20Afghanistan%20and%20Pakistan%20UPDATE_FINAL.pdf

Crockatt, R. (2003). *America Embattled: September 11, Anti-Americanism, and the Global Order*. London: Routledge.

Cronin, A. (2009). *How Terrorism Ends: Understanding the Decline and Demise of Terrorist Campaigns*. Princeton, NJ: Princeton University Press.

De Goede, M. (2008). The Politics of Preemption and the War on Terror in Europe. *European Journal of International Relations, 14*(1), 161–185.

De Londras, F. (2014). Guantanamo Bay, the Rise of the Courts, and the Revenge of Politics. In D. Jenkins, A. Jacobsen, & A. Henriksen (Eds.), *The Long Decade: How 9/11 Changed the Law* (pp. 155–167). Oxford: Oxford University Press.

Dunér, B. (2005). Disregard for Security: The Human Rights Movement and 9/11. *Terrorism and Political Violence, 17*(1–2), 89–104.
Dunne, T. (2007). The Rules of the Game Are Changing: Fundamental Human Rights in Crisis After 9/11. *International Politics, 44*(2–3), 269–286.
Dyer, C., White, M., & Travis, A. (2004). Judges' verdict on terror laws provokes constitutional crisis. *The Guardian*. Retrieved May 10, 2019, from https://www.theguardian.com/uk/2004/dec/17/terrorism.humanrights3
ECHR. (1998). *European Convention on Human Rights*. Retrieved May 10, 2019, from https://www.echr.coe.int/Documents/Convention_ENG.pdf
Engin, F. I., & Rygiel, K. (2007). Abject Spaces: Frontiers, Zones, Camps. In E. Dauphinee & C. Masters (Eds.), *The Logics of Biopower and the War on Terror; Living, Dying, Surviving* (pp. 181–204). Hampshire: Palgrave Macmillan.
Ericson, R. V. (2008). The State of Preemption: Managing Terrorism Risk Through Counter Law. In L. Amoore & De M. Goede (Eds.), *Risk and the War on Terror* (pp. 57–76). Taylor and Francis eBooks. Retrieved from http://www.tandfebooks.com/isbn/9780203927700
Evangelista, M. (2008). *Law, Ethics, and the War on Terror*. Cambridge: Polity.
Fitzpatrick, J. (2003). Rendition and Transfer in the War against Terrorism: Guantanamo and Beyond. *Loyola of Los Angeles International and Comparative Law Review, 25*(3–4), 457–492.
Forsythe, D. P. (2006). United States Policy Toward Enemy Detainees in the "War on Terrorism". *Human Rights Quarterly, 28*(2), 465–491.
Gambari, I. A. (2006). *A Multilateral Response to Terrorism*. Commonwealth Ministers Reference. Retrieved May 10, 2019, from http://www.unis.unvienna.org/pdf/Gambari.pdf
Gearty, C. (2005). 11 September 2001, Counter-terrorism, and the Human Rights Act. *Journal of Law and Society., 32*(1), 18–33.
General Assembly. (1970). *Basic Principles for the Protection of Civilian Populations in Armed Conflicts, General Assembly Resolution 2675*. Retrieved May 10, 2019, from http://daccessdds.un.org/doc/RESOLUTION/GEN/NR0/349/40/IMG/NR034940.pdf?OpenElement
General Assembly. (2006). *Protection of Human Rights and Fundamental Freedoms While Countering Terrorism*. Retrieved May 10, 2019, from https://www.un.org/en/ga/search/view_doc.asp?symbol=A/RES/65/221
Gonzales, A. R. (2002). Memorandum for the President: Decision Re Application of the Geneva Conventions on Prisoners of War, 25 January

2002. In K. Greenberg & J. Dratel (Eds.), *The Torture Papers: The Road to Abu Ghraib*. New York: Cambridge University Press.

Grabosky, P. (2008). Community policing in an age of terrorism. *Crime, Law and Social Change, 50*(1–2), 1–5.

Green, P. (2002). A Question of State Crime. In P. Scraton (Ed.), *Beyond September 11th: An Anthology of Dissent* (pp. 71–76). London: Pluto Press.

Green, P., & Ward, T. (2004). *State Crime: Governments, Violence and Corruption*. Retrieved October 15, 2015, from https://www.dawsonera.com/readonline/9781849641197

Halliday, J. (2016, March 20). Almost 4,000 People Referred to UK Deradicalisation Scheme Last Year. *The Guardian*.

Hamm, M., & Spaaij, R. (2015). *Lone Wolf Terrorism in America: Using Knowledge of Radicalization Pathways to Forge Prevention Strategies*. Washington, DC: National Institute of Justice.

Happold, M. (2003). Security Council Resolution 1373 and the Constitution of the United Nations. *Journal of International Law, 16*(3), 593–610.

Hare, I., & Weinstein, J. (2009). *Extreme Speech and Democracy*. Oxford: Oxford University Press.

Harrelson-Stephens, J., & Callaway, R. L. (2009). "The Empire Strikes Back": The US Assault on the International Human Rights Regime. *Human Rights Review, 10*(3), 431–452.

Henderson-King, D., Henderson-King, E., Bolea, B., Koches, K., & Kauffman, A. (2004). Seeking Understanding or Sending Bombs: Beliefs as Predictors of Responses to Terrorism. *Peace and Conflict: Journal of Peace Psychology, 10*(1), 67–84.

Herold, M. (2017). A Dossier on Civilian Victims of United States Aerial Bombings of Afghanistan. *Cursor*. Retrieved May 10, 2019, from http://www.cursor.org/sotries/civilian_deaths.htm

Hersh, S. M. (2004). Torture at Abu Ghraib: American Soldiers Brutalized Iraqis. How Far Does the Responsibility Go? *The New Yorker*. Retrieved May 10, 2019, from http://www.newyorker.com/magazine/2004/05/10/torture-at-abu-ghraib

Hirsh, B. M., & Isikoff, M. (2004). The Roots of Torture. *Newsweek International*. Retrieved May 1, 2018, from http://www.msnbc.msn.com/id/4989481/

Hoffman, P. (2004). Human Rights and Terrorism. *Human Rights Quarterly, 26*, 932–955.

Holloway, D. (2013). *9/11 and the War on Terror.* Edinburgh University Press. Retrieved From https://www-cambridge-org. /core/books/911-and-the-war-on-terror/33D506A2854663A7E2F08CB7F714D30C

House of Commons. (2012). *Roots of Violent Radicalisation Nineteenth Report of Session 2010–12.* London: The Stationery Office Limited.

Hoyle, C., Bradford, A., & Frenett, R. (2015). Becoming Mulan? Female Western Migrants to ISIS. Institute for Strategic Dialogue. Retrieved October 21, 2016, from http://www.strategicdialogue.org/ISDJ296

Human Rights First. (2018). Guantanamo by the Numbers. Retrieved May 1, 2019, from https://www.humanrightsfirst.org/resource/guantanamo-numbers

Human Rights Watch. (2009). *Cruel Britannia British Complicity in the Torture and Ill-treatment of Terror Suspects in Pakistan.* Retrieved October 21, 2016, from https://www.therenditionproject.org.uk/documents/RDI/091124-HRW-Cruel-Britannia.pdf

Hunt Jr., B. A. (2016). Locke on Equality. *Political Research Quarterly, 69*(3), 546–556.

ICRC. (2003). *ICRC Advisory Service on International Humanitarian Law, International Humanitarian Law and International Human Rights Law.* Retrieved October 28, 2016, from https://www.icrc.org/en/document/icrc-advisory-services-international-humanitarian-law

ICRC. (2014). *The Geneva Conventions of 1949 and their Additional Protocols.* Retrieved October 28, 2016, from, https://www.icrc.org/en/document/geneva-conventions-1949-additional-protocols

Ignatieff, M. (2002). Human Rights, Sovereignty and Intervention. In N. Owen (Ed.), *Human Rights, Human Wrongs* (pp. 49–88). Oxford: Oxford University Press.

Joint Committee on Human Rights. (2005). *Counter-Terrorism Policy and Human Rights: Draft Prevention of Terrorism Act 2005.* Joint Committee on Human Rights. Retrieved June 28, 2016, from https://publications.parliament.uk/pa/jt200506/jtselect/jtrights/jtrights.htm

Joint Committee on Human Rights. (2015). *Legislative Scrutiny: Counter-Terrorism and Security Bill.* Retrieved October 28, 2016, from https://publications.parliament.uk/pa/jt201415/jtselect/jtrights/86/86.pdf

Kauzlarich, D. (2007). Seeing War as Criminal: Peace Activist Views and Critical Criminology. *Contemporary Justice Review, 10*(1), 67–85.

Khan, A. (1991). Report to the Secretary-General dated 15 July 1991 on humanitarian needs in Iraq prepared by a mission led by the Executive

Delegate of the Secretary-General for humanitarian assistance in Iraq. Retrieved from http://www.casi.org.uk/info/undocs/s22799.html

Klausen, J. (2009). British Counter-Terrorism After 7/7: Adapting Community Policing to the Fight Against Domestic Terrorism. *Journal of Ethnic and Migration Studies, 35*(3), 403–420.

Kramer, R. C., & Michalowski, R. J. (2005). War, Aggression and State Crime: A Criminological Analysis of the Invasion and Occupation of Iraq. *The British Journal of Criminology, 45*(4), 446–469.

Leffler, M. (2004). Bush's Foreign Policy. *Foreign Policy, 144*, 22–28.

Legislation.gov.uk. (2004). Civil Contingencies Act 2004. Retrieved May 10, 2019, from http://www.legislation.gov.uk/ukpga/2004/36/pdfs/ukpga_20040036_en.pdf

Legislation.gov.uk. (2012) Protection of Freedoms Act 2012. Retrieved May 10, 2019, from http://www.legislation.gov.uk/ukpga/2012/9/part/4/enacted

Lemu, M. N. (2016). Notes on Religion and Countering Violent Extremism. In H. Abadi (Ed.), *Countering Daesh Propaganda: Action-Oriented Research for Practical Policy Outcomes* (pp. 43–50). Atlanta: The Carter Center.

Lewis, A. (2005). Introduction. In A. Lewis, K. Greenberg, & J. Dratel (Eds.), *The Torture Papers: The Road to Abu Ghraib* (pp. Xiii–Xvi). Cambridge: Cambridge University Press. https://doi.org/10.1017/CBO9780511511127.001

Liberty. (2011). Liberty's Committee Stage Briefing on the Terrorism Prevention and Investigation Measures Bill in the House of Lords. Liberty. Retrieved May 10, 2019.

Liberty. (2014). Liberty's Written Evidence to the Select Committee on Extradition Law. Retrieved May 10, 2019, from https://www.libertyhuman-rights.org.uk/sites/default/files/Liberty%27s%20written%20evidence%20to%20the%20House%20of%20Lords%20Select%20Committee%20on%20Extradition%20%28Sept%202014%29.pdf

Lyon, D. (2007). National ID Cards: Crime-Control, Citizenship and Social Sorting. *Policing, 1*(*1*), 111–118.

Manderson, D. (2008). Another Modest Proposal: In Defence of the Prohibition against Torture. In M. Gani & P. Mathew (Eds.), *Fresh Perspectives on the War on Terror* (pp. 27–44). ANU E Press. Retrieved from https://www.jstor.org/stable/j.ctt24hf7j

Mathew, P. (2008). Black Holes, White Holes and Worm Holes: Pre-emptive Detention in the 'War on Terror'. In M. Gani & P. Mathew (Eds.), *Fresh Perspectives on the War on Terror* (pp. 159–188). ANU E Press. Retrieved from https://www.jstor.org/stable/j.ctt24hf7j

McGrew, A., & Held, D. (2002). Introduction. In A. McGrew & D. Held (Eds.), *Governing Globalization: Power, Authority and Global Governance* (pp. 1–25). Cambridge: Polity Press.
McInnes, C. (2003). A Different Kind of War? September 11 and the United States' Afghan War. *Review of International Studies, 29*(2), 165–184.
Michalowski, R. J. (2009). Power, Crime and Criminology in the New Imperial Age. *Crime, Law, Social Change, 51*(3), 303–325.
Milne, S. (2009). *Terrorism and Counter-Terrorism: Ethics and Liberal Democracy.* Oxford: Blackwell Publishers.
Moeckli, D. (2008). *Human Rights and Non-discrimination in the 'War on Terror'.* Published to Oxford Scholarship Online. Retrieved June 10, 2018, from https://doi.org/10.1093/acprof:oso/9780199239801.001.0001
Mutimer, D. (2007). Sovereign Contradictions: Maher Arar and the Indefinite Future. In E. Dauphinee & C. Masters (Eds.), *The Logics of Biopower and the War on Terror; Living, Dying, Surviving* (pp. 159–180). Hampshire: Palgrave Macmillan.
Mythen, G., Walklate, S., & Peatfield, E. (2016). Assembling and Deconstructing Radicalisation in PREVENT: A Case of Policy-Based Evidence Making? *Critical Social Policy.* https://doi.org/10.1177/0261018316683463
Nye, J. S. (2002). The American National Interest and Global Public Goods. *International Affairs, 78*(2), 233–244.
OHCHR. (1987). *Convention against Torture and Other Cruel, Inhuman or Degrading Treatment or Punishment.* Retrieved May 10, 2019, from https://www.ohchr.org/en/professionalinterest/pages/cat.aspx
Oliverio, A., & Lauderdale, P. (2005). Terrorism as Deviance or Social Control: Suggestions for Future Research. *International Journal of Comparative Sociology, 46*(1–2), 153–169.
Orakhelashvili, A. (2008). The Interaction Between Human Rights and Humanitarian Law: Fragmentation, Conflict, Parallelism, or Convergence? *European Journal of International Law, 19*(1), 161–182.
Peirce, G. (2010). *Dispatches From the Dark Side: On Torture and the Death of Justice.* London: Verso.
Perezalonso, A. (2010). The Message of Torture: Biopolitics and Bare Life in the US Discourse of the War on Terror. *Global Discourse, 1(2)*, 147–165.
Piazza, J. A. (2008). Incubators of Terror: Do Failed and Failing States Promote Transnational Terrorism? *International Studies Quarterly, 52*(3), 469–488.
Pliger, J. (2002). *The New Rulers of the World.* London: Verso.

Post, J. M., Sprinzak, E., & Denny, L. (2003). The Terrorists in Their Own Words: Interviews with 35 Incarcerated Middle Eastern Terrorists. *Terrorism and Political Violence, 15*(1), 171–184.

Provost, R. (2002). *International Human Rights and Humanitarian Law*. New York: Cambridge University Press.

Ragazzi, F. (2017). Countering Terrorism and Radicalisation: Securitising Social Policy? *Critical Social Policy, 37*(2), 163–179.

Rashid, A. (2008). *Taliban: Islam, Oil and the New Great Game in Central Asia*. London: I.B. Taurus & Co..

Rasool, E. (2016). Preventing the Synapse: Transmission of Daesh Religious Signals in Search of Receivers. In H. Abadi (Ed.), *Countering Daesh Propaganda: Action-Oriented Research for Practical Policy Outcomes* (pp. 38–42). Atlanta: The Carter Center.

Rasul et al. v. Bush, President of the United States. (2004). Retrieved May 10, 2019, from https://caselaw.findlaw.com/us-supreme-court/542/466.html

Rawls, J. (1971). *A Theory of Justice*. Cambridge, MA: Harvard University Press.

Rees, W., & Aldrich, R. J. (2005). Contending Cultures of Counterterrorism: Transatlantic Divergence or Convergence? *International Affairs, 81*(5), 905–923.

Rehman, J. (2007). Islam, "War on Terror" and the Future of Muslim Minorities in the United Kingdom: Dilemmas of Multiculturalism in the Aftermath of the London Bombings. *Human Rights Quarterly, 29*, 831–878.

Roberts, A. (2007). Review Essay: Torture and Incompetence in the 'War on Terror'. *Survival, 49*(1), 199–212.

Ruggiero, V. (2007). War, Crime, Empire and Cosmopolitanism. *Critical Criminology, 15*(3), 211–221.

Ruperez, J. (2006). The United Nations in the Fight Against Terrorism. United Nations. Retrieved May 10, 2019, from https://www.un.org/sc/ctc/wp-content/uploads/2017/01/2006_01_26_cted_lecture.pdf

Saurette, P. (2005). Humiliation and the Global War on Terror. *Peace Review: A Journal of Social Justice, 17*(1), 47–54.

Scheinin, M. (2005). Promotion and Protection of Human Rights: Report of the Special Rapporteur on the promotion and protection of human rights and fundamental freedoms while countering terrorism. United Nations. Retrieved May 10, 2019, from https://undocs.org/E/CN.4/2006/98

Scherrer, A., & Bigo, D. (2015). Will the Democratic Debate Over Counterterrorism Gain the Edge in Battle? Open Democracy. Retrieved May 10, 2019, from https://www.opendemocracy.net/can-europe-make-it/amandine-scherrer-didier-bigo/will-democratic-debate-over-counterrorism-gain-edge

Schmitt, C. (1996). *The Concept of the Political.* London: The University of Chicago Press.

Schutz, A. (1967). *The Phenomenology of the Social World.* Evanston, IL: Northwestern University Press.

Schwenk, E. H. (1945). Legislative Power of the Military Occupant Under Article 43, Hague Regulations. *The Yale Law Journal., 54*(2), 393–416.

Shepherd, A. (2017). Extremism, Free Speech and the Rule of Law: Evaluating the Compliance of Legislation Restricting Extremist Expressions with Article 19 ICCPR. *Journal of International and European Law, 33*, 62–83.

Simons, G. (1998). *The Scourging of Iraq: Sanctions, Law and Natural Justice.* Hampshire: Palgrave; Macmillan Press.

Simons, G. (2002). *Targeting Iraq: Sanctions and Bombings in US Policy.* London: Saqi Books.

Speckhard, A., & Akhmedova, K. (2005). Talking to Terrorists. *The Journal of Psychohistory, 33*(2), 125–156.

Stanton, G. H. (2007). Could the Rwandan Genocide Have Been Prevented? *Journal of Genocide Research, 6*(2), 211–228.

Statutory Instruments. (2011). *Prevention and Suppression of Terrorism.* The Terrorism Act 2000. Retrieved May 10, 2019, from https://assets.publishing.service.gov.uk/government/uploads/system/uploads/attachment_data/file/97940/terrorism-act-remedial-order.pdf

Steyn, J. (2004). Guantanamo Bay: The Legal Black Hole. *International & Comparative Law Quarterly, 53*(1), 1–15.

Stigall, D. E., Blakesley, C. L., & Jenks, C. (2009). Human Rights and Military Decisions: Counterinsurgency and Trends in the Law of International Armed Conflict. University of Pennsylvania. *Journal of International Law, 30*(4), 1379–1381.

Stohl, M. (2008). The Global War on Terror and State Terrorism. *Perspectives on Terrorism.* Retrieved June 10, 2018, from http://www.terrorismanalysts.com/pt/index.php/pot/article/view/48/html

The Guardian. (2009). Anti-terrorism, Crime and Security Act 2001. Retrieved May 10, 2019, from https://www.theguardian.com/commentisfree/liberty-central/2009/jan/13/anti-terrorism-act

Thomas, P. (2016). Youth, Terrorism and Education: Britain's Prevent Programme. *International Journal of Lifelong Education, 35*(2), 171–187.

Thornton, P. (2005). Iraq's Oil: The Spoils of War. *The Independent*. Retrieved April 18, 2019, from http://news.independent.co.uk/world/middle_east/article328526.ece

TPIMA. (2011). Terrorism Prevention and Investigation Measures Act 2011. Retrieved May 19, 2019, from http://www.legislation.gov.uk/ukpga/2011/23/pdfs/ukpga_20110023_en.pdf

Turner, I. (2016). A Communitarian Justification for Measures to Prevent Terrorism in the UK. *Perspectives on Terrorism, 10*(5), 68–82.

Turton, D., & Marsden, P. (2002). *Taking Refugees for a Ride? The Politics of Refugee Return to Afghanistan*. Afghanistan Research and Evaluation Unit. Retrieved June 21, 2017, from https://www.refworld.org/pdfid/47c3f3cb1a.pdf

UDHR. (1948). *Universal Declaration of Human Rights*. Retrieved June 21, 2017, from https://www.un.org/en/universal-declaration-human-rights/

UN. (1948). *Universal Declaration of Human Rights*. Retrieved June 21, 2017, from https://www.un.org/en/universal-declaration-human-rights/

UN. (2005). *Resolution 1624 (2005)*. United Nations. Retrieved June 1, 2019, from https://www.un.org/en/ga/search/view_doc.asp?symbol=S/RES/1624%20%282005%29

UN. (2006). *UN Charter: Full Text*. Accessed May 1, 2019, from https://www.un.org/en/sections/un-charter/un-charter-full-text/

UN. (2008). *The Protection of Human Rights and Fundamental Freedoms While Countering Terrorism*. Retrieved May 10, 2019, from https://unispal.un.org/UNISPAL.NSF/0/549DE4D8937F3459852574DE0052C973

UN. (2018). *UN Global Counter-Terrorism Strategy*. Retrieved June 21, 2019, from https://www.un.org/counterterrorism/ctitf/en/un-global-counter-terrorism-strategy

UNHR. (1966). *International Covenant on Civil and Political Rights*. Retrieved June 21, 2017, from https://www.ohchr.org/Documents/ProfessionalInterest/ccpr.pdf

UNICEF. (1998). *Situation Analysis of Children and Women in in Iraq*. Baghdad: UNICEF. Retrieved 1 May 2019, from http://www.casi.org.uk/info/unicef/irqpt2a.pdf

UNICEF. (1999a). *The Situation of Children and Women in South and Central Iraq*. UNICEF. Retrieved May 1, 2019, from https://www.unicef.org/iraq/situation/sit-sou-cen.htm

UNICEF (1999b). *The Situation of Children and Woman in Northern Iraq*. UNICEF. Retrieved May 1, 2019, from https://www.unicef.org/iraq/situation/sit-north.htm

Weissbrodt, D., & Hallendorff, M. (1999). Travaux Preparatoires of the Fair Trial Provisions--Articles 8 to 11--of the Universal Declaration of Human Rights. *Human Rights Quarterly, 21*, 1061–1096.

Welch, M. (2008). Ordering Iraq: Reflections on Power, Discourse, & Neocolonialism. *Critical Criminology, 16*(4), 257–269.

Williams, P. J. (2001). By Any Means Necessary. *The Nation*. Retrieved June 21, 2019, from https://www.thenation.com/article/any-means-necessary-1/

Wilson, R. J. (2003). United States Detainees at Guantánamo Bay: The Inter-American Commission on Human Rights Responds to a "Legal Black Hole". *Human Rights Brief, 10*(3), 1–5.

Ysseldyk, R., Matheson, K., & Anisman, H. (2010). Religiosity as Identity: Toward an Understanding of Religion from a Social Identity Perspective. *Personality and Social Psychology Review, 14*(1), 60–71.

Zulaika, J. (2009). *Terrorism: The Self-fulfilling Prophecy*. London: University of Chicago Press.

4

The Case of Al-Qaeda: From Allies to Enemies

This chapter charts the rise of al-Qaeda (AQ), the group largely believed to have committed the acts of 9/11 which provided the impetus for the 'war on terror' (Halliday, 2002). This chapter starts by assessing the factors which influenced the emergence of AQ, and their motivations and aims as a terrorist organization. The second half of this chapter explores the emergence of AQ from a critical perspective, which considers the role of the United Kingdom and the United States in the emergence of the AQ. Of great importance in this discussion is the demonstration of geopolitical power in constructing terrorism. This chapter explores how AQ was not labelled as a terrorist organization when it was using violence to counter the threat of communism in Afghanistan, and how it was redefined as a terrorist organization when it started to use violence against western states. This demonstrates how terrorism is a political concept because the use of the term has been determined by the entity against which the violence is directed. This chapter therefore reveals the symbiotic relationship between state crime and terrorism in the 'war on terror' through exploring how al-Qaeda were purposely created as a terrorist organization through which the UK and US governments could harm other states. Moreover, this often-omitted part of history will be explored

S. Ahmed, *The 'War on Terror', State Crime & Radicalization*, Palgrave Studies in Risk, Crime and Society, https://doi.org/10.1007/978-3-030-40138-2_4

to document the more nuanced ways in which the US and UK governments were involved in creating al-Qaeda.

This chapter thereby demonstrates the value of considering the history of Islamist terrorist organizations, and the implications of such an analysis for our understanding of the relationship between state crime and terrorism in the 'war on terror'. Using a historical perspective, and one that seeks to question the circumstances in which terrorist groups came to exist also has implications for revealing the root causes of terrorism and therefore, the important processes which gave rise to terrorism. Such an analysis necessitates an exploration of the interactions between the macro-national level, the meso-societal level and the micro-individual-emotional level and therefore, how inter-state crime and intra-state crime facilitate radicalization. In discussing these interconnections, this chapter does not seek to argue that macro-national level state crimes alone facilitate terrorism, rather it seeks to demonstrate how some of the factors which contributed to the existence of terrorism and terrorist groups, in this case AQ, were state crimes.

The Emergence of Al-Qaeda

Although the 'war on terror' has been conceptualized as starting with the attacks of September 11th, it could be argued that most of the state-instigated processes and mechanisms which led to September 11th and the existence of AQ were created before 9/11. When considering the rise of AQ, one must consider how the terrorist group came to exist and the specific factors which shaped the group, its ideology, its motivations and therefore, its existence.

The first factor which facilitated the emergence of AQ is Soviet-style state-communism, and therefore the role of communism and the communist coup in 1978 in transforming Afghanistan. It has been argued that a lack of law and order leads to, and indeed facilitates organized crime and street crime (Aguirre & Herrera, 2013; Van Dijk, 2007; Williams, 1994). Similarly, in the realm of terrorism, the UN (2018) identified a lack of law and order, governance and political instability in contributing to the existence of terrorism. The influx of communism had severe consequences for Afghanistan, in not only causing instant civil disruption, but also in leading to long-term political and social instability and the existence of the factors just highlighted as contributing to terrorism. Prior to the prevalence of communism in Afghanistan, under the rule of King Mohammad Zahir Shah and President Mohammad Daoud Khan, Afghanistan was a safe, stable, freer and more liberal society, especially for women (Braithwaite & Wardak, 2013; Jones, 2010; Maley, 1993).

In 1979, the Soviet Union invaded Afghanistan. The invasion was responded to by a military coalition in which the United States, western Europe, Pakistan, and Saudi Arabia merged with the Mujahideen and Osama bin Laden. Within this nexus, the Mujahideen, which mainly consisted of Afghan and Arab Muslims, became a vessel through which states could counter the communist threat. However, using the Mujahideen to counter the Soviet Union also necessitated the existence of an ideology which could be used to motivate, and indeed unite the Mujahideen to pursue the Soviet Union as an enemy. Of interest is how a group, in this case the Mujahideen, were constructed as a legitimate source through which to combat Soviet communism and how this construction featured many of the facets which would later become so instrumental in the creation, maintenance, growth and existence of Islamist terrorism. It could be argued that if the Mujahedeen were used by coalition states to counter a threat which wasn't a state, then it would be possible to conceptualize the actions of the Mujahedeen as a form of state sponsored terrorism. However, if one deconstructs the actions used by the Mujahedeen in relation to violations of IHRL and IHL, it is still possible to conceptualize these actions as a form of state sponsored warfare, and possibly state crime. On a practical level, it was necessary to create the physical conditions in which the Mujahideen could become a credible force to counter the communist invasion. The coalition constructed communism in relation to discourses of otherization and a lack of commonality, and these macro-national level and meso-societal level variables facilitated radicalization. Where discourses of otherization and a lack of commonality are prevalent, individuals view otherized groups as a binary and it is this lack of belonging and attachment to the group that makes violence against these group possible.

The second factor which facilitated the existence of AQ was the financing of the Mujahideen. The Mujahideen would battle the Soviet Union, and receive financing via the drug trade, the CIA and the oil monarchies of the Gulf (Kepel, 2006; Mamdani, 2002). The US support of the Mujahideen led to a surge in US heroin consumption, with the United States channelling at least $3 billion to Mujahideen groups between 1979 and 1992 and the Saudi dynasty provided the same funds via Islamic charities, and drug-running operations (Parenti, 2002). If one considers the logistical necessities of terrorist groups, finance constitutes a necessity, and therefore it would be plausible to assume that the Mujahideen would not have been able to exist without financial state facilitation. However, what also becomes apparent is the role of geo-political construction in the area of narcotics. On a US national level selling heroin is a crime, as is the transfer of the drug from one country to another, which constitutes the higher criminal offence of drug trafficking. This again demonstrates the importance of identity, because the distribution of narcotics should not be legitimized by virtue of it occurring via states, as opposed to non-state groups. Through providing the Mujahideen with financial assistance, the coalition provided the economic conditions which facilitate terrorism, and this could be conceptualized as meso-societal level facilitation since it provides the economic conditions within which terrorism can emerge.

The third necessity in making the Mujahideen a credible army was the supply of weapons. Under international trade agreements, such as the Consolidated EU and National Arms Export Licensing Criteria, it is illegal for states to sell arms to organizations that may use these arms to cause harm (ATT monitor, 2016; Dunne & Perlo-Freeman, 2003) (see Chap. 6 for a more in-depth discussion on arms). The United States provided the Mujahideen with US-made Stinger anti-aircraft missiles which helped to weaken Soviet air power (Mamdani, 2002; Scraton, 2002). Trucks took weapons to Afghanistan and bought back heroin, with the money from the opium drugs trade helping the Mujahedeen to introduce a 'revolutionary tax' which financed the war against the Soviet Union (Kepel, 2006). The symbiotic relationship between finance, weapons and narcotics was permitted because of who it served: western states. One can instantly note the existence of ideological construction and geo-political power in how these very same actions are criminalized in relation to other groups, such as international organized crime groups. Further, this lack of scrutiny and forethought meant that there was no contemplation of how the processes, in this case the use of narcotics to fund jihadist activities, could continue to exist beyond the communist threat, and come to form one of the essential financing mechanisms through which terrorist groups could emerge and sustain their existence. The transfer of funds by states, via the narcotics trade, constituted one of the meso-societal level grassroots conditions conducive for terrorism. Long term it would become an important factor in creating the economic climate necessary for terrorism and it would therefore remain a meso-societal level factor which directly facilitates terrorism. For example, after the withdrawal of the Soviet Union, an estimated 70% of the Taliban's income came from protection money and the sale of opium (Glaze, 2007) and after 2001, Afghanistan supplied 92% of the world's illicit opium (UN, 2006). States were therefore instrumental in creating the economic conditions and physical conditions necessary for the Mujahideen to exist. However, the state facilitation of terrorism via the Mujahedeen also involved perhaps far darker, and arguably more dangerous mechanisms, such as that of creating and promoting jihadism. The coalitions were therefore also directly involved in creating other meso-societal level conditions which facilitate radicalization, such as the social and the ideological conditions necessary for terrorism.

The previous chapter discussed the UN criminalizing the incitement and glorification of terrorism through creating resolution 1624 (UN, 2005). The duty placed on states was due to a recognition that individuals or groups that promote dangerous ideologies, disperse these ideologies and this dispersal facilitates radicalization. However, dispersing jihadism was one of the main ways in which the coalition facilitated the Mujahideen. Here one can recognize the irony that is prevalent in the 'war on terror', and how historic state actions have facilitated terrorism and created some the processes which now maintain and sustain terrorism. It could therefore be argued that the coalition incited religious hatred and terrorism through inciting jihad against the Soviet Union. As Bronson (2006: 9) states, 'during the 1980s, American leaders believed that bringing down the Soviet Union was worth the costs of empowering religious radicals in

Afghanistan and elsewhere'. Although states can facilitate terrorism through creating the practical conditions necessary for terrorism, they can also facilitate terrorism through creating the ideological factors, such as racism, discrimination and marginalization which constitute the meso-societal level and facilitate radicalization.

The fourth factor that was essential for the emergence of the Mujahideen was ideology. Interestingly, many of the facets that are now associated with Islamist ideology were actively manufactured by states, as part of the state produced Mujahideen jihadist ideology to motivate and legitimize the violence against the Soviet Union (as detailed below). Rapoport's (2012) four waves of terrorism are testimony to the need for ideologies, as well as favourable social and political conditions for the existence of terrorism. It can be argued that dangerous ideologies constitute one of the most dangerous facets of terrorism. These ideologies can become part of mainstream society and when they do, it is then far more difficult to counter ideologies which advocate the marginalization and otherization of entire groups, with evident examples being genocide and apartheid. The somewhat simple, and yet unequivocal idea that underpinned the state manufactured jihadist ideology in the fight against communism was combining religious ideology and political ideology. It was not envisaged that the constructed link between the two would continue to shape and motivate the existence of terrorism well after the defeat of Soviet communism in Afghanistan. The contemporary importance and existence of this link can be witnessed from how religious ideology and political ideology form the backbone of definitions of terrorism, with the Terrorism Act 2006 citing these ideologies as the cause and motivation for terrorists to commit acts of terrorism. Under the Terrorism Act 2006, terrorism is defined as an action or threat designed to influence the government or intimidate the public. Its purpose is to advance a political, religious or ideological cause. The state use of and facilitation of religious ideology was instrumental in forming what would later be called the 'jihad narrative' (Prevent, 2011).

According to Byman (2005a), ideology can also function to support states that seek to export their own political system or want some strategic advantage. The coalition sought a strategic advantage and therefore created an ideology to support securing the means necessary to obtain their desired advantage. The manufactured ideology was formed to construct a common enemy and common grievances (Byman, 2005b; Cline & Alexander, 1986; Hoffman, 2006; Levitt, 2002; Nacos, 2006; Shay, 2005). The main idea exploited in the creation of this ideology was 'the godlessness of communism' (Dupree, 1985; Saikal, 2004). This instantly led to a sharp division of 'us' versus 'them', with religion being the definer of categories and therefore difference. The ideology was praised and embraced by states, with the United States labelling the Mujahedeen as 'freedom-fighters' and President Reagan introducing them as the 'moral equivalents of our Founding Fathers' when they visited the Oval Office (Ahmad, 2008: 5). However, this ideology was not simply dispersed, it was also institutionalized. As Choussudovsky (2001) describes, the United States, Saudi, and Pakistani alliance turned religious madrassas into political schools and thus began the growth of a more formalized version of jihadism amongst young Muslims. As evidenced in Chaps. 5 and 6, the use of schools for training jihadism was perhaps one of the most significant factors which would influence, and indeed guarantee the growth of jihadism for years to come. One can therefore note how states created the macro-national level and meso-societal level conditions necessary for radicalization. They produced the very discourses, binaries and inter-group hostilities which made it possible for the Mujahedeen to feel the emotions required to commit acts of violence against communists.

As this holistic approach to the 'war on terror' reveals, the different factors which contributed to the emergence of AQ were heavily influenced by state actions and therefore, when one considers the role of states in contemporary terrorism, many of the processes which now maintain terrorism can be traced back to state facilitation (see Chap. 6 for a detailed discussion of the educational institutionalization of Islamist ideologies). The establishment of schools and religious madrassas meant that state practices created the meso-societal level grassroot conditions which would facilitate terrorism. Jihadist Islamist ideology became institutionalized in schools and through doing so, it became entrenched in the social conditions within which the society operated.

The emphasis on religion fulfilled another important objective for the coalition, it provided unity and therefore ensured that those of the same religious identity, Muslims would join the jihadist cause. A credible army was required to defeat the communists, and the use of Islam to provide ideological legitimacy and form a facilitator of recruitment can be witnessed from the following data. The Afghanistan war led to the creation of a global network of individuals that brought together between 10,000 and 50,000 volunteers from 40 different Islamic countries, including Indonesia, Algeria, Sudan, Egypt and Saudi Arabia to fight communism (Mamdani, 2002; Rashid, 1999; Scraton, 2002). One can instantly see the continuation of this process through how contemporary Islamist terrorist groups exist as a global network. The value and long-term impact of these processes cannot be under-estimated because although these processes now form taken for granted facets of Islamist terrorism, assessing their origins contributes to a neutral ontological understanding of the factors which caused radicalization. More importantly, it is only through such an approach, where one carves open a space where all factors which contribute to terrorism can emerge, that it will possible to then reduce, and eliminate the conditions which give rise to terrorism. The premise of utilizing religion as an ideology for the furtherance of a political cause was deeply embedded in the fight against communism, and thus became part of a larger psyche and discourse whereby religion became recognized as a means through which to promote political ideologies.

The fifth factor that was influenced by state practices and positively facilitated the existence of Islamist terrorism was the creation of a leader, Osama bin Laden. Bin Laden came from a wealthy family that sponsored scholarships in universities like Yale and Harvard, and was trusted by the Saudi security services, their Pakistani counterparts and the CIA (Gerges, 2015). The CIA assisted bin Laden in creating a major arms depot and a training facility, both of which were instrumental in leading to the creation of al-Qaeda in 1989 (Rashid, 2008). The Soviet war transformed bin Laden in several ways. Through witnessing how religion, political motivation and terrorism/war could be used for the destruction of one of the world's superpowers, bin Laden experienced how these factors could be combined and used against other states (Mozaffri, 2005). This is where the power of religion and use of opium in facilitating political action became a reality, because as previously stated, when the Soviet Union withdrew, these mechanisms remained. The relationship between bin Laden and the coalition broke down in the Gulf war in 1991, when the

Saudi government allowed the United States and its allies to base themselves in Saudi Arabia (Gerges, 2015). Kepel (2003: 97) highlights the significance of the victory over the Soviet Union for the Mujahedeen, stating,

> they saw themselves as the ones who had shattered the Soviet empire in the same way that the first Muslims had destroyed the Sassanid Empire. Now, the Salafi-Jihadists were ready to fight the Byzantium of today: the United States of America.

This period was vital in terms of providing many of the factors which would continue to exist, and influence the existence and continuation of terrorist groups, such as AQ. Bin Laden was given power, shown how to use ideology to form a terrorist group and ultimately trained in how to build a terrorist group by states.

The growth of Islamist terrorism was also influenced by the larger geopolitical context, which involved amongst other events, the Iranian revolution. The revolution incorporated the war between Iran and Iraq, and the invasion of Kuwait by Iraq facilitated 'the rise and radicalization of Islamist movements all over the world' (Mozaffri, 2005: 37). Conflicts in 'Chechnya, Iraq (in the period after the US-led invasion in 2003), Yemen, Libya, Somalia, Mali and others' helped to attract jihadist foreign fighters (Bakker & Zuijdewijn, 2015: 2). Bin Laden also exploited the existence of global injustices through claiming that AQ was fighting global injustices against Muslims, and this further strengthened and combined religion with political motivation to advance the political cause of pursuing jihad, and pursuing justice (Sadiki, 2002). For example, following the Madrid bombings in March 2004, an AQ statement read, 'if you don't stop your injustices, more and more blood will flow and these attacks will seem very small compared to what can occur in what you call terrorism' (Al-Qaeda, 2004). It could be argued that because the idea of achieving justice via war was successful in ousting the Soviet Union, bin Laden then continued to use injustice to mobilize troops and facilitate recruitment.

The Afghan war and the coalition used the concept of godlessness to create a religious binary and this was a powerful ideology because it exploited individuals' religious sentiments to gain political motivation.

They also portrayed terrorism and therefore violence as a legitimate way to counter the threat of godlessness, and the Soviet threat to the existence of religion and Islam. In uniting these concepts, jihad became associated with armed conflict (Alexiev, 2004) and Muslims were radicalized to believe that it is their 'religious and moral obligation to wage Jihad against *kafir* or non-believers' (Githens-Mazer, 2010: 5). Therefore, state practices which facilitated terrorism included creating the economic conditions for terrorism, supplying arms for terrorism, creating an ideology that incorporated religion and politics, the educational institutionalization of jihadist ideologies, use of ideologies to facilitate recruitment into the Mujahideen and the use of terrorism to counter ideologies such as godlessness. Prior to discussing the continuation of these state-instigated factors in the 'war on terror', it is worth noting that whereas during the Afghan war, states controlled the use of these ideology, weapons and finances, following the war, states were no longer able to control these entities and especially the use of the jihadist ideology.

The war and post-war conditions fed into the micro-individual-emotional level through, impacting trauma and other psychological disorders (Shaw, 1986; Speckhard & Akhmedova, 2005; Weenink, 2015), powerlessness (Boyns & Ballard, 2004; Henderson-King, Henderson-King, Bolea, Koches, & Kauffman, 2004; Lemu, 2016; Speckhard & Akhmedova, 2005); promoting a sense of belonging to the group identity (Abdo, 2006; Gould & Klor, 2016; Hamm & Spaaij, 2015; Post, Sprinzak, & Denny, 2003); a perceived binary of Muslim and non-Muslim (Hoyle, Bradford, & Frenett, 2015) and injustice, political oppression and political grievances (Meloy, Roshdi, Glaz-Ocik, & Hoffmann, 2015; Mythen, Walklate, & Khan, 2009; Pape, 2003; Rasool, 2016). As this chapter explores, some of these variables were created as part of countering the Soviet Union and the ideology required to do this; other variables, like trauma, existed due to the war and variables such as powerlessness, injustice, political oppression and political grievances were far more fluid and existed during and after the war.

When one considers the role of states, it is possible to contend that the coalition positively impacted these variables through facilitating the emergence of the Mujahideen. However, states also impacted these very variables through their withdrawal from Afghanistan, which created the meso-societal level grass root conditions which were conducive to terrorism. As previously stated, the UN (2018) highlights the role of prolonged unresolved conflicts, and lack of good governance as being conditions conducive to terrorism. As previously stated political instability has also been recognized, with states having a duty to ensure public safety and order under Article 43 of the Hague Regulations 1907 (Schwenk, 1945). Although the coalition members were under this duty, they failed to ensure public safety and order when they withdrew from Afghanistan and this failure heavily influenced the continuation of terrorism in the country.

> When the Soviets were about to withdraw, the U.S. visionary leader Charlie Wilson, who supported the fight, proposed to the U.S. Congress to fund the rehabilitation of the Afghan and foreign fighters. Having spent $3 billion to fight the Soviets, the U.S. Congress lacked the foresight to invest with a fraction of the amount to rehabilitate the foreign fighters and their families. (Gunaratna, 2016: 86)

As this chapter explores, the immediate challenges were vast and in the absence of foreseeability and authority, democracy and political stability to remedy these challenges, terrorism was able to flourish.

Whereas the Mujahideen and AQ were direct products of the Cold War—'trained, equipped, and financed by the CIA and its regional allies—the Taliban came out of the agony and the ashes of the war against the Soviet Union' (Mamdani, 2002: 772). The conditions after the war continued to facilitate terrorism. These conditions can be conceptualized as constituting the meso-societal level, because they directly created the context within which a terrorist group, the Taliban could emerge. As Keen (2006: 174) states, after a war that had devastated the country, 'its people were crying out for reconstruction'. The war led to large numbers being displaced because the occupying states had failed to facilitate the reconstruction of Afghanistan prior to their withdrawal. More than 1.2 million Afghans lost their lives and the country's 'economic, political, educational and cultural infrastructure was decimated' (Braithwaite & Wardak, 2013: 182). Afghanistan descended into warlordism which was further exacerbated with the decline of funds into the country. These economic, social and political conditions facilitated the emergence of the

Taliban. First, the Taliban were able to disperse their jihadist ideology via schools, with many Afghan civilians and refugees having no choice but to send their children to religious schools, and second, the Taliban were able to provide order in society and a form of stability (Ahmad, 2008). There was a legal duty to provide structure via reconstruction by the coalition. Instead, strain was prevalent in Afghan society through a lack of employment, services and increased levels of poverty, which contributed to individuals joining the Taliban. The Taliban gave individuals hope. To put it crudely, the choice was living in poverty and potentially dying from the existence of inhumane conditions or joining a group that was offering stability and employment. The relationship between state crime and terrorism can therefore be conceptualized as the failure to fulfil a legal duty, and this failure facilitating terrorism.

The country was subjected to two highly centralized state projects: first, Soviet-supported Marxism, and then, CIA-supported Islamization (Ahmad, 1991). Even when the first ideology had been defeated, the second remained part of Afghan life through having been institutionalized in madrassas. The second phase of institutionalization included instilling what Ahmad (1991) calls 'Islamization' in the criminal justice system. States can institutionalize an ideology and the criminal justice system, with its inherent capacity for social control, represents one of the most powerful ways for states to do so. The institutionalization went beyond the education system and, as Barfield (2010) states, by 1994 the Taliban were implementing a system of justice closely tied to their Deobandi ideology. This was the beginning of establishing a Sharia system of law, and by 1998, the Taliban had taken over much of Afghanistan. The extremist jihadist ideology became part of Sharia law, leading to a legal system that committed heinous war crimes and crimes against humanity (Afghanistan Justice Project, 2005; Grossman, 2006). Afghanistan now also provided a place for recruits to be trained and veterans from Bosnia, Chechnya, Algeria, Egypt, Iraq and elsewhere flocked to Afghanistan (Gerges, 2015). However, whereas individuals were flocking to help the coalition defeat communism, and during this time the coalitions were able to mentor these individuals in their battle with the Soviet Union, after the withdrawal, the Taliban gained the power to shape and use this army to defeat their self-proclaimed enemies.

By the time the Soviet Union left Afghanistan in 1989, AQ represented the global jihadist-Salafi ideology and were confident from believing that they had defeated the Soviet Union (Volpi, 2011). Internationally AQ were transforming the jihadi discourse and by the 1990s, AQ existed in many countries with weak states, including Afghanistan and northern Yemen (Halliday, 2002). In 1998, AQ were formally launched and included groups from countries including Algeria, Bangladesh, Egypt and Pakistan, and bin Laden's global jihad was based on countering America (Cronin, 2006; Wright, 2007).

Following the Soviet war,

> 'many Arab countries were reluctant to bring back their nationals, fearing they would seek to replicate the Afghan experience in their home countries' and therefore 'many became destitute, and their anger was harnessed by terrorist groups to fight in Kashmir, Chechnya, Bosnia, and other conflict zones'. (Gunaratna, 2016: 86)

As Halliday (2002) states, the power of today's Islamist movements is a legacy of the Cold War and the past. For example, bin Laden stated,

> what America is tasting now, is something insignificant compared to what we have tasted for scores of years. Our nation (the Islamic world) has been tasting this humiliation and this degradation for more than 80 years. Its sons are killed, its blood is shed, its sanctuaries are attacked, and no one hears and no one heeds. (Bin Laden, 2001)

This division was premised on justice and revenge. It was motivated by dispersing an ideology to counter a dangerous US imperialist ideology. Bin Laden gained support through emphasizing how jihad could combat geo-political US power. Factors which facilitate radicalization through the macro-national level and meso-societal level, such as perceived political oppression, stigma and injustices were all factors which impacted the micro-individual-emotional level, and bin Laden offered individuals a way of dealing with their emotions of anger, betrayal and loss. As his speech reveals, he used these factors to further heighten individuals' beliefs that violence was the only means through which they could stop injustices. Bin Laden utilized contemporary displays of oppressive power and successfully tied international experiences of injustice and oppression to local ones, and through doing so, he was able to mobilize individuals' emotions of fear and vulnerability. It could be argued that bin Laden understood the interconnectedness of the relationships presented in the constitutive theory of radicalization, because he placed the individual as the focus and then sought to understand how society, states and the world impact the individual and their identity, perceptions, beliefs, values and feelings. Through simply recognizing these relationships, he was able to exploit the destruction of the universal level via the 'war on terror' and point out just how self-defeating this war is. He was also able to highlight the binary construction and existence of the world, and some of these divisions, whereby one groups human rights, are used to justify the denial of another groups. His use of legislation which disproportionately targeted Muslims, genocides where the international community failed to act, the manipulation of universal values which are meant to unite humanity, provided him with a platform from which he could take the moderate negative emotions experienced because of the 'war on terror' and heighten these through highlighting other realities within the 'war on terror'. He very successfully not only highlighted macro-national level and meso-societal level factors which impact the micro-individual-emotional level, but was also able to understand the extent to which the super macro-universal level had damaged the community of humanity.

Bin Laden tied all of these factors, events and ideals and the consequences of their destruction to political action and violence. Bin Laden had 'been central to the US-backed Saudi strategy to spread the Saudi version of Islam, Wahhabism, in Afghanistan' (Green, 2002: 74), and globally, dispersing a literalist brand of Islam-puritanical Wahhabism that dismissed all other interpretations of Islam (Sadiki, 2002). As the following chapters demonstrate, Wahhabism became the main driving force behind global terrorism. The coalition therefore both institutionalized jihadism in Afghanistan and globally dispersed Wahhabism. After 2001, AQ and the Taliban continued to exist as a network of individuals that shared similar beliefs and ideologies, but also maintained a degree of independence (Stenersen, 2013). Differences between the groups included the Taliban being concerned with internal Afghan issues and

AQ pursing transnational jihad and justice. Therefore, whereas AQ were concerned with the US occupation of Mecca and Medina, the holiest and most sacred places for Muslims, the Taliban were mainly concerned with national Afghanistan issues (Duyvesteyn, 2004; Grob-Fitzgibbon, 2005; Rice, 2009).

This chapter has explored one of the first instances within the 'war on terror' where states facilitated terrorism via state practices, state crime and state created discourses. Of interest is how the coalition used their power to create and promote jihad. Although tying religion to violence is not a new practice, and there are many historic examples of this, the use of religion by the coalition did influence the creation and perpetuation of a movement and ideology. This ideology of jihad facilitated both the existence of macro-national level state crimes, and the meso-societal level conditions which facilitate state crime. In all these actions, as highlighted above, there were international safeguards that were meant to restrict the existence of these very practices. In the first instance, the violation of these safeguards created a reality whereby states could exercise the misuse of their power, and in the second instance, it further represented the institutionalization of geo-political power. Interestingly, these two features facilitate both the conditions within which radicalization can flourish and they also give layers of legitimacy to claims of geo-political injustice, political oppression and global discriminatory practices. It was in this interplay of geo-political power, religion, violence and state crimes, that bin Laden was successful in carving his own counter discourse to the 'war on terror'. And it was his acute awareness of how to use and exploit the reality that was being created to empower and motivate individuals that he was able to create AQ.

References

Abdo, G. (2006). *Mecca and Main Street: Muslim Life in America after 9/11*. Oxford: Oxford University Press.

Afghanistan Justice Project. (2005). *Casting Shadows: War Crimes and Crimes against Humanity: 1978–2001*. Retrieved May 1, 2019, from http://afghanistanjusticeproject.org/warcrimesandcrimesagainsthumanity19782001.pdf

Aguirre, J., & Herrera, H. A. (2013). Institutional Weakness and Organized Crime in Mexico: The Case of Michoacán. *Trends in Organized Crime, 16*(2), 221–238.

Ahmad, A. (2008). *Islam, Islamisms and the West.* Social Register. https://socialistregister.com/index.php/srv/article/view/5873/2769

Ahmad, E. (1991, April 7). In Afghanistan: Cease Fire Please. *Dawn.* Karachi. Retrieved May 1, 2019, from https://www.hampshire.edu/library/archives-and-special-collections

Al Qaeda. (2004). *Full Text: Al-Qaeda: Madrid Claim.* Retrieved May 1, 2019, from http://news.bbc.co.uk/1/hi/world/europe/3509556.stm

Alexiev, A. (2004, March). *Understanding Sufism and Its Potential Role in US Policy.* Nixon Centre Conference Report. Retrieved May 1, 2018, from http://www.islamawareness.net/Sufism/sufism_us_policy.pdf

ATT Monitor. (2016). *Dealing in Double Standards: How Arms Sales to Saudi Arabia Are Causing Human Suffering in Yemen.* Retrieved May 1, 2019, from https://www.amnesty.org.uk/files/webfm/Documents/issues/att_monitor_case_study_2_-_saudi_arabia_-_final_version.pdf

Bakker, E., & Zuijdewijn, J. R. (2015). *Jihadist Foreign Fighter Phenomenon in Western Europe: A Low-Probability, High-Impact Threat.* The Hague: International Centre for Counter-Terrorism. Retrieved May 1, 2019, from https://www.icct.nl/wp-content/uploads/2015/11/ICCT-Bakker-DeRoyvanZuijdewijn-Jihadist-Foreign-Fighter-Phenomenon-in-Western-Europe-October2015.pdf

Barfield, T. (2010). *Afghanistan: A Cultural and Political History.* Princeton, NJ: Princeton University Press.

Bin Laden, O. (2001). Text: Bin Laden's Statement. *The Guardian.* Retrieved May 2, 2012, from http://www.guardian.co.uk/waronterror/story/0,1361,565069,00.html

Boyns, D., & Ballard, J. D. (2004). Developing a Sociological Theory for the Empirical Understanding of Terrorism. *The American Sociologist, 35*(2), 5–25.

Braithwaite, J., & Wardak, A. (2013). Crime and War in Afghanistan, Part 1: The Hobbesian Solution. *The British Journal of Criminology, 53*(2), 179–196.

Bronson, R. (2006). *Thicker than Oil: America's Uneasy Partnership with Saudi Arabia.* Oxford: Oxford University Press.

Byman, D. (2005a). *Deadly Connections: States that Sponsor Terrorism.* Cambridge: Cambridge University Press.

Byman, D. (2005b). *Confronting Passive Sponsors of Terrorism.* Washington, DC: The Brookings Institution, Center for Middle East Policy. Retrieved

June 21, 2019, https://www.brookings.edu/research/confronting-passive-sponsors-of-terrorism/
Choussudovsky, M. (2001). *Who Is Osama Bin Laden?* Centre for Research for Globalization. Retrieved June 21, 2019, from https://www.globalresearch.ca/osamagate/369
Cline, R. S., & Alexander, Y. (1986). *Terrorism as State-Sponsored Covert Warfare*. Virginia: Hero Books.
Cronin, A. K. (2006). How Al-Qaida Ends: The Decline and Demise of Terrorist Groups. *International Security, 31*(1), 7–48.
Dunne, P., & Perlo-Freeman, S. (2003). *The Impact of a Responsible Arms Control Policy on the UK Economy*. Oxfam. Retrieved June 21, 2019, from http://carecon.org.uk/Users/paul/Oxfamreport7.pdf
Dupree, N. H. (1985). The Conscription of Afghan Writers: An Aborted Experiment in Socialist Realism. *Central Asian Survey, 4*(4), 69–87.
Duyvesteyn, L. (2004). How New Is the New Terrorism? *Studies in Conflict & Terrorism, 27*(5), 439–454.
Gerges, A. F. (2015). *The Rise and Fall of Al-Qaeda*. Oxford: Oxford University Press.
Githens-Mazer. (2010). *Rethinking the Causal Concept of Islamic Radicalisation*. Working Paper. The Committee on Concepts and Methods. Retrieved 21 October 2016, from http://www.concepts-methods.org/Files/WorkingPaper/PC%2042%20Githens-Mazer.pdf
Glaze, J. A. (2007). *Opium and Afghanistan: Reassessing U.S. Counternarcotics Strategy*. US Government. Retrieved May 1, 2018, from https://ssi.armywarcollege.edu/pdffiles/pub804.pdf
Gould, E., & Klor, E. F. (2016). The Long-Run Effect of 9/11: Terrorism, Backlash, and the Assimilation of Muslim Immigrants in the West. *The Economic Journal, 126*(597), 2064–2114.
Green, P. (2002). A Question of State Crime. In P. Scraton (Ed.), *Beyond September 11th: An Anthology of Dissent* (pp. 71–76). London: Pluto Press.
Grob-Fitzgibbon, B. (2005). What Is Terrorism? Redefining a Phenomenon in Time of War. *Peace & Change, 30*(2), 231–246.
Grossman, P. (2006). Truth, Justice and Stability in Afghanistan. In N. Roht-Arriaza & J. Mariezcurrena (Eds.), *Transitional Justice in the Twenty-First Century: Beyond Truth Versus Justice* (pp. 255–277). Cambridge: Cambridge University Press.
Gunaratna, R. (2016). Best Practices: Rehabilitating and Reintegrating Foreign Fighters. In H. Abadi (Ed.), *Countering Daesh Propaganda: Action-Oriented Research for Practical Policy Outcomes* (pp. 84–92). Atlanta: The Carter Center.

Halliday, F. (2002). *Two Hours that Shook the World. September 11 2001: Causes and Consequences*. London: Saqi Books.
Hamm, M., & Spaaij, R. (2015). *Lone Wolf Terrorism in America: Using Knowledge of Radicalization Pathways to Forge Prevention Strategies*. Washington, DC: National Institute of Justice.
Henderson-King, D., Henderson-King, E., Bolea, B., Koches, K., & Kauffman, A. (2004). Seeking Understanding or Sending Bombs: Beliefs as Predictors of Responses to Terrorism. *Peace and Conflict: Journal of Peace Psychology, 10*(1), 67–84.
Hoffman, B. (2006). *Inside Terrorism*. New York: Columbia University Press.
Hoyle, C., Bradford, A., & Frenett, R. (2015). *Becoming Mulan? Female Western Migrants to ISIS*. Institute for Strategic Dialogue. Retrieved October 21, 2016, from http://www.strategicdialogue.org/ISDJ296
Jones, S. G. (2010). *In the Graveyard of Empires: America's War in Afghanistan*. London: W. W. Norton & Company, Inc.
Keen, D. (2006). *Endless War? Hidden Functions of the 'War on Terror'*. Pluto Press. Retrieved June 21, 2019, from https://www.dawsonera.com/abstract/9781849642774
Kepel, G. (2003). The Origins and Development of the Jihadist Movement: From Anti-Communism to Terrorism. *Asian Affairs, 34*(2), 91–108.
Kepel, G. (2006). *Jihad: The Trail of Political Islam*. London: I.B Tauris.
Lemu, M. N. (2016). Notes on Religion and Countering Violent Extremism. In H. Abadi (Ed.), *Countering Daesh Propaganda: Action-Oriented Research for Practical Policy Outcomes* (pp. 43–50). Atlanta: The Carter Center.
Levitt, M. (2002). *Targeting Terror: U.S. Policy Toward Middle Eastern State Sponsors and Terrorist Organizations, Post-September 11*. Washington, DC: Washington Institute for Near East Policy. Retrieved June 21, 2019, from https://www.washingtoninstitute.org/uploads/Documents/pubs/TargetingTerror.pdf
Maley, W. (1993). The Future of Islamic Afghanistan. *Security Dialogue, 24*(4), 383–396.
Mamdani, M. (2002). Good Muslim, Bad Muslim: A Political Perspective on Culture and Terrorism. *American Anthropologist, 104*(3), 766–775.
Meloy, J. R., Roshdi, K., Glaz-Ocik, J., & Hoffmann, J. (2015). Investigating the Individual Terrorist in Europe. *Journal of Threat Assessment and Management, 2*(3–4), 140–152.
Mozaffri, M. (2005). Bin Laden, Islamism and Terrorism. *Society, 42*(5), 34–42.

Mythen, G., Walklate, S., & Khan, F. (2009). 'I'm a Muslim, but I'm Not a Terrorist': Victimisation, Risky Identities and the Performance of Safety. *The British Journal of Criminology, 49*(6), 736–754.

Nacos, B. L. (2006). *Terrorism and Counterterrorism*. New York: Pearson Longman.

Pape, R. (2003). The Strategic Logic of Suicide Terrorism. *American Political Science Review, 97*(3), 343–361.

Parenti, C. (2002). America's Jihad: A history of Origins. In P. Scraton (Ed.), *Beyond September 11th: An Anthology of Dissent* (pp. 10–18). London: Pluto Press.

Post, J. M., Sprinzak, E., & Denny, L. (2003). The Terrorists in Their Own Words: Interviews with 35 Incarcerated Middle Eastern Terrorists. *Terrorism and Political Violence, 15*(1), 171–184.

Prevent. (2011). *Prevent Strategy*. London: The Stationery Office Limited.

Rapoport, D. C. (2012). The Four Waves of Modern Terrorism. In J. Horgan & K. Braddock (Eds.), *Terrorism Studies: A Reader* (pp. 41–59). London: Routledge.

Rashid, A. (1999). The Taliban: Exporting Extremism. *Foreign Affairs*. Retrieved June 21, 2019, from https://www.foreignaffairs.com/articles/afghanistan/1999-11-01/taliban-exporting-extremism

Rashid, A. (2008). *Taliban: Islam, Oil and the New Great Game in Central Asia*. London: I.B. Taurus & Co.

Rasool, E. (2016). Preventing the Synapse: Transmission of Daesh Religious Signals in Search of Receivers. In H. Abadi (Ed.), *Countering Daesh Propaganda: Action-Oriented Research for Practical Policy Outcomes* (pp. 38–42). Atlanta: The Carter Center.

Rice, S. K. (2009). *Emotions and Terrorism Research: A Case for a Social-Psychological Agenda. Journal of Criminal Justice, 37*(3), 248–255.

Sadiki, L. (2002). One 'Islam', Many 'Islams': Understanding the Arab-Islamic Perspective on 11 September in a Globalising World. *Irish Studies in International Affairs, 13*(1), 43–60.

Saikal, A. (2004). Islam and the West: Challenges and Opportunities. In V. Hooker & A. Saikal (Eds.), *Islamic Perspectives on the New Millennium* (pp. 19–31). Singapore: ISEAS Publishing.

Schwenk, E. H. (1945). Legislative Power of the Military Occupant under Article 43, Hague Regulations. *The Yale Law Journal, 54*(2), 393–416.

Scraton, P. (2002). Introduction: Witnessing 'Terror', Anticipating 'War'. In P. Scraton (Ed.), *Beyond September 11th: An Anthology of Dissent* (pp. 1–9). London: Pluto Press.

Shaw, E. D. (1986). Political Terrorists: Dangers of Diagnosis and an Alternative to the Psychopathology Model. *International Journal of Law and Psychiatry, 8*(3), 359–368.

Shay, S. (2005). *The Axis of Evil: Iran, Hizballah, and Palestinian Terror*. London: Routledge.

Speckhard, A., & Akhmedova, K. (2005). Talking to terrorists. *The Journal of Psychohistory, 33*(2), 125–156.

Stenersen, A. (2013). The Relationship Between al-Qaeda and the Taliban. In P. Bergen (Ed.), *Talibanistan: Negotiating the Borders Between Terror, Politics, and Religion* (pp. 69–93). Oxford: Oxford University Press.

UN. (2005). *Resolution 1624 (2005)*. United Nations. Retrieved June 1, 2019, from https://www.un.org/en/ga/search/view_doc.asp?symbol=S/RES/1624%20%282005%29

UN. (2006). *Afghanistan Opium Survey 2006: United Nations Office on Drugs and Crime*. Retrieved June 21, 2019, from https://www.unodc.org/pdf/research/AFG05%20_full_web_2006.pdf

UN. (2018). *UN Global Counter-Terrorism Strategy*. Retrieved June 21, 2019, from https://www.un.org/counterterrorism/ctitf/en/un-global-counter-terrorism-strategy

Van Dijk, J. (2007). Mafia Markers: Assessing Organized Crime and Its Impact Upon Societies. *Trends in Organized Crime, 10*(4), 39–56.

Volpi, F. (2011). Introduction: Critically Studying Political Islam. In F. Volpi (Ed.), *Political Islam: A Critical Reader* (pp. 1–8). London: Routledge.

Weenink, A. (2015). Behavioral Problems and Disorders among Radicals in Police Files. *Perspectives on Terrorism, 9*(2), 17–33.

Williams, P. (1994). Transnational Criminal Organisations and International Security. *Survival, 36*(1), 96–113.

Wright, L. (2007). *The Looming Tower: Al Qaeda's Road to 9/11*. London: Penguin Books.

5

From the Humanitarian Crisis to a State of Emergency

This chapter continues to examine the presence of state crimes in the 'war on terror' and how these state crimes have facilitated terrorism. The Paris terrorist attacks in 2015 had a profound impact on the 'war on terror'. This chapter also explores the impact of the terrorist attacks in Paris on the 'war on terror'. It details how states responded to these attacks through extending the boundaries of the criminal justice system, notably through the declaration of a state of emergency in France, and how such measures marked the increased securitization of Europe, and the further eradication of civil liberties and due process.

The chapter also critically considers the dominant discourses used to legitimize these state actions, and the implications of these actions and their associated discourses on the radicalization process. It further reveals the self-defeating nature of the 'war on terror' in claiming to defend and maintain universal values, and yet, introducing discourses and mechanisms which disintegrate these very values. It also reveals how the 'war on terror' continued to create a dichotomy of humanity through claiming to protect some populations, and at the same time, abandoning the humanity of other populations, namely refugees. The chapter displays how an increase in securitization, based on the constructed threat of terrorism

S. Ahmed, *The 'War on Terror', State Crime & Radicalization*, Palgrave Studies in Risk, Crime and Society, https://doi.org/10.1007/978-3-030-40138-2_5

and need to protect populations from terrorism, led some countries to abandon their legal and moral duty towards other human beings, even though the world was witnessing, and is still witnessing, the largest humanitarian crisis since the Second World War—with millions of individuals at risk of starvation and death (EC, 2015). Thus, the perpetuation of the dehumanization process, which is evident in both the actions of terrorists and state crimes, is explored within the 'war on terror'. In demonstrating the more nuanced invisible forms of state power which form vessels through which dangerous ideologies are maintained, reinforced and acted upon, the chapter elucidates the role of states in maintaining the 'war on terror' through facilitating radicalization. UK domestic policies and legislation following the Paris attacks are considered as part of this synergy, as well as the UK role in the Syrian war and the refugee crisis. As the chapter and the book demonstrate, the 'war on terror' has become a self-defeating discourse. It claims to protect universal values and seeks to eradicate the very factors which facilitate terrorism, but through trying to meet this aim, it introduces state practices which create, sustain and facilitate terrorism.

Terrorism as a State of Emergency?

Since its inception in 2001, the 'war on terror' has been reconfigured on numerous occasions, with terrorist attacks, constructed threats and global wars continuing to shape the ever-changing boundaries of the discourse. The 2015 Paris terrorist attacks were instrumental in re-defining the boundaries of the 'war on terror'. The terrorist attacks on 13 and 14 November 2015 were remarkable in the level of planning and sophistication they displayed. They involved 7 coordinated strikes which led to the death of 130 people with 350 injured (Lequesne, 2016; Oksanen et al., 2018; Walklate & Mythen, 2016). The use of 'soft targets' represented the evolution of terrorism and, rather than terrorists relying on suicide attacks and bombs, terrorism evolved to include the use of handguns and vehicles. This use of 'soft targets' also led to an increased sense of insecurity amongst populations which in turn produced a 'global reaction of solidarity and support for France' (Tatchell, 2015). The global reaction was as much about wanting to show solidarity with France, as it was about states recognizing that they too could be victims of such attacks. Two hours after the terrorist attacks, the French President declared a state of emergency, which involved the closure of borders and the deployment of the Army in the capital. As stated in previous chapters, the declaration of a state of emergency leads to states obtaining a considerable amount of power, which becomes possible through the derogation of laws designed to curtail the use of state power against individuals. This declaration politically framed the Paris attacks as a series of attacks that necessitated the need for such measures.

The growing influence of ISIS also shaped the state response to the Paris terrorist attacks. When considering the type of terrorist threat and the level of terrorist threat during this time, the number of terrorist attacks in Europe from 2007 to 2015 highlighted the increasing threat and presence of ISIS. According to Europol, there was a decrease in the number of terrorist attacks failed, foiled or completed in the period 2007–2013 (Europol, 2016). However, in 2015 there was a twofold increase in the number of terror-related arrests in Europe, with a total of 1077 arrests (Renard, 2016). And the majority of terrorist incidents (around 60%) and fatalities (around 80%) were in the following five countries: 'Syria, Iraq, Afghanistan, Pakistan and Nigeria' (Renard, 2016: 3). Therefore, most acts of terrorism occurred in Muslim majority countries. When one considers the worst single attack of terrorism in western countries, it was committed by Anders Breivik in 2011, a Christian ultra-Zionist extremist who killed 77 individuals, mostly teenagers. These figures reveal the significant contrast between the actual threat of terrorism, and the constructed threat of terrorism as being committed in western countries by Islamist terrorists after September 11th. And as is increasingly evident, within the 'war on terror' the state construction of terrorism tends to serve an ideological purpose, and it is neither neutral in conception, nor free from exploitation.

The existence and use of the terrorist threat as an ideological ruse is further evident when one considers the existence of terrorism before 9/11. 'From the mid-1970s until the mid-1990s, more than 150 persons died every year from terrorism in Europe. Even with the Paris attacks, there were still fewer fatalities from terrorism in Europe in 2015 than in an average year of the late twentieth century' (Renard, 2016: 3). Renard (2016: 3) goes onto contend that 'today's fear of terrorism has more to do with psychology—how people perceive and live with terrorism—than with the actual threat'. The difference between reality and perception, between 'old terrorism' and 'new terrorism' is about how new terrorism has been constructed, which subsequently shapes perceptions, beliefs and knowledge. However, although the overall incidents of terrorism have decreased, Islamist terrorism is one form of terrorism that has increased.

> More people have been killed by jihadi violence in Western Europe in 2014–2016 (273 people) than in all previous years combined (267 people). This is due to a small number of highly deadly incidents: The Paris attack on 13 November 2015 (130 killed), the Brussels bombing in March 2016 (32 killed) and the Nice truck attack in July 2016 (84 killed). (Nesser, Stenersen, & Oftedal, 2016: 3)

The increase in Islamist terrorism is also reflected in arrest figures. 'Europol reported that between 2011 and 2015, 1579 individuals were arrested in connection with Islamist terrorism investigations. The figure for the previous five-year period (2006–2010) was 937' (Hegghammer, 2016: 160). The increase in Islamist terrorism has also been fuelled by ISIS, with Interpol circulating a list of 173 Islamic state fighters it believes could have been trained to mount suicide attacks in Europe (Tondo, Wintour, & Messina, 2017). Where the United Kingdom is concerned, 'between 2011/12 and 2015/16 there were 1199 terrorism-related arrests' (compared with 932 in the previous five-year period) (House of Commons, 2016: 14). Where Islamism-related terrorism is concerned, 'in the 2001–2012 period, 88% of the people arrested in the UK in terrorism-related cases were Muslims' (House of Commons, 2016: 20).

- 'In the six years after the introduction of the *Terrorism Act 2000*, there were a large number of arrests made, with an approximate average of 200 arrests made under this legislation each year' (Allen & Dempsey, 2018: 12).
- 'Of those arrested for terrorism related offences between 2001/02 and 2016/17, 40% were reported as being of Asian appearance, 30%

White, 12% Black, and 18% Other or Not Known' (Allen & Dempsey, 2018: 15).

- 'Data suggests that increasingly over the years, those arrested for terrorism related offences are of Asian ethnic appearance, whereas the proportion of those who are White or Other has declined' (Allen & Dempsey, 2018: 16).
- 'Between 1 September 2001 and 31 August 2012, there were 2297 people arrested for terrorism related offences, of which 1066 (46%) self-declared to be Muslim' (Allen & Dempsey, 2018: 19).
- 'On 31 March 2017 105 (57%) of the prisoners in custody for terrorism related offences defined themselves as Asian or Asian British and only 38 (21%) White. The majority (90%) of prisoners in custody for terrorism related offences on 31 March 2017 declared themselves as Muslim' (Allen & Dempsey, 2018: 24).

The Paris terrorist attacks were framed as a form of new terrorism. The use of the phrase 'new terrorism' has served to further fuel the perception that new measures are required to counter terrorism and that old measures are inadequate. The creation of 'new', by virtue of the identity of the enemy, growth in the number of attacks, and increasing number of actions used by terrorists to cause death have combined to maintain the belief that new aggressive security measures are required. In this socio-political context, states that are, and perceive that they are, the target of terrorist attacks are more likely to enact domestic political changes that restrict the freedom of the population, with the media pushing policy makers into more aggressive actions (Donohue, 2008; Pape, 2003; Weinberg, 2008; Wilkinson, 1977, 2006). However, given the radicalizing impact of many of the measures introduced as part of the 'war on terror', and their violation of safeguards that exist to protect individuals' human rights, it seems worth asking if they have been counter-productive in the fight against terrorism? It then seems plausible to ask, and argue, that if terrorism was constructed as a continuum, with the similarities between old terrorism and new terrorism forming the continuities, would Islamist terrorists form a distinctive category that are inhumane, and therefore deserve subhuman status? Or instead, would they simply form another category of terrorism, in much the same way as animal rights-based terrorism and far-right instigated terrorism? And would such a classification have served to maintain the civil liberties of suspects? And therefore, not contributed to the existence of the micro-individual-emotional level variables which facilitate radicalization? However, just as 9/11 and the 'war on terror' fed into the micro-individual-emotional level variables of injustice, political oppression and political grievances, the state response to the Paris terrorist attacks further fuelled the power of these variables in radicalizing individuals.

The day after the attacks in Paris, President Hollande declared that France was at war. The warfare paradigm renders possible certain counter-terrorism measures that would be impossible during peace times, and it also accelerates the pursuit of security through military action and the denial of civil liberties. As Buzan, Wæver, and de Wilde (1998) state, security facilitates the process by which extraordinary measures are created as a necessity. A state of emergency was announced which allowed the restriction of civil liberties, in order to implement measures to protect the state without the need for approval from the judicial system (Zedner, 2009). The security measures introduced included the 'temporary closure of France's borders, the deployment of 1,500 troops into the Paris area', 'the implementation of curfew, and detention without charge' and the possibility to put suspects under house arrest after their return from conflict areas in Syria and Iraq (Tatchell, 2015: 1–2). Although the state of emergency was meant to be a temporary measure, on 19th and 20th November, the French Senate voted almost unanimously to extend the state of emergency for three months, and since then it has been extended several more times (Boutin & Paulussen, 2016). The use of a state of emergency reality predisposes state actions, which in non-state emergency situations would constitute state crimes. And as stated in previous chapters, the principles of necessity and proportionality are important in determining if the declaration of a state of emergency is legitimate. The legitimization of a state of emergency also raises questions about the circumstances which led to the declaration, and whether these circumstances warrant the abandonment of state obligations under IHRL and IHL. However, the wider implications of such measures are that where they are perceived as being legitimate, and are therefore likely to be perceived as being illegitimate, unjust and as in violation of human rights and the rule of rule, they are likely to facilitate radicalization. The manipulation of power by the state impacts the super macro-universal level through tarnishing the values of protection, human rights and security present at this level, and it is the macro-national actions of the state which lead to these values being destroyed and perceptions of inequality, injustice and so on, which promote radicalization.

In the first few days of the implementation of a state of emergency, 168 raids were conducted by the police without judicial orders, and there were 23 arrests and 104 home arrests (Lichfield, 2015). In the weeks following the terrorist attack, the Minister of the Interior announced that French security services had carried out 1072 raids in which they placed 119 people in custody (Nossiter, 2013). The New York Times (2016a, 2016b) noted that between 14 November 2015 and 13 May 2016, approximately 3600 warrantless searches and 400 house arrests were made. France therefore used various forms of power that would require judicial oversight in a non-state of emergency context. Further, the question of necessity is essential because if the state of emergency was not warranted and legitimate, through being disproportionate to the threat that existed, then the use of a state of emergency constitutes state crime. This is because it violates UDHR (1948) Article 2 that states,

> everyone is entitled to all the rights and freedoms set forth in this Declaration, without distinction of any kind, such as race, colour, sex, language, religion, political or other opinion, national or social origin, property, birth or other status.

The measures also violate UDHR (1948) Article 9, which states no one shall be subjected to arbitrary arrest, detention or exile. The powers attributed to states through the declaration of a state of emergency were therefore widely used and, although a state of emergency may have been required immediately after the terrorist attacks, the question of necessity exists around the extension of the period. Here it can be noted that the extension of the state of emergency and the raids, arrests and home arrests conducted under this declaration constitute macro-national level intra-state crime and facilitate terrorism through impacting the rule of law, human rights and ethnic, national and religious discrimination, all factors identified by the UN (2018) as being conducive to terrorism.

The existence of ethnic, national and religious discrimination was most prevalent where places of worship were concerned. In conjunction with the raids and arrests, measures used in the state of emergency included the power to close suspicious public places, including mosques that were believed to be promoting dangerous ideologies. Three mosques and four prayer rooms were closed because they were believed to be promoting extremist ideologies (Rubin, 2015). The closure of these places violates Article 2 of the UDHR (UN, 1948). The measures also violate Article 18, which states:

> everyone has the right to freedom of thought, conscience and religion; this right includes freedom to change his religion or belief, and freedom, either alone or in community with others and in public or private, to manifest his religion or belief in teaching, practice, worship and observance. (UN, 1948)

Research by Amnesty International (2016a) which involved interviewing several witnesses revealed that the police were using unnecessary violence, such as breaking and damaging residents' properties, violent language and actual physical aggression for no apparent reason. Additionally, they found that interventions were poorly explained to the residents, with counter-terrorism powers being misused for non-terrorism offences (Amnesty International, 2016a). The question of whether the closure of the places mentioned above constituted legitimate measures is even more questionable when one considers that the Kouachi brothers, who were responsible for the Charlie Hebdo attacks, were radicalized outside of the country's Muslim institutions and were excluded from mosques for their extremist views (Downing, 2015). These measures had a huge capacity to further compound existing perceptions of discrimination, marginalization and discriminatory law enforcement amongst French Muslims that were found to alienate Muslim communities in France's already divided society (Połońska-Kimunguyi & Gillespie, 2016). The emergency measures therefore constituted macro-national level intra-state crime and impacted the micro-individual-emotional level.

The Paris terrorist attacks also led to policy changes on the European level and large-scale surveillance and the monitoring of EU citizens within Europe based on 'risk categories' (Bigo et al., 2015). However, both the

European Parliament and the Court of Justice of the European Union (CJEU) expressed concerns about the necessity, proportionality and fundamental rights of individuals under the large-scale system of (blanket) surveillance that was introduced (Bigo et al., 2015). These measures went against the principle of free movement inside the Schengen area and Schengen rules which state that systematic checks and surveillance of EU citizens are prohibited (Casella-Colombeau, 2017). The use of risk categories leads to profiling which goes against the principle of non-discrimination, which forms the basis of the EU legal system and the EU Charter of Fundamental Rights. Therefore, it is possible to comprehend the concerns of both the European Parliament and the Court of Justice of the European Union (CJEU) at the measures introduced (Carrera & Hernanz, 2015). According to the state centric 'war on terror' narrative, the measures introduced were based on profiling individuals, arresting and monitoring those deemed to fit the 'terrorist profile'. However, one can also note how the use of risk categories exacerbates the prevalence of ethnic, national and religious discrimination which is outlined by the UN (2018) as a condition that is conducive to terrorism. The existence of macro-national level intra-state crime is also likely to impact perceptions of justice and induce powerlessness and therefore feed into several of the variables present at the micro-individual-emotional level (Boyns & Ballard, 2004; Henderson-King, Henderson-King, Bolea, Koches, & Kauffman, 2004; Lemu, 2016; Speckhard & Akhmedova, 2005).

It should also be stated that these state crimes are likely to impact perceptions of discrimination, social exclusion, marginalization, justice, human rights and the rule of law. Therefore, the introduction of new counter-terrorism measures does not just impact one variable associated with radicalization, rather it feeds into the plethora of perceptions, experiences and lived realties which feed into the radicalization process in multiple ways. Moreover, the counter-terrorism measures which were introduced in France were also likely to be perceived alongside the measures introduced in the United States, with research by Ahmed (2015, 2016) demonstrating how the 'war on terror' has led to transnational and thus, localized and global understandings of injustice, suffering and marginalization via Muslims' Islamic identity.

A Truly Global Destruction of the Universal to 'Protect' Humanity

The United States also continued to pursue terrorists in ways which deviated from the rule of law. President Obama came into power in 2009, after the wars in Iraq and Afghanistan. In 2011, the Washington Post reported that no President in US history has ever relied so extensively on the secret killings of individuals to advance the nation's security goals (Miller, 2011). However, although the Obama administration had used drones to kill individuals, claiming that drones are precise, a New York University School of Law and Stanford University Law School research report published in 2012 noted that Obama's drone war often used the strategy of hitting the same target multiple times, thereby also killing the rescuers and humanitarian workers who go to help the injured (Greenwald, 2012). The *New York Times* noted that Obama's method for counting civilian deaths caused by drone strikes was incorrect because it counted all military-age males in a strike zone as combatants, therefore implying guilt by association and severely underestimating the number of civilian deaths (Becker & Shane, 2012). Between 2004 and 2012, approximately 3100 people were reported to have been killed by US drone strikes, including at least 800 innocent civilians (Milne, 2012). In 2012, the UN stated that drone strikes may constitute 'war crimes' and that the use of drone strikes and 'targeted killings' has been found to be 'immensely attractive' to other states in the world, and thus, such practices 'weaken the rule of law' as they 'fall outside the scope of accountability' (Bowcott, 2012). Similarly, Ian Seiderman, the Director of the International Commission of Jurists, noted that as a result of the global drone war, 'immense damage was being done to the fabric of international law' (Bowcott, 2012).

It appears that within the 'war on terror' and on the international level, mechanisms of accountability are less of a priority than the 'war on terror' mechanisms constructed as maintaining security. The use of drones by the United States constitutes a war crime through violating several concepts designed to uphold the rule of law when states engage in warfare.

1. Under the IHL, parties to any conflict must, at all times, 'distinguish between civilians and combatants', especially in that 'attacks may only be directed against combatants' and 'must not be directed against civilians'.[1]
2. The continued use of drones aimed at the same targets not only contributed to the death of civilians, but also represents an intentional attack on civilians, which is a war crime.[2]
3. The repeated use of drones on the same area also violates the principle of proportionality, because IHL prohibits disproportionate attacks, which are those 'which may be expected to cause incidental loss of civilian life, injury to civilians, damage to civilian objects, or a combination thereof, which would be excessive in relation to the concrete and direct military advantage anticipated'.[3]
4. Intentionally launching an indiscriminate attack resulting in death or injury to civilians, or a disproportionate attack (i.e. knowing that the attack will cause excessive incidental civilian loss, injury or damage) constitutes a war crime.[4]
5. The protection of the civilian population and civilian objects is further underpinned by the requirement that all parties to a conflict take precautions in attack.[5]
6. The parties must choose means and methods of warfare with a view to avoiding, and in any event to minimizing, incidental loss of civilian life, injury to civilians and damage to civilian objects.[6]
7. Everything feasible must be done to verify that targets are military objectives, to assess the proportionality of attacks, and to halt attacks if it becomes apparent, they are wrongly directed or disproportionate.[7]
8. Where circumstances permit, parties must give effective advance warning of attacks which may affect the civilian population.[8]

---

[1] Protocol I & II additional to the Geneva Conventions 1949 (ICRC, 2014).

[2] Rome Statute of the International Criminal Court, 1998 (ICRC, 2014).

[3] Protocol I, Articles 51(5)(b) and 57. Protocol II and Amended Protocol II to the Convention on Certain Conventional Weapons (ICRC, 2014).

[4] Protocol I & II additional to the Geneva Conventions 1949 (ICRC, 2014).

[5] Protocol II, Article 13(1) (ICRC, 2014).

[6] Customary IHL, Rule 17 (ICRC, 2003).

[7] Customary IHL, Rules 16-19 (ICRC, 2003).

[8] Customary IHL, Rules 20 (ICRC, 2003).

From the above principles of IHL, it is clear that the use of drones constitutes a war crime on several grounds, drones are not only disproportionate but, under IHL, their use should have been discontinued in the light of the number of civilian causalities. States are under a legal obligation to protect civilians and exercise their power with caution, and this also involves giving advance warnings. However, as Greenwald (2012) stated, many drones killed the rescuers and humanitarian workers who went to help the injured.

The clear violations of IHL suggest that the international level remains tied to sovereignty and protecting the nation-state. IHRL and IHL are meant to exist above the state, echoing universality and humanity through human rights, and yet their role, importance and values have been severely undermined in the 'war on terror'. Here one can make the link between the three orders and how the violation of rules at the super macro-universal level leads to macro-national level intra-state crimes and intra-state crimes and these collectively create the lack of law and political instability and thus the social conditions which facilitate terrorism. However, the violations of these laws also serve a much more powerful and sinister narrative and that is the AQ narrative. It demonstrates how, within the 'war on terror', the deaths of thousands of Muslims are worth nothing compared to the death of one US soldier which legitimizes the kind of questions Lemu (2016) identified, extremists ask. Therefore, just as the 'war on terror' narrative exploits universal values of humanity, freedom, democracy and so on, to further its cause, so does the AQ narrative, and both are equally as dangerous in using mechanisms which diminish the very values they claim to be defending.

However, the narratives also feed into each other, thereby creating the 'war on terror' as a vicious cycle. As previously stated, this is because the state-created mechanisms used as part of a 'war on terror', given the AQ narrative legitimacy in its claims of inequality, political oppression, discrimination and so on. In doing so, they further radicalize individuals which then leads to more terrorist acts, which in turn leads to more state counter-terrorism mechanisms. It could therefore be argued that the super macro-universal level operates according to geo-political power and this bias and manipulation of power is used by states to progress and disperse their power. However, the inequality that is the result of geopolitical power not only undermines the international laws designed to protect citizen's human rights but, in doing so, it further fuels extremist claims of there being a war against Islam, and Muslims must therefore engage in a global jihad.

The damage to IHRL and IHL and the inherent human rights, liberalism and humanity they convey, harm humanity and the very values which exist to constitute a binding force for humanity. The values create and shape beliefs of fairness, justice, equality and a just world (Correia, Vala, & Aguiar, 2001) but, because these values are not maintained, their existence produces harmful impacts. Here one can ask the question, that if these values did not exist and individuals were socialized to know and believe inequality, injustice and so on is prevalent, would they still experience injustice, grievance, powerlessness and so on? Within the 'war on terror', the super macro-universal level exists as a mechanism through which states enact their power and violate human rights, rather than a level which maintains and upholds human rights. In making claims to protect this level and these very entities, states produce the mechanisms which destroy these entities.

One could also ask the question, would it be better to have values and rights at the super macro-universal level which are being violated, or not have values and rights at all? The answer must include a consideration of the power and the damage that is inflicted from rights being broken and damaged, and how these feed into injustice and break individuals' notions of humanity and universalism. If individuals suffer secondary victimization due to their negative experiences involving criminal justice institutions, with these experiences recognized as diminishing their existing beliefs in such organizations and justice (Elliott, Thomas, & Ogloff, 2012; Wemmers, 2013), then surely the 'war on terror', with its vast implications for justice, human rights, equality and so on, also constitutes secondary victimization? Research by Ahmed (2015, 2016) found that British Muslims had pre-existing beliefs regarding human rights and the universal level, and within the 'war on terror' they had experienced the erosion of rights and values which they believed would always exist. The destruction of these values tested their belief in humanity, with many struggling to understand and accept how the security inherent in these values could be undermined (Ahmed, 2015, 2016). The research demonstrated how some values were fluid, but those at the universal level were understood as being sacred because they were perceived as the binding force of humanity, and as values that gave humanity meaning (Ahmed, 2015, 2016). It therefore follows that the erosion of these values in the 'war on terror' has vast implications for individual's understanding of their place within humanity and their beliefs regarding humanity.

As with the 9/11 terrorist attacks, the Paris terrorist attacks led to the introduction of new counter-terrorism legislation in the United Kingdom. On 12 February 2015, the UK government enacted the Counter Terrorism and Security Act 2015. As mentioned in Chap. 3, the Act introduced measures that allow authorities to seize passports and travel documents from persons suspected of involvement in terrorism. Under this Act, British citizens returning to the United Kingdom can have their passport seized, and those believed to have been involved in terrorism can be excluded from re-entering the United Kingdom (Legislation.gov.uk, 2015). The removal of citizenship is also prevalent in the Asylum and Nationality Act 2006.

> Under section 40 of the British Nationality Act of 1981, as amended by the Immigration, Asylum and Nationality Act of 2006, citizenship can be removed a) from those who had acquired it fraudulently; or b) where the Secretary of State is satisfied that the person has done something seriously prejudicial to the vital interests of the U.K., provided, as is made clear by section 40(4), that revocation of citizenship would not render him stateless. (Esbrook, 2016: 1258)

The House of Lords rejected the initial legislation through which individuals could be rendered stateless. The threshold that passed was one of the Secretary of State having 'reasonable grounds for believing that the person is able, under the law of a country or territory outside the United Kingdom, to become a national of such a country or territory' (Legislation.gov.uk, 2014). As with other forms of UK counter-terrorism legislation, the burden of proof is the concept of 'reasonableness' and thus, as Hale-Ross (2015: 12) states, 'mere suspicion that a citizen has engaged with terrorist activity is the required threshold'.

These powers have been extensively used. From 2003 to 2012, Britain revoked the citizenship of 27 people (Parsons, 2014). In 2013, Britain stripped another 20 people of their citizenship on national security grounds and, in 2014, 17 individuals with dual nationality saw their British nationality being revoked, although it is not clear how many of these cases were related to national security (Parsons, 2014). As of 2017, more than 150 suspected jihadists and criminals had been stripped of their citizenship and banned from returning to the United Kingdom and more than 40 dual nationals, including British-born people with parents of different nationalities, had their right to a passport removed (The Guardian, 2017b). Although these powers have been extensively used, the most high-profile case was that of Shamima Begum. Shamima left the United Kingdom to join ISIS in 2015 and in February 2019, she had her British citizenship revoked, after she was found at a refugee camp in Syria (Busby, 2019). It was believed that Shamima was of dual nationality and could therefore claim citizenship in Bangladesh.

The 1954 Convention relating to the Status of Stateless Persons and the 1961 Convention on the Reduction of Statelessness are the key international conventions addressing statelessness and they are complemented by international human rights treaties and provisions relevant to the right to a nationality (UNHCR, 2019). The Council of Europe's 1997 European Convention on Nationality also legislates against the provision of statelessness. Together these conventions make it unlawful to deprive someone of citizenship, if this deprivation of British citizenship would render a person stateless (Anderson, 2016). Interestingly, in his paper on 'Citizenship removal resulting in statelessness', David Anderson QC, the Independent Reviewer of Terrorism Legislation stated, that citizenship deprivation power is ineffective and counter-productive against terrorism, in that:

(a) It amounts to a policy of catch and release, setting up today's convicts as tomorrow's foreign fighters' and exporting them to places where they can do more damage because (unlike at home) they cannot be monitored.
(b) The power encourages 'the dangerous delusion that terrorism is (or can be made into) a foreign threat and problem', diminishing the incentive to deal with it domestically.

(c) Exercise of the power may result in complex and costly legal battles about whether human rights concerns (in particular, the prohibition against delivering people to torture abroad) prevent deportation to the remaining country of citizenship. (Anderson, 2016: 12)

This legislation challenges the Kantian philosophy of proportionality through legitimizing a form of punishment through which individuals can be rendered stateless. It also has vast implications for radicalization with research by Ahmed (2016) demonstrating that discriminatory counter-terrorism policies are negatively impacting British Muslims sense of belonging to their British identity. This legislation is inherently discriminatory and violates the following articles within the UDHR. It violates

> Article 3 everyone has the right to life, liberty and security of person,
>
> Article 7 all are equal before the law and are entitled without any discrimination to equal protection of the law,
>
> Article 13 1. Everyone has the right to freedom of movement and residence within the borders of each State. 2. Everyone has the right to leave any country, including his own, and to return to his country and
>
> Article 15 1. everyone has the right to a nationality 2. no one shall be arbitrarily deprived of his nationality nor denied the right to change his nationality. (UN, 1948)

Within these articles, everyone should have the protection of the law, and yet only those individuals that are of dual nationality are not afforded the protection of the human rights enshrined in the laws and conventions stated above. This is yet another example of how the 'war on terror' divides humanity and in this case, it divides humanity based on one's identity. Research by Ahmed (2015) demonstrated that British Muslims view their rights in relative terms and having reduced human rights was severely undermining their commonality with British non-Muslims. Therefore, rather than maintain security, such measures as Anderson (2016) rightly contends, are likely to be counter-productive in fighting terrorism and moreover, they are likely to impact the discrimination, lack of human rights, powerlessness and so on which are all associated with facilitating the radicalization process.

The Investigatory Powers Act was introduced in 2016 and gave UK intelligence agencies and police, sweeping surveillance powers, which included a range of tools for snooping and hacking by the security services. Jim Killock, the Executive Director of Open Rights Group, said: 'the state has unprecedented powers to monitor and analyse UK citizens' communications regardless of whether we are suspected of any criminal activity' (MacAskill, 2017). It could be argued that UK counter-terrorism legislation completely undermines human rights through measures which include mass surveillance, deporting individuals to countries where there is a risk of torture, stripping people of their nationality, and controlling their movement and detaining them without charge or due process (Bowcott, 2017). However, the usefulness of these measures raises some interesting questions. They are based on security and a belief that intelligence and security can pre-empt threats and British Muslims require closer surveillance. However, as Warsi points out, in all three recent UK terrorist attacks, Muslim community members had come forward to warn the authorities that the perpetrators had exhibited extremist behaviour, she says 'in all cases they reported them [the terrorists]; it was obvious to them who was radicalised' (Townsend, 2017).

It can be argued that the 'war on terror' has increasingly exploited the space above nations and between nations, to extend its power. On a super macro-universal level, there has been an absence of measures to restrict the state extension of power or state violation of existing safeguards, and this has led to vast increases in state power. However, the 'war on terror' has also exploited the space between nations to utilize spaces where existing human rights safeguards do not apply, and they have also used this space in rendering citizens as stateless and creating Guantánamo Bay. Under existing safeguards, citizens that have had to leave their nation-state have protected refugee status under the 1951 Refugee Convention (UNHCR, 2016). However, within the 'war on terror', international invasions in Syria, Iraq and Afghanistan and internal counter-terrorism measures have created a population that has not only had to leave their nation-state due to wars and counter-terrorism legislation, but also been constructed as a risk and as not warranting the same protection and status afforded to refugees. As the next section demonstrates, the 'war on terror' has not only created a mass population of refugees, through the invasions in Iraq, Afghanistan and Syria but then constructed these very same refugees as potential terrorists. And here one can note the use of geo-political power, and identity in claims that coalition countries face such a threat of terrorism that they should invade other countries. Yet, when this very same threat leaves millions stateless, trying to escape terrorist groups such as ISIS, they are constructed as potential threats and the very threat that they have faced is selectively rendered invisible.

This chapter has thus far explored some of the significant developments of the 'war on terror' following the Paris terrorist attacks. Of interest is how 9/11 and the Paris terrorist attacks were catalysts for spurring a series of international and national measures, all of which increased the power of states to violate and deviate from establish safeguards. This represents a worrying trend because it demonstrates that acts of terrorism are harmful in leading to the death of innocent civilians, but the counter-terrorism measures to reduce these threats are also damaging, through permanently changing the exercise of state power and reducing the capacity of safeguards which exist to protect human rights. Perhaps the most worrying feature of this is how this process has been normalized in the 'war on terror'.

As mentioned in Chap. 1, the event focused 'war on terror' places states as reactors to acts of terrorism, with such a perspective failing to even acknowledge or create a space where one can discuss how states facilitate terrorism. Acts of terrorism are being used to extend the sovereign power of the state. This raises serious concerns about how the 'war on terror' was constructed and continues to be maintained. This is because within this construction, attention and privilege are not attributed to the victims of state power, or the victims of countries devastated through invasions. Instead, all consequences of state practices following terrorist attacks are neutralized because the focus is on the damage and harm of the terrorist attack. Such a focus legitimizes all responses to acts of terrorism. By denying the damage of these state actions, although the loss of life in terrorist acts is recognized, dehumanization and loss of life is given no place when it forms part of states' responses to terrorism. Therefore, the 'war on terror' discourse, with its attribution of power, attention and humanity to attacks of terrorism, continues to mask over and make invisible war crimes, state crimes and the plethora of suffering in the form of death, starvation, and torture that the 'war on terror' legitimizes. It is also plausible to contend that given the way the 'war on terror' has been constructed, terrorist attacks will continue to mark the erosion of civil liberties. This book demonstrates the power of the 'war on terror' in all its guises, and therefore one must include the power of the 'war on terror' to diminish universal human rights and universal safeguard mechanisms to ensure the protection of all life. In such a climate, and as this book seeks to evidence, claims of securitization also have similarities with nationalism, whereby nationalism and security are prioritized at the expense of universality and humanity.

The next section seeks to document the development of the super macro-universal level, via IHRL and IHL, so that the direct consequences of the 'war on terror' and its destruction of the universal level can be contextualized. An analysis of the 'war on terror' must be read according to the history of universal human rights, because it is only through a historical reading that the severe implications and consequences of increased state power, nationalism and sovereignty can be understood. And further, it can be appreciated that human rights were formed through the deaths of millions of individuals and therefore these are the very consequences of not maintaining these safeguards.

The Development of International Human Rights Law (IHRL) and International Humanitarian Law (IHL)

An understanding of the development of IHRL and IHL facilitates an appreciation of the impact of the 'war on terror' on universal human rights. International responses to the Holocaust can still be noted as the most significant activity of states acting beyond their own territory to mould and shape universal values and human rights. The event demonstrated the immense power of a sovereign state, and how power and ideology could be united to justify and motivate the killing of other groups based on their identity. The world witnessed the damage of genocide, leading to international developments aimed at ensuring that such harmful exercises of power, even in the name of nationalism and sovereignty, could never again be a reality. The Holocaust was therefore significant in uniting interpretations and understandings of what would constitute legitimate and illegitimate state practices. By providing a threshold and criteria of what was acceptable and unacceptable, it allowed shared beliefs to form unity amongst nations at the international level. In 1948, the United Nations Convention on Genocide was adopted by the UN General Assembly.

The Convention contained the following three articles:

> Article I 'confirmed that genocide whether committed in time of peace or in time of war, is a crime under international law'.
>
> Article II stated that genocide includes 'any of the following acts committed with intent to destroy, in whole or in part, a national, ethnical, racial or religious group, as such: (a) Killing members of the group; (b) Causing serious bodily or mental harm to members of the group; (c) Deliberately inflicting on the group conditions of life calculated to bring about its physical destruction in whole or in part; (d) Imposing measures intended to prevent births within the group; (e) Forcibly transferring children of the group to another group'.
>
> Article III specified that the following 'acts shall be punishable: (a) Genocide; (b) Conspiracy to commit genocide; (c) Direct and public incitement to commit genocide; (d) Attempt to commit genocide; (e) Complicity in genocide. Notably there are no quantitative thresholds set for the behaviors listed under Article II'. (Leitenberg, 2006: 16)

In 2004, this Convention was reinforced by the introduction of a Special Adviser on Genocide Prevention following the 'Preventing Genocide: Threats and Responsibilities' conference in 2004.

It would be plausible to assume that given the introduction of the Convention on Genocide in 1948, the commitment given by states to maintain such international standards of human rights, and the horrors and long-term consequences of the Holocaust, that there have either been no violations of the convention, or that violations have been adequately punished, thereby upholding the international rule of law. However, this has not been the case, with genocides occurring in countries including Somalia, Kosovo, Rwanda and Bosnia in which the international community has failed to adequately intervene. The following testimony to a US Congressional Committee by Holly Burkhalter of Human Rights Watch on 16 September 1992 regarding Somalia reveals what this lack of intervention means:

> it seems to me a great tragedy and a scandal that things have to get to the point of 2,000 deaths a day for the people that really make decisions in this town to notice that something is desperately wrong. Because Andrew Natsios and others were calling this the worst humanitarian disaster in the world 10 months ago. The UN has known what the problems are. Indeed, the Secretary General of the UN has been begging on his knees for the last year for attention to Somalia. (Burkhalter, 1992: 30–33)

However, Somalia is not an isolated example. A lack of state intervention has also been manufactured through language, with states being reluctant to even acknowledge the genocide that was occurring in Bosnia. Instead, the acts by the Serbs were labelled as 'almost indescribable', 'an atrocious set of acts', and 'tantamount to genocide' by the US Secretary of State Warren Christopher (cited Power, 2002). There was also an implicit denial to acknowledge the Rwandan genocide. As Leitenberg (2006: 27) states, 'as the numbers reached 200,000, then 500,000, then 700,000, they were all reported in the media, week by week, but the U.S. Department of State ordered its staffers not to use the term "genocide"' in describing the events'. After the genocide, President Clinton apologized for the inaction of the United States, and in December 1999, UN Secretary General Kofi Annan apologized on behalf of the UN for the lack of UN action (Annan, 1999; Carroll, 2004). However, this was too late for those that lost their lives and one must remember that such deaths could have been prevented through intervention. The right and duty to intervene was used by states to legitimize their lack of intervention. One can instantly note the readiness of states to intervene internationally and nationally within the 'war on terror' to extend their own power and their lack of action in other spheres where there is human suffering. This selective action, which heavily impacted the death count in Somalia, Kosovo, Rwanda, and Bosnia, led to questions regarding the use of humanitarian intervention in cases of genocide. And it is also worth noting that this 'double standard', as it is perceived in the AQ narrative is exploited by extremists to radicalize individuals. 'The UN Charter both generally prohibited the use of force and guaranteed a state's right to be free from intervention, except for measures authorized by the Security Council under its Chapter VII powers or through state actions taken in self-defense' (Williams, Worboys, & Ulbrick, 2012: 477).

The lack of clarity over the use of humanitarian intervention to genocide was raised internationally. In 2001, the question of intervention was addressed by the International Commission on Intervention and State Sovereignty (ICISS), an independent, Canadian-sponsored commission. The Commission concluded that 'state sovereignty' includes 'a state's responsibility to protect its own citizens' which became known as 'the responsibility to protect, or R2P' (ICISS, 2001 cited Williams et al., 2012: 481). The ICISS proposed that states had three separate duties under the responsibility to protect. The first duty was that 'individual states were primarily responsible for protecting their populations' (ICISS, 2001 cited Williams et al., 2012: 482). ICISS categorized this as a state's responsibility to prevent, mainly though eliminating the root causes of mass atrocities (ICISS, 2001 cited Williams et al., 2012).

The second duty was the responsibility of the international community to protect a state's population, 'where a state either fails to protect its population-or is the driving force behind mass atrocities' (ICISS, 2001 cited Williams et al., 2012: 482). The duties specified put populations centre stage in advocating that they should be protected either by states or, where this isn't possible then, by the international community. The ICISS therefore recognized the right and duty of the international community to intervene to ensure the protection of citizens and recognized that such a right should be used where there is a misuse of sovereign state power against civilians. One can therefore notice how the duties created went beyond categorizing state power as an entity tied exclusively to the geographic territory of the sovereign state. The outlook was international, and thus reaffirmed the international level as a terrain to challenge and curtail the exercise of abusive state power. Such developments have facilitated the existence of the super macro-universal level as a level that can both reduce state power, or as has been evident in the 'war on terror', and increase state power through the introduction of resolutions.

The third duty created pertained to states assisting post-conflict states to rebuild and reconstruct following mass atrocities, thereby reaffirming the dangers of political instability (ICISS, 2001 cited Williams et al., 2012). This 'responsibility to rebuild', as it is also known, requires that the international community pays attention to address the causes of harm. The ICISS provided a detailed six-part test for determining whether the use of force for humanitarian purposes is warranted. According to this test, for intervention to be legitimate: (1) the action must be authorized by a legitimate authority; (2) the assistance with intervention must be a last resort; (3) the states concerned must have rightful intentions; (4) the action must be proportional to the humanitarian crisis; (5) the action must have reasonable prospects of success; (6) there must be a just cause (ICISS, 2001).

In 2005 representatives from 170 states met at the World Summit to discuss how to tackle global threats. The World Summit concluded that force could only be used to protect populations if peaceful measures had failed, and if the use of force was in accordance with the UN Charter's Chapter VII framework and therefore authorized by the Security Council (ICISS, 2001). However, the power of nations to veto interventions means that there could be no intervention, even in the most extreme cases of genocide and crimes against humanity, such as in Syria. In 2012, the UN Human Rights Council found that the Syrian crisis was being driven by state-approved war crimes and crimes against humanity, including the deliberate killing and torture of civilians, including children and women (OHCHR, 2012; UNHCR, 2015a, 2015b). However, regardless of the mass atrocities taking place in Syria, intervention was vetoed by Russia and China (The Guardian, 2017a).

The 'war on terror' has not only exposed the selective use of power at the international level—indeed demonstrating the preoccupation with providing resolutions which empower states against civilians, and a lack of enforcement against states that harm civilians and violate international law—but also exploited the space between states. The Universal Declaration of Human Rights affirms that 'everyone has the right to a nationality, thereby acknowledging the legal and practical importance of nationality for the enjoyment of human rights' (UNHCR, 2004: 2). Therefore, international human rights exist via states and, within the 'war on terror', increasing numbers of individuals exist outside the state. As already stated, counter-terrorism measures have introduced the punishment of statelessness into the counter-terrorism framework. States such as the United States have also exploited the space between states, utilizing places like Guantánamo Bay to punish suspected terrorists. The spaces between states and outside states are therefore becoming increasingly used within the 'war on terror', and these spaces represent areas where there is a severe reduction of human rights. Therefore, it appears that although the 'war on terror' is based on the securitization of states, it is increasingly using a space outside states to engage in actions which contribute to individuals not even having a basic standard of human rights. It could then be argued that although the concept of human security is central to ensuring that people have the right to live in freedom and dignity, free from poverty and despair and free from fear and want (UN General Assembly, 2005), the 'war on terror', on the one hand seeks to defend and uphold this position through introducing security measures aimed at preserving human security, and yet on the other hand, it is a discourse that is being used to subject an increasing number of individuals to have no human security. It could therefore be argued that the 'war on terror' is polarizing humanity and creating those that deserve human security and human rights, and those that are undeserving of human security and human rights. In this way, the 'war on terror' arguably has similarities to warfare, since it too involves killing, torture, rendition, invasions and wars, detention, and displacement. It could be stated that it is also similar to genocide, since these very actions are based on identity, with the 'war on terror' creating spaces where there are no human rights, (which is similar to the creation of areas of warfare) and within these spaces groups possessing a different identity are afforded a complete reduction of human rights. One must also remember that a principle of legitimizing warfare and genocide is the claim by nations that such acts are a form of self-defence against a risk that threatens the life of a nation, and such a threat warrants the denial of human rights. It could therefore be argued that on an abstract level the super macro-universal level has increasingly developed measures to decrease the prevalence of genocide. However, at the same time powerful and dangerous discourses such as the 'war on terror' not only lead to the global mass discrimination of the

Muslims, but also incorporate multiple forms of IHLR and IHL violations and continue to emanate destructive features of warfare and genocide.

The Dehumanization of Outsiders for the Protection of Insiders

This section explores how the 'war on terror' shaped the refugee crisis, and the implications of this for terrorism. The definition of a refugee includes contextual factors as contributing to this status. A refugee according to the Convention of 1951 includes persons who are 'unable or unwilling to return to their country of origin' on the grounds of 'being persecuted for reasons of race, religion, nationality, membership of a particular social group, or political opinion' (UNHCR, 2010a). 'Refugees should not be penalized for their illegal entry or stay' (UNHCR, 2010a). The definition of a stateless person is

> a person who is not considered as a national by any State under the operation of its law. Statelessness can occur for several reasons, including discrimination against particular ethnic or religious groups, or on the basis of gender; the emergence of new States and transfers of territory between existing States; and gaps in nationality laws. (UNHCR, 2017)

As stated, within the 'war on terror' statelessness has become a major problem because wars and new legislation have legitimized the expulsion of citizens from a given territory. These actions are dangerous because they strip a person of belonging to a state, and thus the very essence through which they obtain human rights. Unlike those that are rendered stateless, refugees are protected by international law. The 1951 Refugee Convention defines who is a refugee and outlines the basic rights which States should afford to refugees. One of the most fundamental principles laid down in international law is that refugees should not be expelled or returned to situations where their life and freedom would be under threat (UNHCR, 2016). However, although such conventions exist to provide civilians with protection, just as concepts of security and threat within the 'war on terror' have rendered IHRL and IHL as invisible, they have also quashed state duties to refugees.

The invasions of Syria and Iraq not only led to the death of innocent people but also the displacement of millions of people (see Chap. 5 for a discussion of these wars). A post-conflict society can fuel and give rise to terrorism and the cases of Syria and Iraq have parallels with what happened with Afghanistan following the Soviet invasion. The refugee crisis following these invasions has been labelled as the 'largest global humanitarian crisis' of our time by the European Commission (EC, 2020: 1). The 2003 invasion of Iraq led to the displacement of an estimated two million refugees (UNHCR, 2010b). Some estimates suggest that between 1.2 million and 1.4 million Iraqis went to Syria, 450,000 to 500,000 Iraqis sought refuge in Jordan and smaller numbers went to Egypt, Iran, Lebanon and Gulf countries (FAFO, 2007; Fagen, 2009; UNHCR, 2007; The Brooking Institute, 2019). The Syrian conflict began to produce refugees in April 2011 (Yazgan, Utku, & Sirkeci, 2015), with 'over 700,000 Syrians registering as refugees with the United Nations High Commissioner for Refugees (UNHCR) in 2014 alone, and an average of approximately 70,000 Syrians fleeing their country every month (UNHCR, 2015a, 2015b). By 2015, more than 50% of Syria's population was displaced and around 220,000 people had been killed with 12.8 million in urgent need of humanitarian assistance inside Syria (Amnesty International, 2015). The number of civilians killed in Iraq between 2003 and 2020 is at least between 184,986 and 207,907 (Iraq Body Count, 2020). More than 400,000 have died because of the Syrian conflict since 2011, with five million seeking refuge abroad and over six million displaced internally (HRW, 2017).

The 'war on terror' has shaped how the refugee crisis has been perceived and constructed. On 19 September 2016, the UN General Assembly met to discuss how to share responsibility for the world's 21 million refugees, of which half—12 million—live in just 10 of the 193 countries in the world (Amnesty International, 2016b). Little progress was made and as of mid-2016, governments had pledged less than 48% of the amount needed by aid agencies to support refugees from Syria (Shetty, 2016). Although the 'war on terror' has created a populist discourse in which western countries are perceived to have a higher intake of refugees, this is in fact untrue. The Middle East has the highest number of refugees and internally displaced persons (IDPs) in the world (UNHCR, 2010c). According to a UNHCR report, 2.1 million registered Syrians are in Egypt, Iraq, Jordan and Lebanon, more than 24,000 Syrian refugees are registered in North Africa and there are 1.95 million registered Syrians in Turkey (UNHCR, 2015a, 2015b). In Jordan, a country of approximately 6.5 million, Syrian refugees are now equivalent to roughly 9–10% of the population (UNHCR, 2014). In Lebanon, the refugee population is equivalent to '26 percent of the Lebanese population' (Berti, 2015: 42), with Turkey hosting the world's largest community of displaced Syrians (UNHCR, 2015a; UNHCR, 2015b). The refugee crisis led to questions about the role of the European Union in responding to the crisis and the number of refugee's European countries should accept. 'Europe has only taken in a small part (2.9 percent) of the overall Syrian refugee population, which represents just a fraction of the 2,301,533 Syrian refugees that Lebanon, Jordan, Turkey, Iraq, and Egypt' sheltered over the period of March 2011 and December 2013 (Fargues, 2014: 2). The refugee crisis became infused with the 'war on terror' thereby influencing state discourses on the refugee crisis.

The book has thus far explored how states responded to perceived threats and risks within the 'war on terror' and how these have extended state power. This section explores the threat and risk to those outside the sovereign territory. Although the 'war on terror' is constructed as a discourse to uphold humanity, freedom and liberal values, this vision is only extended to those within the nation-state, with their rights and freedom being used to legitimize the criminalization and dehumanization of those outside the nation-state. In this way, the 'war on terror' was and is producing a binary of the world, which can be likened to colonialist and imperialist projects which constructed far away territories and people as less deserving of freedom, human rights, autonomy and dignity than those within the nation-state.

Fassin (2011) argues that the 'politics of compassion/or humanitarianism' and the vocabulary of suffering, compassion, assistance and responsibility forms part of our political life. However, although our common humanity is the sole criterion through which responsibility and ethics combine, leading to a politics of compassion, in reality discourses which render invisible our shared humanity and make difference the sole criterion lead to politics of marginalization, discrimination, otherization and oppression. Discourses also function to label humans into categories of underserving victims and deserving victims (Richardson & May, 1999). As Holmes and Castaneda (2016: 16) state, 'international conventions establish refugees as *involuntarily* displaced by political circumstances, including war and violence (as well as natural and anthropogenic disasters); they are thus framed as deserving'. In such a construction, refugees are constructed as deserving sympathy, because contextual factors are recognized as contributing to their victim status. Although there is always an innate tension between state interests and the ethics of hospitality (Derrida, 2001), the refugee crisis did produce an emotional response. As Aziz (2016: 56–57) contends, the '13.6 million people that have been forced to leave their homeland due to the civil wars in Syria and Iraq are not just numbers, but sentient mortals who feel the pangs of hunger, pain and strive to maintain their self-respect'. The most emotive point in the crisis was the death of Aylan Kurdi. Aylan Kurdi was a three-year-old boy who was found on a Turkish beach. The image reverberated across the globe, with broadsheet and tabloid newspapers showing his body on the front page. Although these images caused an outpouring of public sympathy, Germany was one of the few countries to welcome refugees and display an ethics of responsibility (Holmes & Castaneda, 2016). Excluding Germany and Sweden, the remaining 26 EU countries pledged around 8700 resettlement places, which amounted to around 0.2% of Syrian refugees (Amnesty International, 2015). Of interest is how the 'war on terror' was used by states to respond to the refugee crisis. Research on the use of categories in the media found that 'both Germany (91.0%) and Sweden (75.3%) overwhelmingly used the terms 'refugee' or 'asylum seeker', and in contrast migrant was the most used term in Italy (35.8%) and especially the United Kingdom (54.2%) (Berry, Garcia-Blanco, & Moore, 2015: 7–8). Discussions of refugees and migrants as a cultural threat or a threat to community cohesion was most prevalent in British (10.8%) newspapers, as was the creation of them being a threat to 'welfare/health systems in the UK press (18.3%) and being linked to crime (8.2%)' (Berry et al., 2015: 8).

The Paris terrorist attacks in 2015 also influenced and shaped how the refugee crisis was constructed. This construction focused on the potential threat of refugees, as opposed to the circumstances or state actions which led to the displacement of people from Iraq and Syria. As stated previously, the normative 'terrorist attack—state response' dichotomy became active. European countries constructed every refugee and migrant as a potential terrorist. It was feared that terrorists would disguise themselves as migrants and enter the country, even though 'there was no concrete evidence that terrorist travellers systematically use the flow of refugees to enter Europe unnoticed' (Europol, 2016). For example, in Hungary, the Prime Minister Viktor Orbán stated that all terrorists are migrants, thereby making a link between terrorism and the inflow of Muslim refugees into Europe (Kaminski, 2015). In the United Kingdom, Mike Hookem, the UKIP defence spokesman, argued that the horrific acts of terrorism in Brussels demonstrate that Schengen free movement and lax border controls are a threat to our security (Mason, 2016). Populist political forces (such as the National Front in France and the United Kingdom's Independence Party) exploited the fears perpetuated by the media to delegitimize migration (De Galbert, 2015), with the fear of migration constituting a crucial part of the Brexit campaign (Rodriguez, 2016). As Friis (2015: 737) argues, there was a reframing of the conflict in Iraq and Syria from a humanitarian crisis '*requiring* a humanitarian response to a "national security" issue *requiring* a military response and intensified counterterrorism efforts'. However, as Rodriguez (2016: 7) contends, the anger and rejection towards migrants and asylum seekers coming to Europe was the reaction ISIS wanted because by creating anger and rejection towards refugees, 'the latter would feel that they are not welcomed in Europe and that their only solution is to remain in Syria under the protection of the Islamic caliphate'.

As previously stated, macro-national level practices also include the creation of dangerous discourses and through facilitating discrimination and racism, they positively impact radicalization (Abdo, 2006; Ahmed, 2016; Blaker, 2015; Gould & Klor, 2016; UN, 2018). According to Rodriguez (2016), the manipulation of the refugee crisis promoted both radicalization and ISIS. In terms of safeguards, the treatment of refugees violated many of the safeguards which exist to protect individuals from discrimination. For example, in the Convention on the Elimination of All Forms of Racial Discrimination (1965), 'racial discrimination' is defined as any distinction, exclusion, restriction or preference based on race, colour, descent or national or ethnic origin which has the purpose or effect of nullifying or impairing the recognition, enjoyment or exercise, on an equal footing, of human rights and fundamental freedoms in the political, economic, social, cultural or any other field of public life (UNHR, 1965). This Convention was violated through Syrian and Iraqi refugees being constructed as a threat and risk based on their ethnic identity, and this then leading to differential treatment, which impaired their recognition and thus their enjoyment and/or exercise of human rights. The Convention clearly specifies that groups should be treated equally, and here one can question if refugees from other countries, non-Islamic countries would also have been constructed as terrorists? Similarly, the UDHR proclaims that all human beings are born free and equal in dignity and rights and that everyone is entitled to all the rights and freedoms set out therein, without distinction of any kind, in particular as to race, colour or national origin (UN, 1948). Based on the International Covenant on Economic, Social and Cultural Rights, which was created in 1966, the UN Committee on Economic, Social and Cultural Rights stated that refugees, stateless persons and asylum seekers, and other disadvantaged and marginalized individuals and groups should enjoy equal treatment in access to non-contributory social security schemes, including reasonable access to health care and family support (UN, 1966). Again, the emphasis is on equal treatment of refugees and stateless persons. These are just a few of the safeguards which exist to protect individuals against discrimination, and of interest is how the 'war on terror' was used by states to violate these obligations.

As the book is demonstrating, within the 'war on terror' the discourses made to legitimize state actions to preserve universal values are damaging the very values they claim to be protecting. It could also be argued that they are damaging these values on a far more destructive and corrosive level. Here one must remember that states, as all the legislation in the book has demonstrated, should protect individuals, maintain equality and trust. It is this legitimacy which makes it possible for states to exercise power and criminalize individuals that break the values and norms of society, and damage society. Therefore, although damage is inflicted when individuals violate social norms, these violations themselves cannot damage the fabric of society, or the existence of justice and humanity, because state actions, through the pursuit of justice and punishment maintain these values. However, when the body and entities that are meant to preserve these values, states, and equally as importantly, the super macro-universal level do not maintain justice, then the very foundations on which society is based are damaged. And when the super macro-universal level, which ought to be the creator, facilitator and regulator of these values, fails to do so or does so as an expression of geo-political power, then there is nothing left to maintain these values. Ideas of humanity can only exist and have meaning if they represent the values they claim to uphold.

In this way, when states claim that terrorism threatens to violate universal values and indeed damage these values, this construction is simply an exploitation of fear to gain power. If it is not, then one must ask, can terrorist groups change the laws, procedures and values on which core institutions, such as the criminal justice system are based? Can they change the values of society? Or the values of the super macro-universal level? It therefore appears that within the 'war on terror' states are states are not only damaging universal values through introducing mechanisms which deviate from established human rights safeguards, but the very construction of terrorism is equally as corrosive. This is because it falsely manipulates individuals into fearing and believing that terrorists can change societal, national and universal values. The construction of terrorists as having the ability to violate these values and the use of fear by states to influence political action, then leads one to ask: do state actions within the 'war on terror' not fall into the definition of terrorism and therefore constitute terrorism? Terrorism is defined as the use or threat of action where the use or threat is designed to influence the government or to intimidate the public or a section of the public, and the use or threat is made for the purpose of advancing a political, religious, racial or ideological cause (Legislation.gov.uk, 2000). States use fear to gain approval for methods that polarize humanity and destroy the values that form the essence of humanity and, through doing so, it could be argued that they commit the vast and widespread forms of terrorism.

Michalowski (2013) contends that states combine militarized actions with restrictive immigration policies which create human suffering on many different levels. What becomes apparent is how a revisionist discourse operates to first, deny the contextual factors which give rise to terrorism and within this, the role of state invasions in contributing to the refugee status and asylum seeker status of individuals. Second, denying these groups hospitality contributes to delegating them to a possible statelessness status, whereby joining a terrorist organization might represent their only opportunity to live. Third, such populist discourses omit the obvious fact that these individuals are escaping war-torn countries which have been destroyed by groups such as ISIS and are therefore victims of terrorism. In this way, not only do invasions contribute to creating the meso-societal political, social, economic and ideological conditions which give rise to terrorism, but then reactions to such conditions further induce individual's capacity to join terrorist organizations through states offering them little hope of an alternative. One can note the interactions between the three levels in how states violate the super macro-universal level and the safeguards present at the international level and how, through committing inter-state crime, states facilitate terrorism and create the meso-societal conditions for terrorism. One can also note the similarities between Afghanistan, Iraq and Syria, and how the invasion of these countries led to political, social and economic instability, which facilitated the rise of terrorist groups in these countries (see Chaps. 4–6 for discussions on instability and the rise of AQ and ISIS).

It seems surprising that although the UK counter-terrorism strategy includes the need to reduce factors which make individuals vulnerable to radicalization, this same logic is not extended to refugees because European policies include measures which make individuals vulnerable to terrorism. Refugees and displaced persons become trapped on the other sides of borders (Fargues, 2014) and their vulnerability makes them susceptible to terrorism. This is because, as Tom Porteous (2007) the Director of Human Rights Watch contends, 'unless this crisis is addressed, we may well look back in ten years' time and see the seeds of the next generation of terrorists'. An evident example of the vulnerability of Syrian refugees is their need to turn to smugglers to reach safe countries, with the number jumping from 14.7% in 2011 to 44.7% in 2013 (Fargues, 2014). Although there is a wealth of legislation to protect individuals from discrimination, in 2017, President Trump banned Syrian refugees from the United States and effectively prevented anyone (including refugees) from Iran, Iraq, Libya, Somalia, Sudan and Yemen from entering the United States. 'These seven countries have two main things in common: they are predominantly Muslim, and they are the countries from where the majority of people seeking asylum from serious human rights violations like persecution or torture are trying to escape' (Shetty, 2017). As Shetty (2017) goes on to state,

> it is ludicrous because there is no data to support the view that refugees—Muslim or otherwise—pose more risk of committing acts of terrorism than citizens. A refugee is not a person who commits acts of terrorism. It is someone fleeing people who commit acts of terrorism.

The creation of suffering on these different levels through discriminatory policies only helps to fuel terrorist claims of inequality and injustice and further exacerbates the construction of a Muslim-non-Muslim world binary, where jihad is required to defend the interests and lives of Muslims.

The media and political domain not only created a discourse that framed the crisis, but this discourse was heavily present in policies. On the European level, at the G20 meeting on 15 November 2015, President of the European Commission, Jean-Claude Juncker argued

> the one who is responsible for the attacks in Paris cannot be put on an equal footing with real refugees, with asylum-seekers and with displaced people. These are criminals and not refugees or asylum-seekers. The cynics who exploit the suffering of Paris have not understood that those who perpetrated the attacks are precisely those whom the refugees are trying to flee. (Juncker, 2015)

In 2015, EU Member States were allocated new obligations under the EU temporary relocation system, which introduced a new criteria considering factors such as population size, total GDP, average number of asylum applications per one million habitants and unemployment rate in the allocation of refugees (Carrera, Blockmans, Gros, & Guild, 2015; Holmes & Castaneda, 2016). Chancellor Angela Merkel announced that Germany would admit Syrian refugees, even if they did not claim asylum in the first EU country they entered (as was the requirement under the Dublin Regulation), thereby suspending the key EU procedure known as the Dublin Regulation (Merkel, 2015). In suspending these procedures, Merkel (2015) argued that, 'if Europe fails on the question of refugees, its close connection with universal civil rights will be destroyed'. Here Merkel recognized that claims to these values mean that actions must contour to these values because, where they go against these values, there is no legitimacy in claiming to be part of these values. In the months that followed, Germany admitted more refugees than any other country in Europe, with the German president Joachim Gauck arguing that Germany had a 'moral duty' to provide safe refuge because Germans were refugees themselves after World War II' (Holmes & Castaneda, 2016: 15). However, the voices which point out the potential damage of state practices which go against universal values are few, and form such a minority that such appeals become silenced.

This chapter has discussed the implications of the 'war on terror' continuing to become a prevalent and powerful discourse in society. It demonstrated how the refugee crisis, a humanitarian crisis became securitized and the implications of such an approach for the self-defeating nature of the 'war on terror'. The post-Paris terrorist attacks era marked the further institutionalization of European and national profiling methods and in doing so, it led to the existence of both macro-national and meso-societal realities which facilitate radicalization. This era can therefore be conceptualized as involving mechanisms which further eroded the values at the super-macro level, and this invariably influenced the macro-national and meso-societal levels.

However, one can also question how the refugee crisis represented an opportunity to correct some of the damage that has occurred to the international level since the 'war on terror'. States could have not only maintained their legal obligations under IHRL, but through doing so, they could have highlighted how refugees are victims of terrorism and therefore how terrorism transcends religions and ethnicity. Events such as this represent opportunities for universal values to be reinforced and such advocacy can positively advance beliefs pertaining to humanity. It therefore appears that within the 'war on terror', the universal level has been used and exploited to promote the rights of some groups over other groups, with identity forming the criteria of differentiation. However, there has been a complete lack in using universalism to unite humanity. Within the 'war on terror' each terrorist attack and humanitarian crisis can be framed in terms of its impact on the whole of humanity, and in terms of our responsibility, empathy and compassion to each other. However, each event has been constructed in terms of divisions and thus binaries, and it is these very processes which facilitate both Islamist and far-right forms of extremism. One can therefore note how the evolution of the 'war on terror' has marked the facilitation of not only Islamist terrorism, but also other forms of terrorism.

References

Abdo, G. (2006). *Mecca and Main Street: Muslim Life in America After 9/11*. Oxford: Oxford University Press.

Ahmed, S. (2015). The Emotionalization of 'War on Terror': Counter-Terrorism, Fear, Risk, Insecurity and Helplessness. *Criminology and Criminal Justice, 15*(5), 545–560.

Ahmed, S. (2016). Citizenship, Belonging and Attachment in the 'War on Terror'. *Critical Criminology, 24*(1), 111–125.

Allen, G., & Dempsey, N. (2018). *Terrorism in Great Britain: The Statistics*. House of Commons. Retrieved July 19, 2019, from https://researchbriefings.parliament.uk/ResearchBriefing/Summary/CBP-7613#fullreport

Amnesty International. (2015). *Syria's Refugee Crisis in Numbers*. Retrieved July 19, 2019, from https://www.amnesty.org/en/latest/news/2015/09/syrias-refugee-crisis-in-numbers/

Amnesty International. (2016a). *Upturned Lives: The Disproportionate Impact of France's State of Emergency*. Retrieved March 1, 2018, from https://www.amnesty.org/download/Documents/EUR2133642016ENGLISH.pdf

Amnesty International. (2016b). *Tackling the Global Refugees: From Shirking to Sharing Responsibility*. Retrieved March 1, 2018, from https://amnesty.org.

pl/wp-content/uploads/2016/02/28.09-FINAL-Tackling-the-Global-Refugee-Crisis_final.pdf

Anderson, D. (2016). *Citizenship Removal Resulting in Statelessness*. Government Publication. Retrieved July 1, 2019, from https://assets.publishing.service.gov.uk/government/uploads/system/uploads/attachment_data/file/518390/David_Anderson_QC_-_CITIZENSHIP_REMOVAL__print_pdf

Annan, K. (1999). *Report of the Independent Inquiry into the Actions of the United Nations During the 1994 Genocide in Rwanda*. Retrieved July 19, 2019, https://reliefweb.int/report/rwanda/report-independent-inquiry-actions-united-nations-during-1994-genocide-rwanda

Aziz, S. (2016). Rise of ISIS and Security Implications for Middle East. *CISS Insight: Quarterly News and Views*, pp. 49–59.

Becker, J., & Shane, S. (2012). Secret 'Kill List' Proves a Test of Obama's Principles and Will. *The New York Times*. Retrieved June 9, 2018, from http://www.nytimes.com/2012/05/29/world/obamas-leadership-in-war-on-al-qaeda.html?pagewanted=all

Berry, M., Garcia-Blanco, I., & Moore, K. (2015). *Press Coverage of the Refugee and Migrant Crisis in the EU: A Content Analysis of Five European Countries*. United Nations. Retrieved June 9, 2018, from http://www.unhcr.org/56bb369c9.pdf

Berti, B. (2015). The Syrian Refugee Crisis: Regional and Human Security Implications. *Strategic Assessment, 17*(4), 51–53.

Bigo, D., Brouwer, E., Carrera, S., Guild, E., Guittet, E., Jeandesboz, J., et al. (2015). *EU Counter-Terrorism Policy Responses to the Attacks in Paris: Towards an EU Security and Liberty Agenda*. Brussels: Centre for European Policy Studies. Retrieved June 9, 2018, from https://www.ceps.eu/system/files/LSE81Counterterrorism.pdf

Blaker, L. (2015). The Islamic State's Use of Online Social Media. *Military Cyber Affairs, 1*(1), 1–9.

Boutin, B., & Paulussen, C. (2016, July 1). *From the Bataclan to Nice: A Critique of France's State of Emergency Regime*. T.M.C. Asser Institute for International & European Law, Policy Brief 2016-01. Retrieved July 19, 2019, from https://papers.ssrn.com/sol3/papers.cfm?abstract_id=2811602

Bowcott, O. (2012). Drone Strikes Threaten 50 Years of International Law, Says UN Rapporteur. *The Guardian*. Retrieved October 21, 2016, from http://www.theguardian.com/world/2012/jun/21/drone-strikes-international-law-un

Bowcott, O. (2017). UK Counter-Terror Laws Most Orwellian in Europe, Says Amnesty. *The Guardian*. Retrieved July 19, 2019, from https://

www.theguardian.com/uk-news/2017/jan/17/uk-counter-terror-laws-most-orwellian-in-europe-says-amnesty

Boyns, D., & Ballard, J. D. (2004). Developing a Sociological Theory for the Empirical Understanding of Terrorism. *The American Sociologist, 35*(2), 5–25.

Burkhalter, H. (1992, September 16). *House Committee on Foreign Affairs, Subcommittee on Africa.* Hearing on the Crisis and Chaos in Somalia (pp. 30–33). 102nd Cong, 2nd Sess.

Busby, M. (2019). Shamima Begum Would Face Death Penalty in Bangladesh, Says Minister. *The Observer*. Retrieved July 19, 2019, from https://www.theguardian.com/uk-news/2019/may/04/shamima-begum-would-face-death-penalty-in-bangladesh-says-minister

Buzan, B., Wæver, O., & de Wilde, J. (1998). *Security: A New Framework for Analysis*. London: Lynne Rienner.

Carrera, S., Blockmans, S., Gros, D., & Guild, E. (2015). *The EU's Response to the Refugee Crisis: Taking Stock and Setting Policy Priorities*. Brussels: Centre for European Policy Studies. Retrieved October 21, 2016, from https://www.ceps.eu/wp-content/uploads/2015/12/EU%20Response%20to%20the%20 2015%20Refugee%20Crisis_0.pdf

Carrera, S., & Hernanz, N. (2015). Re-Imagining Mobility and Identity Controls: The Next Generation of the EU Migration Management Toolkit. *Journal of Borderlands Studies, 30*(1), 69–84.

Carroll, R. (2004). US Chose to Ignore Rwandan Genocide. *The Guardian*. Retrieved July 19, 2019, from https://www.theguardian.com/world/2004/mar/31/usa.rwanda

Casella-Colombeau, S. (2017). Policing the Internal Schengen Borders—Managing the Double Bind Between Free Movement and Migration Control. *Policing and Society, 27*(5), 480–493.

Correia, I., Vala, J., & Aguiar, P. (2001). The Effects of Belief in a Just World and Victim's Innocence on Secondary Victimization, Judgements of Justice and Deservingness. *Social Justice Research, 14*(3), 327–342.

De Galbert, S. (2015). *The European Union's Refugee Crisis*. American Foreign Policy Council. Retrieved October 21, 2016, from https://www.afpc.org/uploads/documents/defense_dossier_november_2015.pdf

Derrida, J. (2001). *On Cosmopolitanism and Forgiveness (Thinking in Action)*. London: Routledge.

Donohue, L. K. (2008). *The Cost of Counterterrorism: Power, Politics, and Liberty*. Cambridge: Cambridge University Press.

Downing, J. (2015). *Paris Attacks: Why France Must Avoid Viewing Its Muslim Population as a Security Threat*. EUROPP: European Politics and Policy. Retrieved October 21, 2016, from http://blogs.lse.ac.uk/europpblog/2015/11/16/paris-attacks-why-france-must-avoid-viewing-its-muslim-population-as-a-security-threat/

EC. (2020). *ECHO Factsheet: Syria Crisis. Humanitarian Aid and Civil Protection, European Commission*. Retrieved April 01, 2020, from https://ec.europa.eu/echo/where/middle-east/syria_en

Elliott, I., Thomas, S. D. M., & Ogloff, J. R. P. (2012). Procedural Justice in Contacts with the Police: The Perspective of Victims of Crime. *Police Practice and Research, 13*(5), 437–449.

Esbrook, L. (2016). Citizenship Unmoored: Expatriation as a Counter-Terrorism Tool. *University of Pennsylvania Journal of International Law, 37*(4), 1273–1329.

Europol. (2016). *Changes in Modus Operandi of Islamic State Terrorist Attacks*. The Hague: Europol.

FAFO. (2007). *Iraqis in Jordan: Their Numbers and Characteristics*. Retrieved October 21, 2016, from https://www.unhcr.org/47626a232.pdf

Fagen, P. W. (2009). *Iraqi Refugees: Seeking Stability in Syria and Jordan*. Institute for the Study of International Migration, Georgetown University. Retrieved October 21, 2016, from https://repository.library.georgetown.edu/bitstream/handle/10822/558297/CIRSOccasionalPaper1PatriciaFagen2009.pdf?sequence=5

Fargues, P. (2014). *Europe Must Take on Its Share of the Syrian Refugee Burden, But How?* European University Institute. Retrieved October 15, 2015, from http://cadmus.eui.eu/bitstream/handle/1814/29919/MPC_PB_2014_01.pdf

Fassin, D. (2011). *Humanitarian Reason: A Moral History of the Present*. London: University of California Press.

Friis, S. M. (2015). 'Beyond Anything We Have Ever Seen': Beheading Videos and the Visibility of Violence in the War Against ISIS. *International Affairs, 91*(4), 725–746.

Gould, E., & Klor, F. K. (2016). The Long-Run Effect of 9/11: Terrorism, Backlash, and the Assimilation of Muslim Immigrants in the West. *The Economic Journal, 126*(597), 2064–2114.

Greenwald, G. (2012). New Stanford/NYU Study Documents the Civilian Terror from Obama's Drones. *The Guardian*. Retrieved July 19, 2019, from http://www.theguardian.com/commentisfree/2012/sep/25/study-obama-drone-deaths

Hale-Ross, S. (2015). *The European Union Should Introduce Legislation to Harmonise Anti-Terror Laws in the 28 Member States*. Retrieved March 6, 2016, from http://researchonline.ljmu.ac.uk/1662/3/Conference%20Paper%202015.pdf

Hegghammer, T. (2016). The Future of Jihadism in Europe: A Pessimistic View. *Perspectives on Terrorism, 10*(6), 156–170.

Henderson-King, D., Henderson-King, E., Bolea, B., Koches, K., & Kauffman, A. (2004). Seeking Understanding or Sending Bombs: Beliefs as Predictors of Responses to Terrorism. *Peace and Conflict: Journal of Peace Psychology, 10*(1), 67–84.

Holmes, S. M., & Castaneda, H. (2016). Representing the "European Refugee Crisis" in Germany and Beyond: Deservingness and Difference, Life and Death. *American Ethnologist, 43*(1), 12–24.

House of Commons. (2016). *Terrorism in Great Britain: The Statistics*. Briefing Paper No. 7613. Retrieved 19 May 2018. Retrieved 26 October 2019, from http://researchbriefings. parliament.uk/ResearchBriefing/Summary/CBP-7613

HRW. (2017). *Syria Events of 2017*. Human Rights Watch. Retrieved July 19, 2019, from https://www.hrw.org/world-report/2018/country-chapters/syria

ICISS. (2001). *The Responsibility to Protect: Report of the International Commission on Intervention and State Sovereignty*. Retrieved October 21, 2016, from http://responsibilitytoprotect.org/ICISS%20Report.pdf

ICRC. (2003). *ICRC Advisory Service on International Humanitarian Law, International Humanitarian Law and International Human Rights Law*. Retrieved October 28, 2016, from https://www.icrc.org/en/document/icrc-advisory-services-international-humanitarian-law

ICRC. (2014). *The Geneva Conventions of 1949 and Their Additional Protocols*. Retrieved October 28, 2016, from https://www.icrc.org/en/document/geneva-conventions-1949-additional-protocols

Iraq Body Count. (2020). Iraq Body Count: Tally Through September 2018. Retrieved July 19, 2019, from https://www.iraqbodycount.org/

Juncker, J.-C. (2015). European Approach to Migration. *Malta Independent Online*. Retrieved March 6, 2016, from http://independent.com.mt/articles/2015-11-22/blogs-opinions/A-European-approach-tomigration-learning-the-lessons-of-Malta-6736145635

Kaminski, M. (2015). *All the Terrorists Are Migrants*. POLITICO. Retrieved May 28, 2018, from http://www.politico.eu/article/viktor-orban-interview-terrorists-migrants-eu-russia-putin-bordersschengen/

Legislation.gov.uk. (2000). *Terrorism Act, 2000*. Retrieved March 25, 2002, from https://www.legislation.gov.uk/ukpga/2000/11/contents/enacted

Legislation.gov.uk. (2014). *Immigration Act, 2014*. Retrieved March 6, 2016, from http://www.legislation.gov.uk/ukpga/2014/22/contents/enacted

Legislation.gov.uk. (2015). *Counter-Terrorism and Security Act 2015*. Retrieved October 21, 2016, from http://www.legislation.gov.uk/ukpga/2015/6/contents/enacted

Leitenberg, M. (2006). *Deaths in Wars and Conflicts in the 20th Century*. Cornell University Peace Studies Program. Retrieved March 6, 2016, from https://www.clingendael.org/sites/default/files/pdfs/20060800_cdsp_occ_leitenberg.pdf

Lemu, M. N. (2016). Notes on Religion and Countering Violent Extremism. In H. Abadi (Ed.), *Countering Daesh Propaganda: Action-Oriented Research for Practical Policy Outcomes* (pp. 43–50). Atlanta: The Carter Center.

Lequesne, C. (2016). French Foreign and Security Challenges After the Paris Terrorist Attacks. *Contemporary Security Policy, 37*(2), 306–318.

Lichfield, J. (2015). Paris Attacks: Francois Hollande Warns Europe Must Control Borders to Prevent 'Dismantling of the EU'. *The Independent*. Retrieved June 21, 2017, from https://www.independent.co.uk/news/world/europe/paris-terror-francois-hollande-announces-plans-to-extend-anti-terror-powers-a6736771.html

MacAskill, E. (2017). 'Extreme Surveillance' Becomes UK Law with Barely a Whimper. *The Guardian*. Retrieved July 19, 2019, from https://www.theguardian.com/world/2016/nov/19/extreme-surveillance-becomes-uk-law-with-barely-a-whimper

Mason, R. (2016). Cameron Criticises Ukip for Linking Brussels Attacks to Immigration. *The Guardian*. Retrieved May 28, 2018, from https://www.theguardian.com/politics/2016/mar/22/cameron-criticises-ukip-for-linking-brussels-attacks-to-immigration

Merkel, A. (2015). The Guardian View on Europe's Refugee Crisis: A Little Leadership, at Last. *The Guardian*. Retrieved May 28, 2018, from https://www.theguardian.com/commentisfree/2015/sep/01/guardian-view-on-europe-refugee-crisis-leadership-at-last-angela-merkel

Michalowski, R. (2013). The Masters Tools: Can Supranational Law Confront Crimes of Powerful States? In E. Stanley & J. McCulloch (Eds.), *State Crime and Resistance* (pp. 201–224). London: Routledge.

Miller, G. (2011). Under Obama, an Emerging Global Apparatus for Drone Killing. *The Washington Post*. Retrieved May 28, 2018, from http://articles.washingtonpost.com/2011-12-27/national/35285416_1_drone-program-drone-campaign-lethal-operations

Milne, S. (2012). America's Murderous Drone Campaign is Fuelling Terror. *The Guardian*. Retrieved May 28, 2018, from http://www.theguardian.com/commentisfree/2012/may/29/americas-drone-campaign-terror

Nesser, P., Stenersen, A., & Oftedal, E. (2016). Jihadi Terrorism in Europe: The IS-Effect. *Perspectives on Terrorism, 10*(6), 3–24.

New York Times. (2016a). *France's Real State of Emergency*. Retrieved August 30, 2016, from http://nyti.ms/2aQ8eZf

New York Times. (2016b). *France's Permanent Emergency State*. Retrieved August 25, 2016, from http://nyti.ms/2api3wV

Nossiter, A. (2013). Paris Attacks Spur Emergency Edict and Intense Policing in France. *New York Times*. Retrieved August 30, 2016, from http://www.nytimes.com/2015/11/24/world/europe/in-france-some-see-the-police-security-net-as-too-harsh-paris-attacks.html

OHCHR. (2012). *Independent International Commission of Inquiry, Report of the Independent International Commission of Inquiry on the Syrian Arab Republic*. United Nations General Assembly. Retrieved March 6, 2016, from http://www.ohchr.org/Documents/HRBodies/HRCouncil/RegularSession/Session21/A-HRC-21-50_en.pdf

Oksanen, A., Kaakinen, M., Minkkinen, J., Räsänen, P., Enjolras, B., & Steen-Johnsen, K. (2018). Perceived Societal Fear and Cyberhate After the November 2015 Paris Terrorist Attacks. *Terrorism and Political Violence*. https://doi.org/10.1080/09546553.2018.1442329

Pape, R. (2003). The Strategic Logic of Suicide Terrorism. *American Political Science Review, 97*(3), 343–361.

Parsons, V. (2014). Government Release Number Deprived of British Citizenship Since 2013. *The Bureau of Investigative Journalism*. Retrieved August 30, 2016, from http://www.thebureauinvestigates.com/2014/12/19/government-release-number-deprived-of-british-citizenship-since-2013/

Połońska-Kimunguyi, E., & Gillespie, M. (2016). Terrorism Discourse on French International Broadcasting: France 24 and the Case of *Charlie Hebdo* Attacks in Paris. *European Journal of Communication, 31*(5), 568–583.

Porteous, T. (2007). Where Will Iraq—and Its Refugees—Go Next? *Reuters*. Retrieved May 28, 2018, from http://www.alertnet.org/db/blogs/1264/2007/05/22-162514-1.htm

Power, S. (2002). *"A Problem From Hell": America and the Age of Genocide*. New York: Basic Books.

Renard, T. (2016). *Fear Not: A Critical Perspective on the Terrorist Threat in Europe*. Security Policy Brief. Retrieved June 21, 2017, from http://aei.pitt.edu/86893/1/SPB77.pdf

Richardson, D., & May, H. (1999). Deserving Victims? Sexual Status and the Social Construction of Violence. *The Sociological Review, 47*(2), 308–331.

Rodriguez, J. F. (2016). *Paris, Berlin, Ankara: A Deal Driven by Populism*. Institute of European Democracies. Retrieved June 21, 2017, from https://www.iedonline.eu/download/2016/schengen/FERRO-RODRIGUEZ.pdf

Rubin, A. J. (2015). France Shuts Three Mosques and Four Muslim Prayer Rooms. *New York Times*. Retrieved July 19, 2019, from https://www.nytimes.com/2015/12/03/world/europe/france-shuts-down-three-mosques-and-four-muslim-prayer-rooms.html

Shetty, S. (2016). *Tackling the Global Refugee Crisis: Sharing, Not Shirking Responsibility*. Amnesty International. Retrieved July 19, 2019, from https://www.amnesty.org/en/latest/campaigns/2016/10/tackling-the-global-refugee-crisis-sharing-responsibility/

Shetty, S. (2017). *The US War on Muslim Refugees*. Amnesty International. Retrieved March 1, 2018, from https://www.amnesty.org/en/latest/news/2017/01/the-us-war-on-muslim-refugees/

Speckhard, A., & Akhmedova, K. (2005). Talking to terrorists. *The Journal of Psychohistory, 33*(2), 125–156.

Tatchell, A. (2015). *Liberty and Security: The Price of Peace After Paris*. The London School of Economics and Political Science. Retrieved June 21, 2017, from http://blogs.lse.ac.uk/lseupr/2015/12/01/323/

The Brookings Institution. (2019). *Resolving Iraqi Displacement: Humanitarian and Development Perspectives*. Retrieved June 21, 2017, from https://www.brookings.edu/wp-content/uploads/2016/06/0216_iraqi_displacement.pdf

The Guardian. (2017a). Russia and China Veto UN Resolution to Impose Sanctions on Syria. Retrieved July 19, 2019, from https://www.theguardian.com/world/2017/mar/01/russia-and-china-veto-un-resolution-to-impose-sanctions-on-syria

The Guardian. (2017b). UK 'Has Stripped 150 Jihadists and Criminals of Citizenship'. Retrieved July 19, 2019, from https://www.theguardian.com/uk-news/2017/jul/30/uk-has-stripped-150-jihadists-and-criminals-of-citizenship

Tondo, L., Wintour, P., & Messina, P. (2017). *Interpol Circulates List of 173 Suspected Members of Isis Suicide Brigade*. Retrieved July 19, 2019, from https://www.theguardian.com/world/2017/jul/21/isis-islamic-state-suicide-brigade-interpol-list

Townsend, M. (2017). Britain Needs to Reset Relations with Its Muslims, Insists Warsi. *The Guardian*. Retrieved July 19, 2019, from https://www.theguardian.com/politics/2017/jun/10/baroness-warsi-britain-must-hit-reset-muslims-relationship

UN. (1948). *Universal Declaration of Human Rights*. Retrieved June, 21 2017, from https://www.un.org/en/universal-declaration-human-rights/

UN. (1966). *International Covenant on Economic, Social and Cultural Rights*. United Nations Human Rights Office of the High Commissioner. Retrieved March 1, 2018, from https://www.ohchr.org/EN/ProfessionalInterest/Pages/CESCR.aspx

UN. (2018). *UN Global Counter-Terrorism Strategy*. Retrieved June 21, 2019, from https://www.un.org/counterterrorism/ctitf/en/un-global-counter-terrorism-strategy

UN General Assembly. (2005). *Resolution Adopted by the General Assembly on 16 September 2005: 60/1. 2005 World Summit Outcome*. Retrieved June 21, 2017, from https://www.un.org/en/development/desa/population/migration/generalassembly/docs/globalcompact/A_RES_60_1.pdf

UNHCR. (2004). *Protecting the Rights of Stateless Persons: The 1945 Convention Relating to the Status of Stateless Persons*. Retrieved July 19, 2019, from https://www.unhcr.org/uk/protection/statelessness/519e20989/protecting-rights-stateless-persons-january-2014.html

UNHCR. (2007). *Statistics on Displaced Iraqis Around The World*. UN High Commissioner for Refugees. Retrieved June 21, 2017, from https://www.unhcr.org/461f7cb92.pdf

UNHCR. (2010a). *Convention and Protocol Relating to the Status of Refugees*. UN High Commissioner for Refugees. Retrieved June 21, 2017, from https://www.unhcr.org/uk/protection/basic/3b66c2aa10/convention-protocol-relating-status-refugees.html

UNHCR. (2010b). *Iraq Country Profile*. UN High Commissioner for Refugees. Retrieved June 21, 2017, from https://www.unhcr.org/uk/iraq.html

UNHCR. (2010c). *UNHCR Global Appeal 2010–2011: Populations of Concern to UNHCR*. UN High Commissioner for Refugees. Retrieved June 21, 2017, from https://www.unhcr.org/4b04002b9.html

UNHCR. (2014). *2014 Syria Regional Response Plan*. UN High Commissioner for Refugees. Retrieved June 21, 2017, from https://www.unhcr.org/syriarrp6/midyear/

UNHCR. (2015a, September). *Syrian Refugees Inter-Agency Regional Update*. United Nations High Commissioner for Refugees. Retrieved June 21 2017, from http://www.refworld.org/docid/562611cf4.html

UNHCR. (2015b). *Syria Regional Refugee Response*. UN High Commissioner for Refugees. Retrieved June 21, 2017, from https://data2.unhcr.org/en/situations/syria

UNHCR. (2016). *UNHCR Viewpoint: 'Refugee' or 'Migrant'—Which Is Right?* UN High Commissioner for Refugees. Retrieved June 21, 2017, from http://www.unhcr.org/55df0e556.html

UNHCR. (2017). *Understanding Statelessness*. UN High Commissioner for Refugees. Retrieved June 21, 2017, from http://www.unhcr.org/uk/stateless-people.html

UNHCR. (2019). *UN Conventions of statelessness*. UN High Commissioner for Refugees. Retrieved June 21, 2017, from https://www.unhcr.org/uk/un-conventions-on-statelessness.html

UNHR. (1965). *International Convention on the Elimination of All Forms of Racial Discrimination*. United Nations Human Rights Office of the High Commissioner. Retrieved June 21, 2017, from https://www.ohchr.org/en/professionalinterest/pages/cerd.aspx

Walklate, S., & Mythen, G. (2016). Fractured Lives, Splintered Knowledge: Making Criminological Sense of the January 2015 Terrorist Attacks in Paris. *Critical Criminology, 24*(3), 333–346.

Weinberg, L. B. (2008). Democratic Responses to Terrorism. In L. B. Weinberg (Ed.), *Democratic Responses to Terrorism* (pp. 1–12). Oxon: Routledge.

Wemmers, J.-A. (2013). Victims' Experiences in the Criminal Justice System and Their Recovery from Crime. *International Review of Victimology, 19*(3), 221–233.

Wilkinson, P. (1977). *Terrorism and the Liberal State*. London: Macmillan.

Wilkinson, P. (2006). *Terrorism Versus Democracy: The Liberal State Response*. Oxon: Routledge.

Williams, P. R., Worboys, J., & Ulbrick, J. T. (2012). Preventing Mass Atrocity Crimes: The Responsibility to Protect and the Syria Crisis. *Case Western Reserve Journal of International Law, 45*(1), 472–503.
Yazgan, P., Utku, D. E., & Sirkeci, I. (2015). Syrian Crisis and Migration. *Migration Letters, 12*(3), 1–12.
Zedner, L. (2009). *Security*. London: Routledge.

6

ISIS: The Special Relationship Between the United States, United Kingdom and Saudi Arabia

This chapter examines ISIS and how its interpretation of Islam and its motivation to establish a caliphate have made this group different from previous Islamist terrorist groups. As with previous chapters, this chapter also explores the relationship between the terrorist group and states by discussing how the invasion of Iraq and Syria facilitated the emergence of ISIS. It therefore locates the emergence and growth of ISIS in state practices and state crimes that have formed part of the counter-terrorism measures introduced in the 'war on terror'.

The second half of the chapter explores the relationship between Saudi Arabia, the United States, United Kingdom and ISIS. When examining this relationship, this chapter critically explores the significance of financial deals involving arms between the United States, United Kingdom and Saudi Arabia, and the role of the United States and United Kingdom in sustaining the state crimes committed by Saudi Arabia against Lebanese citizens and Saudi citizens. This chapter then elucidates how Saudi Arabia facilitated the existence of ISIS through firstly, embracing and validating the Wahhabism practiced by ISIS and secondly, through financially supporting the actions of ISIS. This

S. Ahmed, *The 'War on Terror', State Crime & Radicalization*, Palgrave Studies in Risk, Crime and Society, https://doi.org/10.1007/978-3-030-40138-2_6

chapter therefore discusses the vast number of state practices and state crimes that have positively influenced the emergence of ISIS and sustained terrorism within the 'war on terror'.

Vested State Interests, Oil and Ideologies

Although the book has considered the role of states in the emergence of Islamist terrorist groups, such as the Taliban and AQ, it is also worth exploring how the relationship between states also facilitates terrorism. At the forefront of this analysis must be a consideration of how the relationship between Saudi Arabia, the United States and the United Kingdom has impacted the emergence of Islamist terrorism. When exploring the relationship between these states, it is important to go back to the establishment of Saudi Arabia. The origins of Saudi Arabia demonstrate its dependency on oil and this provides an understanding of its contemporary relationship with the United States. In 1932, the Kingdom of Saudi Arabia was founded by King Abdul-Aziz Ibn Saud after a prolonged military campaign, which included British support via arms and finance (Aburish, 2005). Oil was discovered in Bahrain by the Standard Oil Company of California (SoCal, now Chevron) (Peck, 2014). In 1933, the United States recognized the new country with King Saud granting SoCal an exclusive 66-year concession for oil exploration and production in the al-Ahsa region (Peck, 2014). In 1936, SoCal joined with Texaco to form the California-Arabian Standard Oil Company (Casoc), and the king extended Casoc's original concession to cover a 440,000 square mile area of Saudi Arabia (Sampson, 1975). The Saudi authorization of the US exploration of oil meant that the United States had a vested interest in the country, and this led President Roosevelt to charge the US Secretary of State with the role of protecting US interests in the Saudi oil concession (Jaffe & Elass, 2007). Following the subsequent discovery of three more major oil fields, Casoc was renamed Aramco (the Arabian-American Oil Company) in 1944 and by 1950, President Truman had publicly committed the United States to the independence of Saudi Arabia (Bronson, 2006; Peck, 2014). Thus, a symbiotic geo-political relationship developed where both countries became reliant on each other to promote their own interests. The United

States relied on Saudi Arabia for oil and the Saudi regime relied on the US support to establish their territory and exist as a sovereign state. However, the political and economic advantages of this reciprocal relationship meant that potentially dangerous religious ideologies, which manifested as part of Saudi governance and expansion, were omitted from scrutiny and critique. As this chapter argues, the consequences of this were, and continue to be, that the Wahhabism that emerged in the eighteenth century continues to inform contemporary Salafism. Here one can identify a direct relationship between state practices and radicalization. It would be plausible to conceptualize the Saudi regime as inciting and glorifying terrorism through dispersing a dangerous ideology which supports terrorism, in much the same way as the coalition did with the Mujahideen to counter the threat of the Soviet Union in Afghanistan.

An exploration of the synergies between Wahhabism and Salafism interpretations of Islam demonstrates the influence of Wahhabism on Salafism. 'Wahhabism draws its name from an eighteenth-century religious reformer known as Muhammad Ibn Abd al-Wahhab (1703–91) who preached in central Arabia' (Denoeux, 2011: 59). Abd al-Wahhab advocated a return to the monotheism that Islam had once introduced which involved a strict, narrow and literal interpretation of the Quran (Volpi, 2011). Wahhabism dismissed all other interpretations of Islam and became increasingly powerful when in 1932, Abd al-Aziz Ibn Saud unified the tribes of Arabia into what became the Kingdom of Saudi Arabia with Wahhabism becoming the country's state-sanctioned ideology (Denoeux, 2011; Hashemi, 2016). However, Wahhabism was also institutionalized, thereby becoming an ideology that informed the internal policies of the country and becoming the governance system of Saudi Arabia (Allhussein, 2018). Saudi governance and politics therefore became infused with Wahhabism, with Wahhabism becoming the dominant ideology to govern all policies and laws. The political elite protected Wahhabism through restricting the space within which other religious ideologies could exist and punished anyone that didn't strictly adhere to Wahhabism. Wahhabism was used to create a legal system that authorized extreme acts of brutality, which included 'public floggings for crimes such as listening to music, shaving beards, wearing silk or gold (for men), smoking, playing chess, backgammon or cards or failing to uphold strict rules of gender segregation' (Hashemi, 2016: 12). In terms of contemporary influence, even with only 1–2% of the world's Muslims, the Saudi regime controls some 90% of the world's Islamic institutions, and most importantly educational institutions (Wright, 2007). This influence is not only based on the country being home to the two most important mosques within Islam, Mecca and Medina (Cordesman, 2006), but the influence is also maintained through inter-state relationships with the United States and United Kingdom. And these inter-state relationships greatly influence the international dispersal of Wahhabism which positively facilitates the existence of terrorism, human rights abuses and state crimes.

The role of Islam within education has become even more prominent with the religious awakening, which combined the teachings of Abd al-Wahhab with the ideology of the Egyptian Muslim Brotherhood (Allhussein, 2018; Vertigans, 2008). One can also draw parallels with Afghanistan following the Soviet invasion and how religion and education combined to create a new generation of jihadists. As Milne (2015: 2) states,

> this US and Western habit of playing with jihadi groups, which then come back to bite them, goes back at least to the 1980s war against the Soviet Union in Afghanistan, which fostered the original al-Qaida under CIA tutelage.

As already stated, Wahhabism remains a powerful foundation of power in the Saudi Kingdom, with the religious ideology still informing the existence of strict rules which govern every sphere of life, including education, law and the economy. Saudi Wahhabism maintains intolerance for non-Wahhabi, non-Arab Muslims, and like Iran and Sudan, the other two nations that maintain Sharia Law, Saudi Arabia has one of the worst human rights records in the world because it practices a strict form of Islamic extremism (Gaffney, 2011; Scheuer, 2011). Although the country maintains a legal system that ignores 'the rule of law, freedom of speech and assembly, the right to travel, women's rights, and religious liberties' (Pipes, 2011: 20), its influence extends beyond its own territory. Wahhabism has become an international geo-political ideology that influences contemporary international Salafism, with both ideologies advocating an extremist interpretation of Islam.

During the mid-twentieth century, Salafism gradually became infused with Wahhabism and, like Wahhabism, Salafism emphasizes a return to the early Muslim community and a rejection of other interpretations of Islam (Hashemi, 2016; Haykel, 2009). The 1973 oil boom provided the Saudi regime with the revenue to promote and disperse Wahhabism, and what became known as Salafism, to counter Iran's Shiite regime and curb Iranian influence in the Gulf (Hasan, 2008; Rohmaniyah & Woodward, 2012). The establishment of the Islamic Republic of Iran in 1979, a modern theological Shiite state, provided the Saudi regime with the perfect enemy. This sectarian conflict tied religion with politics, just as had happened in Afghanistan, thereby fuelling the ideological construction of a 'holy war'. The holy war was as much about fighting for political influence, as it was about promoting authentic Islam, with both Saudi Arabia and Iran constructing their ideology as the authentic Islam and thereby constructing the opposing side as infidels. The Saudi regime engaged in publicity campaigns to radicalize citizens into fighting the infidels (Hamid, 2016; Vassiliev, 2000). Religion, politics, nationalism and self-preservation became infused with the Saudi regime claiming that all Saudi citizens had a responsibility to defend the Ummah, which was under threat from infidels (Hegghammer, 2008). The conveyed sense of responsibility exploited Saudi citizens' duty to protect the Ummah, whilst also constructing other interpretations of Islam as false. Thus, a binary was created whereby most Saudi citizens supported Saudi Arabia's self-proclaimed status as defenders of the Muslim faith (Byman, 2005). One can note the similarities here between the unison of politics and religion in Afghanistan by the coalition to motivate jihadists, and the unison of these ideologies to unite Saudi citizens by Saudi Arabia. As stated previously, more nuanced invisible forms of state power also form vessels through which dangerous ideologies are maintained, reinforced and acted upon in the 'war on terror'. And, macro-national-level facilitators of radicalization also consist of the creation of dangerous discourses.

Saudi Arabia has also funded madrassas and mosques to propagate their version of Islam around the world. In many cases they have exploited the poverty and instability prevalent in countries such as Pakistan,

Indonesia, the Philippines, Malaysia, Thailand, India and parts of Africa, by providing a source of much-needed finance to these countries. This funding has allowed them to disseminate Wahhabist literature, provide generous scholarships for the training of imams, pay foreign preachers, and build mosques, schools and study centres (Butt, 2015; Hubbard & Sheikh, 2015). Having the financial means is therefore vital in allowing this ideology to be exported, just as it was vital for the coalition during the Soviet invasion in Afghanistan. According to official Saudi information, 'Saudi funds have been used to build and maintain over 1,500 mosques, 202 colleges, 210 Islamic Centers wholly or partly financed, and almost 2,000 schools for educating Muslim children in non-Islamic countries in Europe, North and South America, Australia and Asia (Silverberg, 2003). Similarly, madrassas (religious schools) have been built in a plethora of places, from Lahore to London, and from Morocco to Malaysia' (Denoeux, 2011: 59) which has ensured the international growth of Wahhabism.

The next section considers the relationship between Wahhabism and terrorism. When exploring this relationship, it is important to remember that resolution 1624 required states to introduce legislation to prevent the incitement and glorification of terrorism (UN, 2005). This subsequently led to the Terrorism Act 2006, which was introduced into the UK law, the offence of encouraging terrorism, which criminalized statements that are likely to be understood as a direct or indirect encouragement of terrorist acts. This legislation suggests a link between terrorist discourses and terrorism to the extent of criminalizing those that encourage such acts. However, as the discussion now demonstrates, this link and its very construction are prevalent only where non-state actors are concerned. This is because, even though states are under a duty to prevent terrorism (UN resolution 1373), where there is evidence of states dispersing these very ideologies, there is a lack of action. It therefore appears that within the 'war on terror' the very factors that are recognized as feeding and facilitating radicalization are neglected when the perpetrators are states. As this chapter demonstrates, such ignorance is purposeful, as it serves geo-political interests and, further, it permeates into a plethora of states crimes involving weapons, war crimes and human rights abuses. This demonstrates the link between the super macro-universal level, and how this operates on the basis of geo-political interests and how the neglect of violations on this level leads to macro-national-level state crimes which facilitate radicalization.

Wahhabism and Terrorism's Shared Ideology

There is evidence to suggest that the type of Islam being exported by the Saudi regime is consistent with extremist interpretations of Islam that legitimize terrorism. Research into Saudi-funded Wahhabi-led schools revealed that these schools promote the hatred of Shi'ite Muslims, Jewish individuals, and homosexuals, and they advocate the need to establish an Islamic caliphate (Bar, 2008). Similarly, Admon (2007) highlights how the document entitled, 'Educational Policy', which was published by the Saudi Education Ministry, has the following two goals as part of its educational policy. The first is to equip students for jihad, and the second is to ensure that the spirit of Islamic jihad is used to fight enemies. In 2005, a report by the Center for Religious Freedom revealed how the material printed with the Saudi support in US mosques between 2003 and 2004 included intolerant and violent material which demonstrated evidence of Wahhabi indoctrination within the United States (Centre for Religious Freedom, 2005). In May 2006, the Center for Religious Freedom, together with the Institute for Gulf Affairs, released a ground-breaking report where they analysed the literature in approximately 15 randomly selected Muslim schools within the United States. Their findings were that every school had highly intolerant, hate-infested, Wahhabi literature that had been exported to American Islamic mosques by Saudi Arabia (Shea, 2006). A larger study was conducted involving 100 randomly selected mosques, to measure the correlation between Sharia adherence and dogma calling for violence against non-believers. Of the 100 mosques surveyed, 51% had texts on site rated as severely advocating violence, 30% had texts rated as moderately advocating violence and 19% had no violent texts. Mosques that presented as Sharia adherent were more likely to feature violence-positive texts on site than non-Sharia adherent mosques (Kedar & Yerushalmi, 2011).

When exploring the relationship between ideology and terrorism, a 2014 opinion poll, conducted via social networking sites found that 92% of Saudi citizens believe that ISIS follows the true version of Islam and Islamic law (Crooke, 2015). This opinion poll indicates the similarity between the Wahhabism prevalent in Saudi Arabia and the ideology espoused by ISIS. To further elucidate and demonstrate this link, 'when ISIS needed textbooks for its school curricula, it downloaded books from the Ministry of Education in Saudi Arabia' (Hashemi, 2016: 15). As Hashemi (2016) argues, Wahhabi texts were a perfect ideological match, given the shared Salafist theological bases between the two political entities. Hashemi (2016) goes on to say that if you are a young Muslim in Cairo, Karachi, Toronto or London and want to connect with your religion, the chances of exposure to a Wahhabi version of Islam are high.

In terms of assessing the influence of Saudi Wahhabism on Islamic extremism, a Brookings Institution study based on a sample size of 20,000 participants concluded that ISIS supporters on twitter disproportionately came from Saudi Arabia (Berger & Morgan, 2015). A study by Sageman (2004) found that 97% of the jihadists studied became increasingly devoted to highly Sharia-adherent Salafist Islam on their path to radicalization, despite adhering to various devotional levels during their youth. According to Middle East Monitor (2014), where ISIS is concerned, more foreign fighters have joined ISIS from Saudi Arabia than any other country, with Saudi fighters having undertaken many of the suicide operations in ISIS-controlled territory. Similarly, when exploring the nationality of those involved in the 2003 Iraq war, the *Los Angeles Times* reported that nearly half of foreign fighters in the country were Saudi, and that fighters from Saudi Arabia are thought to have carried out more suicide bombings than those of any other nationality (Parker, 2007).

The link between Saudi Arabia and terrorism is multi-faceted. Of these facets, the predominant similarity is ideology, and as evidenced above, this means that Saudi citizens are more likely to believe that ISIS is legitimate in its ideology and quest, and therefore join ISIS. However, this link also shows that the Saudi regime has practices that are facilitating terrorism. This facilitation is so powerful that terrorism cannot be countered unless the mechanisms which sustain terrorism, such as this, are eradicated. These mechanisms, amongst other things, include Saudi financing, the dispersal of Wahhabism and the discrimination of other forms of Islam.

Wahhabism suppresses free speech and independent critical inquiry (Stern & Shideler, 2011) and, through delegitimizing other interpretations of Islam, it promotes the discrimination against other non-Wahhabi Muslims as well as non-Muslims. This lack of exposure to more moderate and progressive interpretations of Islam facilitates the perception that there is only one interpretation of Islam. As Mansour al-Hadj, a human rights activist who was raised in Saudi Arabia, states, 'I grew up with the view that I, as a Saudi, am the only one that is right in this world. If we cannot make people understand that there are rules of human rights, and that every human being must be respected, then you can never counter terrorism'. And therefore, it is possible to contend that the regime violates all safeguards which exist to protect individuals against discrimination, such as the Declaration on the Elimination of All Forms of Intolerance and of Discrimination Based on Religion or Belief (1981) and, through doing so, it is also guilty of human rights violations and state crime.

Saudi Arabia has also directly influenced other Muslim countries, with the decrease in tolerance and increase in discrimination in these countries being directly attributed to Saudi influence (Hashemi, 2016). Saudi Arabia uses inhumane practices which include silencing individuals who oppose their human rights record. The Saudi government defined terrorism as any act with a criminal motive that directly or indirectly undermines public order and the state's security and stability or endangers national unity (Al Arabiya, 2014). The introduction of new counter-terrorism legislation by the Saudi regime has been used to justify the human rights abuse of those who oppose the regime and/or promote human rights. For example, the Saudi blogger, Raif Badawi, received a punishment of 1000 lashes over 20 weeks for running a liberal website promoting the freedom of speech (Butt, 2015). Amnesty International has recorded a worrying increase in death sentences against political dissidents in Saudi Arabia since 2013, including at least 34 members of Saudi Arabia's Shi'a community, all of whom are accused of activities deemed a 'risk to national security' (Amnesty International, 2017a). Yussuf al-Mushaikass was executed, along with three other men for terror-related offences in connection with their participation in anti-government protests in the Shi'a majority Eastern Province between 2011 and 2012. His execution was based on an unfair trial which hinged largely on a 'confession' obtained through torture (Amnesty International, 2017b). As previously stated, the right to a fair trial is an absolute human right, which exists in Article 10 of the UDHR (Weissbrodt & Hallendorff, 1999), with the ICCPR and Geneva Convention both prohibiting torture, cruel, inhuman or degrading treatment (UNHR, 1966). The regime is therefore committing macro-national-level intra-state crimes through violating human rights safeguards.

Given the similarities between the regime and ISIS, it is not surprising that they share similar human rights violations. In 2014, ISIS broadcast the beheadings of five foreign hostages and in 2016, Saudi Arabia carried out at least 87 executions, beginning with a mass execution of 47 prisoners, including a prominent Shi'a cleric (Human Rights Watch, 2016; The Guardian, 2015; Tufft, 2015). Although the Saudi regime does not disseminate videos of its public executions, videos showing public beheadings can be found on video-sharing sites, such as LiveLeak, with the executions frequently taking place in public spaces like sports stadiums (Friis, 2015). Similarly, the conduct of ISIS towards civilians under its control frequently violates fundamental IHRL and IHL safeguards. Civilians are killed if they try to flee ISIS-controlled areas and they are used to shield ISIS fighters from attack, which is a war crime (Amnesty International, 2017c: 43). Since both Saudi Arabia and ISIS adhere to Wahhabism, it is to be expected that there are other similarities between them. For example, the list of punishments enforced by ISIS is nearly identical to the crime and punishment provisions routinely implemented in Saudi Arabia (Butt, 2015; Donaghy & Atkinson, 2015; Hashemi, 2016). One could therefore argue that the Saudi regime is simply a more established version of ISIS and, because it exists as a state, it is able to violate IHRL and IHL. As this chapter explores, human rights abuses by the Saudi regime tend to be omitted from international scrutiny and actions due to trade deals, most notably those involving oil and arms. As Webb (2007: 11) contends, Ronald Reagan encouraged the Saudis to buy arms from Britain, which led to the '1985 Al-Yamamah agreement and, from then on, British governments turned a blind eye to the human rights abuses in Saudi Arabia, where beheadings, the hacking off of hands, floggings and torture are normal practice'.

Saudi Arabia's Financing of ISIS

This chapter has explored the relationship between Saudi Arabia and ISIS via ideology, and although this formed an integral part of the emergence of ISIS, on a practical level this relationship also involved financial assistance. In terms of financing, the amount spent on exporting Wahhabism reveals the Saudi dedication to establishing Wahhabism as the dominant version of Islam in the world. According to Butt (2015), the Saudi regime has spent more than $100 billion exporting Wahhabism to poorer Muslim countries over the past three decades, whereas the Soviet Union spent around $7 billion spreading communism from 1921 to 1991. Money and power are inextricably linked, and the financing of Salafism has led many smaller organizations to align themselves with Salafists (Starr, 2012). The financing of Wahhabism has been directly linked to the growth of terrorism. Saudi Arabia has provided funds that have been spent on funding terrorist organizations and dispersing extremist ideologies in mosques, prisons and educational institutions (Baran, 2008; Levey, 2005). And what Gaffney (2011: 42) terms, 'financial jihad' has been used to increase violent methods that support the growth of Islamic Wahhabism. Although the Saudi regime has directly financed terrorism through education centres and schools, they have also indirectly financed terrorism through funding charitable organization.

The regime exploits one of the five pillars of Islam, zakat, which is giving money to charity.

> Some Islamic finance funds apply 2.5 percent of their proceeds to zakat, translating into many hundreds of millions— if not billions— of dollars flowing to their favored charities which are also jihadist Islamist organizations and three of the largest Muslim charities in the United States were all shut down by the federal government due to their ties to terrorism financing. (Gaffney, 2011: 49)

According to the State Department International Narcotics Control Strategy Report on money laundering, Saudi Arabia 'continues to be a significant jurisdictional source for terrorist financing worldwide' (United States Department of State, 2009). Crooke (2015) conceptualizes this export as the manifestation of soft power. This soft power allows the Saudi regime to quash those who oppose their ideology. In this way, the regime does not have to directly use violent tactics abroad (although it has no qualms in doing so) because the export of soft power creates the conditions for more extremist exercises of power.

One can make the link between the Saudi regime and imperialism. Imperialism works to export ideologies that allow states to have indirect control over territories, and the export of Wahhabism achieves this objective (Reid, 2005; Stabile & Kumar, 2005). Interestingly one can also make the link between political instability and ideology. For example, Saudi Arabia exploits states that suffer immense poverty and political instability and through finance, they reconstruct such countries according to their own vision. Considering the vast damage of colonialism, the Fourth Geneva Convention (1949) clearly bans an occupying power from restructuring the economy according to their own vision and imperialism is now held as being morally wrong (Jenkins, 2011; Jouannet, 2007). However, one can argue that the Saudi regime engages in imperialism, especially when one considers how Saudi Arabia influences educational institutions in other countries and therefore ensures that generations will be socialized to follow their ideology and a religious system which dictates every area of their life. This form of imperialism, which has both economic and ideological dimensions, can therefore be conceptualized as macro-national-level inter-state crime.

However, as is becoming apparent, geo-political power and influence shapes and constructs IHRL and IHL violations and, within this context, interstate relationships with their inherent vested interests can act to conceal these very violations. The US support of Saudi Arabia has meant that the link between Saudi financing and terrorism has been dismissed. In 2003, Saudi Arabia criminalized money laundering and enforced procedures to prevent terrorist financing and domestic terrorism (Allam, 2010). However, it appears that this stance is ideological since the regime has used these measures to criminalize opponents of the regime, rather than stem the Saudi financing of terrorism (Ehrenfeld, 2011). Similarly, a 2009 General Accounting Office (GAO) report on Saudi efforts to stop terror financing noted that Saudi financial institutions demonstrated a continued unwillingness to freely share information with western authorities (United States General Accounting Office, 2009). The Saudi regime is believed to have spent around $100 billion promoting a violent, intolerant and puritanical Wahhabist sect of Islam, sponsoring Sunni Salafism and giving rise to violent Sunni Salafi groups such as AQ, ISIS, and Boko Haram (Hussain, 2014). However, as Ehrenfeld (2011: 135) states,

> 'when it comes to Saudi investments or contributions in the United States, the American government does not disclose information, making it difficult to discover the true extent of the Saudi financial, political, educational, and social influence in America'... with successive U.S. administrations demonstrating a 'willful blindness and recklessness vis- à- vis Saudi Arabia's cultivation of Islamic radicalism and terrorism financing activities'.

The Wiki-leaks scandal demonstrated how this ignorance exists at the highest levels of government, including American presidents, with a leaked cable from former Secretary of State, Hilary Clinton, stating how AQ, Hamas and other jihadist groups obtain millions of dollars from Saudi sources during Hajj and Ramadan and Saudi Arabian donors are the predominant sources of Sunni terrorist funding worldwide (Handley, 2010). This link has also been made by former Vice President Biden, who stated:

> Our allies in the region were our largest problem in Syria. The Turks were great friends... [and] the Saudis, the Emirates, etcetera. What were they doing?.... They poured hundreds of millions of dollars and tens of tons of weapons into anyone who would fight against Assad—except that the people who were being supplied, [they] were al-Nusra, and al-Qaeda, and the extremist elements of jihadis who were coming from other parts of the world. (cited Butt, 2015)

The secrecy is even more apparent when one considers the 9/11 terrorist attacks. Fifteen of the 19 plane hijackers of the terrorist attacks of 9/11 were Saudi Arabian. A 900-page report entitled 'Joint Inquiry into Intelligence Community Actions Before and After the Terrorist Attacks of September 11th 2001' has been classified. The lead author of the report, former Florida Senator Bob Graham, explained that the report is hidden because it points 'a very strong finger at Saudi Arabia as the principal financier' of the 9/11 hijackers (cited Butt, 2015). He goes on to say, 'ISIS…is a product of Saudi ideals, Saudi money and Saudi organizational support, although now they are making a pretense of being very anti-ISIS' (cited Butt, 2015). Similarly, the US National Commission on Terrorist Attacks upon the United States (the 9/11 Commission) report, which was released in 2004, described Saudi Arabia as having been 'a problematic ally in combating Islamic extremism' (Prados & Blanchard, 2007: 9–10).

What becomes apparent is how the inter-state relationship between Saudi Arabia and the United States serves Saudi interests in exporting Wahhabism. It could therefore be argued that this inter-state relationship maintains the conditions which give rise to terrorism. There is also the non-ideological direct support of terrorism, whereby the Saudi regime directly supplies terrorist organizations with arms. When one considers the roles of states in facilitating terrorism, the list includes, providing finance, ideology, weapons, creating political and social instability, denying individuals' humanity, using torture and so on; the list is extensive and some of these facets were also present during the invasion of Afghanistan. However, this list omits all the variables which emerge due to invasions and counter-terrorism measures, such as those pertaining to injustice, powerlessness, discrimination and so on. It could therefore be argued that within the 'war on terror', states facilitate terrorism in two ways. The first is directly through financial assistance, weapons and ideology, and the second is through introducing mechanisms as part of countering terrorism which positively impact the micro-individual-emotional level. The list therefore includes many of variables identified by the UN (2018) and those that are the result of both super macro-universal-level and macro-national-level state crimes. As the next section details, it was the invasions of Iraq and Syria which led to the conditions in which ISIS could emerge.

Invasions of Iraq and Syria in the Emergence of ISIS

This section considers the meso-societal-level and states-facilitating terrorism from below through creating the political, social, ideological and economic climate in which terrorism can emerge. Although sectarian violence might form part of the immediate impact of invasions, because as Ramsbotham and Woodhouse (2000) argue, removing stable regional powers can leave a void in which new conflicts emerge, there are also long-term consequences of region instability. The Human Security Centre (2005) elucidates how 'indirect' deaths, such as war-exacerbated disease and malnutrition, account for nearly 90% of war-related deaths. This reveals the long-term impact of conflict and the importance of ensuring that post-conflict societies are rebuilt. The absence of stability not only contributes to terrorism, but it also leads to immense human suffering. The conflicts in Syria and Iraq and the marginalization of Iraqi Sunnis contributed to the emergence of ISIS (Byman, 2016). The Iran-Iraq war (1980–1988) 'destroyed Iraq's main oil terminals, refineries and petrochemical plants and cost Iraq approximately $452 billion', and the Iraq-Kuwait war (1990–1991) led to the United Nations imposing severe economic sanctions under the 'Oil for Food' program, which contributed to 'a sharp increase in malnutrition, infant mortality and disease' during the 1990s (Hashemi, 2016: 4). Iraq has therefore suffered from a plethora of internal state and external state-initiated harms with the 'UN Oil for Food' programme also contributing to the suffering of people in the region (see Chap. 3 for more in-depth discussion).

The 2003 invasion of Iraq by the United States and the United Kingdom led to several hundred thousands of Iraqis being killed and wounded with at least 18,800 killed between 1 January 2014 and 31 October 2015 (OHCHR, 2015). The tactics used by the US-led coalition contributed to deaths. As Amnesty International notes,

> by using explosive weapons with wide area effects and disproportionate airstrikes in densely populated areas, the US-led coalition and Iraqi forces failed to adapt their tactics to the reality on the ground.... Thousands of

> civilian deaths could have been avoided in west Mosul, had the Iraqi forces and the US-led coalition prioritized their protection, as required by international humanitarian law. (Amnesty International, 2017d)

Amnesty International researchers found a pattern of attacks in which the US-led coalition and Iraqi forces appear not to have struck their intended military targets, instead killing and injuring civilians and destroying or damaging civilian objects. In some cases, civilian deaths and injuries appear to have resulted from a choice of weapon that was inappropriate for the circumstances or from a failure to take necessary precautions to verify the target was a military objective (Amnesty International, 2017e). 'According to Airwars, between 19th February and 19th June 2017, attacks launched by Iraqi and coalition forces may have caused the deaths of as many as 5,805 civilians' (Amnesty International, 2017c: 6). As stated in Chap. 5, these actions are illegal under IHL. Everything feasible must be done to verify that targets are military objectives, to assess the proportionality of attacks, and to halt attacks if it becomes apparent, they are wrongly directed or disproportionate. Iraq is a state party to the four Geneva Conventions of 1949 and their Additional Protocol of 1977 relating to the Protection of Victims of International Armed Conflicts (Protocol I) (Amnesty International, 2017c: 41). The rules of customary international humanitarian law are legally binding on all parties, including the US-led coalition, Iraqi armed forces, government-backed militias and ISIS. States have an obligation to investigate possible violations of the laws of war and bring justice to those responsible for war crimes (Amnesty International, 2017c). Therefore, there were several violations of IHL and these violations have the capacity to positively facilitate the variables in the micro-individual-emotional level that lead to radicalization. Acts of aggression such as this also perpetuate the kind of discourses that as Lemu (2016) identified, extremists ask Muslims. They exacerbate the demonstration of a disregard for human life, where such a disregard is based on identity.

The ideological construction is further evident when one considers how in terms of public discourses and those distributed by the media, little attention is paid to how war and conflict in Iraq led to long-term instability which contributes to sectarian violence. These constructions further perpetuate the absence of states in explanation of terrorism. There was no 'al-Qaida in Iraq until the US and Britain invaded' (Milne, 2015: 2). Following the invasion in 2003, the Iraqi Governing Council (IGP) was formed and consisted of 'pro-US Iraqi individuals with sinister sectarian pasts' (Aziz, 2016: 53). However, this US-backed government had difficulty gaining legitimacy among Sunni Muslims (Riedel & Saab, 2008). According to Milne (2015: 2), the United States 'exploited the existence of ISIS against other forces in the region as part of a wider drive to maintain western control'. And, being involved in formulating a pro-US government in Iraq gave the United States considerable power. However, the Maliki administration promoted intolerance and sectarian violence against Sunni protesters which included the killing of eight children (Aziz, 2016). The violence practiced by the government alienated Sunni Muslims and through doing so, it led Sunni Muslims to sympathize with ISIS and see ISIS as the only organization that could offer them protection and represent their interests. The United States was therefore directly involved in producing a reality where sections of the population would feel injustice, political oppression and grievances and these would further exacerbate their radicalization and their perception that joining ISIS was the only way to address these grievances and obtain equality.

The Fourth Geneva Convention outlines the need for 'occupying powers' to rebuild a state prior to complete withdrawal, and the ICISS outlined the responsibility to rebuild and reconstruct following state atrocities (Williams et al. 2012; ICRC, 2014), with both recognizing how a lack of political stability gives rise to violence. Iraq and Syria suffered a complete destruction of their infrastructure, with political instability remaining in these countries following the invasions. Any analysis of the growth and emergence of ISIS must account for the role of the meso-societal level and therefore, how states contributed to an environment where the political, ideological and social conditions that positively facilitate terrorism existed. Had political stability existed, ISIS would not have been able to use its ideologies to create a state. It was only through states creating instability that ISIS could then exploit the vulnerability of the region and people to implement its own aims. As Tomé (2015: 124) states, ISIS has flourished and been effective at 'administering organization in the areas where "state authority" was missing or fragile and by the end of June 2014 it controlled a vast area that ranged from Aleppo in Syria to the Diyala province in Iraq, and a population of nearly 6 million people'.

Populist discourses omit the failure of occupying states to rebuild territories, in this case Iraq and Syria, thereby further fuelling the idea that states do not contribute to the existence of terrorist groups. However, as Hubbard and Sheikh (2015) contend, ISIS has been able to exploit conflict in the region and offer security, jobs and a sense of order in an area overwhelmed by war and conflict. ISIS has provided financial stability in the region through taking over oil assets in eastern Syria and Iraq, and its daily oil revenue was estimated to be between $1 million and $3 million per day (Cronin, 2015; Solomon, Chazan, & Jones, 2015). Extortion, ransoms, illicit taxation systems, smuggling, kidnapping, robberies and the theft and looting of antiquities form other sources of income for ISIS (Drennan, 2014; Gurule, 2016; Johnson & Trindle, 2014). As ISIS went from being a terrorist organization to a state, their capacity to cause harm and suffering increased, because as previously stated, states have the greatest capacity for violence.

The roots of ISIS can therefore be traced back to the chaos and lack of stability that was present in Iraq following the fall of Saddam Hussein and created the 'optimal conditions for the resurgence of ISIS' (Fernandez, 2015: 17). It could be argued that the United States, as the occupying power, failed to ensure the stability of the region prior to its withdrawal and this facilitated the growth of ISIS. The need to establish stability and possible consequences of not doing so have not only been recognized by the United Nations as facilitating terrorism (UN, 2018), but they have also been recognized by the United States. In 2012, a report prepared by the Defense Intelligence Agency predicted the rise of ISIS, noting that al-Qaeda-affiliated groups were the 'major forces driving the insurgency in Syria', and a former Pentagon official also suggested that the United States not only turned a blind eye to its support of such groups, but 'it was a wilful decision' (Marshall, 2015). The United States was also directly involved in the sectarian violence, with a *Guardian* investigation revealing how 'a fearsome paramilitary force' was established in Iraq in 2003, which was designed to counter the Sunni insurgency which had developed in reaction to the US invasion and occupation, running ruthless death squads which further plunged the country into a deep civil war (Mahmood et al., 2013). Although violence in the region had decreased by 2008, Cockburn (2015) notes how this was because most of the ethnic cleansing in Iraq had taken place by then, and the Shia had won.

The Syrian conflict also led to the destruction of Syria which facilitated the emergence of ISIS. In 2013, France, the United Kingdom and United States increased their participation in the Syrian civil war. The United States, France and Britain funded religious extremist sects and trained rebels inside Jordan to fight the Syrian government (Marshall, 2015). One can instantly draw parallels with Afghanistan and the CIA training of extremists to fight the Soviet Union. What becomes apparent is how coalition forces use extremists to further their own agenda, with a total disregard for how their actions, beliefs and tactics constitute state-sponsored terrorism, or how this may contribute to future sectarian violence and terrorism. The conflict in Syria had an enormous impact on the Syrian population. There were more than 250,000 deaths in the Syrian conflict in 2014 alone, life expectancy dropped by 27 years and more than half of Syria's 23 million population became internally displaced or fled the country as refugees (UN, 2015). According to the Syrian Network for Human rights, from March 2011 to October 2015, Syrian regime forces were responsible for 96% of civilian deaths and ISIS was responsible for approximately 1% of civilian deaths (Syria Network for Human Rights, 2015). This led the UN Secretary-General Ban Ki-moon to issue a global warning that Syria is the biggest security and humanitarian crisis of our time (Ki-Moon, 2016). When describing the crisis, Hashemi (2016: 7) states,

> the human rights catastrophe that has engulfed Syria worsens with every passing year. Syria is the primary moral and humanitarian catastrophe of the 21st century. This conflict has produced the world's worst refugee crisis since World War II, a chemical weapons crisis, a rape crisis, a health crisis, a hunger crisis, a torture crisis, a cultural heritage crisis—and, as a consequence of all the foregoing—an ISIS crisis. These quasi-genocidal conditions have created a fertile soil for the rebirth and expansion of radical Islamist militancy in the heart of the Arab world.

The conflict was seized on by Salafi-jihadis. As Englund & Stohl (2015: 3) state, just as in Iraq, 'Jihadis began to occupy towns' to 'enforce compliance with their own version of Islamic Sharia law' and the 'restoration of some order was, at first, frequently welcomed by local population'. Research by Speckhard and Yayla (2015: 95) revealed that

> Syrians who join IS are rewarded with salaried jobs which for young men translates into the ability to marry and for young women the money allows them to save their families from literal starvation. Foreign fighters receive additional rewards: wives, sexual slaves, and sometimes homes and cars.

The lack of political stability in both countries, as was the case with Afghanistan, drives people to join extremist groups and in post-conflict area, such groups have represented the only means through which employment, food and necessities are available.

ISIS was able to gain the confidence of Sunni Muslims and therefore, just as in Iraq, the very factors which facilitate terrorism, isolation, marginalization and vulnerability were fuelling loyalty to ISIS (Barnard & Arango, 2015). Hashemi (2016: 5) points out how 'Iraq and Syria are unique in the sense that these states have been most adversely affected by the twin legacies of political authoritarianism and the consequences that flow from war and state collapse, thus creating a vacuum that has been filled by radical Islamism'... and although the Syrian war has been of 'shorter duration', its 'social effects have been more devastating'. One can therefore note the interplay of state practices and authoritarianism, political instability and terrorism. Both Syria and Iraq require long-term stability which involves, amongst other things, reducing state and non-state violence and creating governments that are pluralistic and do not marginalize and discriminate groups. However, geo-political power and vested state interests are the very things which have prevented political stability in these areas.

The meso-societal level of state facilitated terrorism is dangerous. As the Syrian and Iraqi conflicts highlight, it leads whole populations towards terrorism or becoming refugees who are simply seeking life. The pit of devastation and anarchy which exists in these regions does not afford individuals with the choice of living via other means. Their choice was to simply join ISIS, which has taken over the territory, or travel in the hope of arriving safely in another country. Here the levels interact. It is the fact that the following super macro-universal level safeguards—to protect refugees and allow them passage into safe territories, the duty to ensure the safety of individuals in occupied territories or to ensure political stability, to maintain human rights, to avoid discrimination through dispersing discriminatory ideologies or, worse still, enacting discriminatory policies and so on—were not maintained, which led to macro-national-level state crimes and the meso-societal creation of the social, political, ideological and economic conditions which facilitate terrorism.

In these conditions, extremists manipulate political grievances, injustices, political oppression, suffering and so on. The power of the AQ narrative, and the situations extremists exploit, stems from the very fact that these situations do exist. As research by Ahmed (2015) demonstrated, these situations give rise to very real emotions of vulnerability, helplessness, fear and insecurity that can be manipulated. The plethora of failures, including the failure of the super macro-universal level, together with the failure of invading and occupying states to ensure public safety and political stability, drive individuals towards terrorism. The search for justice and the right to life are our birthright. We cannot judge those who yearn for such basic standards of human rights. They are the victims of geo-political inequality, and a super macro-universal level which fails to give them the rights afforded to refugees, fails to maintain IHRLs and IHLs, and constructs discourses which further perpetuate their inhumanity in order to conceal the myriads of IHRL and IHL violations.

ISIS flourished in the political and economic instability of Iraq and Syria, establishing its headquarters in Mosul and in Raqqa. It was originally established as a part of AQ in 2014, with Abu Musab Zarqawi naming the organization al-Qaeda in Iraq (AQI) and swearing loyalty to Osama bin Laden. The organization instigated attacks against Iraqi Shiites. However, these attacks went against al-Qaeda's major goals, which included 'the expulsion of U.S. forces and the creation of an Islamic emirate in Iraq'. Following the death of Zarqawi in 2006, Ayyub al-Masri, a former member of the Zawahiri's Islamic jihad group in Egypt, took over AQI (Tomé, 2015). However, in October 2006, factions of jihadists created the Islamic State in Iraq (ISI), with al-Baghdadi

Abu Umar becoming the leader of this group. This group existed as an independent organization that aimed to establish an Islamic state and therefore had very different aims from those of AQ. Different names have been used to reflect the different positions and ambitions of the organization. For example, 'ISIS: an acronym for the Islamic State in Iraq and Syria', and 'ISIL to include the whole Levant including Jordan, Lebanon and Palestine' (Shamieh & Zoltán, 2015: 367). The organization then changed its name to the Islamic State (IS) to signify that the group no longer wanted to be defined according to a geographical territory but, instead, wanted to exist as a state. When Abu Omar al-Baghdad (aka al-Baghdadi, Abu Umar) died as a result of a US-led air strike in 2010, Bakr al-Baghdadi became the leader of a very fragile IS (Fishman, 2011; Tomé, 2015). In April 2013, '"Abu Bakr al Baghdadi announced his intent to merge his forces in Iraq and Syria with those of the Syria-based, Al Qaeda affiliated group *Jabhat al Nusra* (Support Front)"... "Jabhat al Nusra and Al Qaeda leaders rejected the merger"... with Al Qaeda's general commander issuing a statement "disavowing the Islamic State in early 2014"' (Blanchard & Humud, 2018: 13). ISIS continued to grow, capturing Fallujah and Ramadi in January 2014, and by the end of the month, ISIS had renamed itself the Islamic State, proclaiming the territory now under its control to be a new caliphate (Cronin, 2015).

As an organization ISIS had a very clear set of objectives. Their first and main objective was to establish a true Islam. ISIS claimed to follow the established 'practice of Islam from the time of the prophet Muhammad and the *sahaba* (Muhammad's companions)' and claimed this as being the only legitimate true version of Islam (Zelin, 2016: 20). The group established their own holy war based on purifying the religion and spreading the true version of Islam through any means necessary. Their claim to be practicing the authentic Islam gave them a self-proclaimed legitimacy to dismiss other Muslims, such as Shi'ite Iranian Muslims, as not being true followers of the faith.

Their second aim was to create a caliphate where pure Islam could be practiced. In his 2 July 2014 speech, Abu Bakr al-Baghdadi formally announced the caliphate and called upon *'ulama* (religious scholars), *fuqaha* (experts in Islamic jurisprudence), *da'i* (callers), especially calling the judges; as well as people with military, administrative, and service expertise and medical doctors and engineers to build the infrastructure required for a new state (Zelin, 2016: 21). The caliphate, now a state, embraced and exploited the idea that all Muslims owe loyalty to the caliphate (Blaker, 2015; Shamieh & Zoltán, 2015). The labelling of the territory as a caliphate was very powerful, with evidence demonstrating how American teenagers were lured by their sense of religious obligation to the caliphate. The number of foreign fighters flocking to Iraq and Syria doubled between the declaration of the new caliphate in June 2014 and the end of 2015 (The Soufan Group, 2015). Interestingly, Fernandez (2015) demonstrates how, through combining Islamic duty with the caliphate, ISIS made some Muslims believe that if they didn't fulfil their religious duty to the caliphate, they would face divine punishment. The exploitation of religious faith underscored the Islamic State's ability to frame its agenda in such a way that it mobilized individuals whose support it required (Robinson, 2017).

ISIS also exploited another idea fundamental to Islam, the coming of the apocalypse. The apocalypse denotes a battle between 'good and evil (Muslims and the unbelievers) that will take place at Dabiq, a city in northern Syria' and, according to ISIS, this battle 'will then bring about the events that will lead to the Day of Judgment where Muslims will be victorious' (Zelin, 2016: 21). This apocalyptic vision supports the organization's claim that there is a clash between true Muslims and non-believers (Blanchard & Humud, 2018). The construction of the apocalypse is therefore based on a binary, with Salafist jihadists utilizing the *takfir* doctrine, which sanctions violence against other Muslims accused of apostasy, unbelief or unfaithfulness (*kafir*) (Bunzel, 2015; Hafez, 2012). ISIS uses and manipulates prophecies from the Quran and the hadith to create legitimacy in their claims, and through doing so, convey the belief that it is only through supporting them that individuals will be granted a place in heaven. Research by Speckhard and Yayla (2015: 95), which was based on interviews with 13 Syrian IS defectors, revealed all 'IS cadres undergo Shariah training in which they are imbued with a takfiri ideology that allows them to deem all others, including Muslims who disagree with IS' extreme ideology, as apostates who should be killed'. And those who have sinned 'are required to go through a process of *tawbah* (repentance), in which they openly have to declare sorrow over past sins and pledge never to repeat them' (Speckhard & Yayla, 2015 :99). As Speckhard and Yayla (2015: 103) contend, ISIS exploits the idea of heaven and hell, claiming that

> 'sacrificing oneself and others in suicide missions' is as a form of "martyrdom" that will lead to the 'rewards of Paradise' and because Islam promotes the concept of a 'horrific hell' for 'anyone whose sins outweigh his or her good deeds on the Day of Judgment'.... 'anyone who has sinned badly may be attracted to carrying out a 'martyrdom' mission in order to gain eternal rewards'.

ISIS disperses its ideologies through the official ISIS online journal *Dabiq*. This name is significant because the hadith states Dabiq as the final place where the apocalypse battle will commence (Hamid, 2016; Rapoport, 2016). Their propaganda reveals the use of important Islamic beliefs and because ISIS is constructed as being synonymous with Islamic principles, values and beliefs, anyone who doesn't join their state is labelled as an unbeliever. In making their claims and objectives, ISIS has combined religion and terrorism, with the need to establish a state. Their exploitation and manipulation of Islamic ideology have facilitated their ability and success in recruiting fighters. According to the International Centre for the Study of Radicalization and Political Violence (ICSR), by 2015 ISIS had recruited 20,730 foreign fighters, and most of these were from North Africa and the Middle East, with approximately 4000 citizens and residents coming from western European countries, 1200 coming from France, 500–600 coming from Germany, 500–600 from the United Kingdom, and 440 from Belgium (Neumann, 2015). Similarly, 'Europol estimates that more than 5,000 Europeans have left to join Islamist fighters in Syria' (Renard, 2016: 3). According to the UN, more than 40,000 foreign terrorist fighters from 110 countries have travelled to join the conflicts in Syria and Iraq (UN, 2017). In terms of membership, ISIS is estimated to have between '50,000 and 100,000 members and at least a million supporters and sympathizers' (Gunaratna, 2016: 84). As Gunaratna (2016: 84) states, these figures are huge in comparison with 'Al-Qaeda, which enjoyed a numerical strength of 2,500 members at its peak'.

The size of ISIS has helped it to realize its ambition of being a state. Although it uses terrorism as a tactic, according to Cronin (2015), it is more like an army-led pseudo-state than a terrorist organization. When one considers the extent to which ISIS has established an infrastructure or indeed, critically considers the extent to which they can be labelled a state, the facts are quite interesting. ISIS has a military of approximately 30,000 fighters who engage in security operations and defend the territory ISIS rule (Cronin, 2015). ISIS functions as a state through controlling the 'political, economic and judicial administration' of the territory it controls, as well as the 'security and military services, medical services, "Islamic education", collection of fees and taxes, issuance of identification documents, printing of its own currency, control of services and resources (mail, transport, telephones, Internet, garbage collection, water, electricity, fuel and energy supply) and, from here, regulation of the economy and society' (Tomé, 2015: 124). Being a state has allowed ISIS to form institutions based on its ideology. ISIS also issues annual reports which outline in numerical and geographical detail its operations—the number of bombings, assassinations, checkpoints, suicide missions, cities taken over and even 'apostates' converted to the ISIS cause (Khalaf & Jones, 2014).

The power derived from such institutionalization is evident when one considers how ISIS 'forces its subjects, i.e. the people under its control, to refer to it as *adDawlah* (the State) and severely punishes people who use other names, including Daesh or IS' (Speckhard & Yayla, 2015: 96). In terms of maintaining fear and conformity, ISIS rules according to the earlier Salafi doctrine mentioned in this chapter, which includes both barbaric and inhumane practices. Many of these practices are similar to those used by Saudi Arabia and are shown on social media. For example, in 2014 the decapitation of journalist James Foley by ISIS was recorded, with other recordings including the killing of Christian, Syrian and Kurdish soldiers (Allen, Hall, Brown, Dolan, & Martin, 2014). In 2013, there were '6362 deaths in Iraq caused by terrorist attacks (an increase of 162% compared to 2012), of which ISIS were responsible for 77%' (IEP Report, 2015: 52). According to the Global Terrorism Index, ISIS was responsible for 6073 deaths in 2014 (GTI, 2015). In 2015, ISIS surpassed Boko Haram as the deadliest terrorist group in the world, undertaking attacks in 252 different cities leading to the death of 6141 people (GTI, 2016: 4). According to Yourish, Watkins, and Giratikanon (2016) by 2016, at least 1200 people have been killed by ISIS outside of Syria and Iraq. The number of deaths from terrorist attacks attributed to ISIS 'fell by 52 per cent in 2017, with total number of incidents falling by 22 per cent' (GTI, 2018: 2). However, the number of terrorist incidents in Europe increased to 282 with ISIS remaining the deadliest global terrorist group in 2017 (GTI, 2018). ISIS frequently uses rape, torture, public beheadings, mass executions, the slaughter of civilians and minorities, including Muslims and violence to maintain fear, with these actions constituting crimes against humanity (Gurule, 2016). One must also investigate the wider state-initiated factors which facilitate the existence of terrorism within the 'war on terror'.

Tacit Support of Terrorism

The wars in Iraq and Syria left the territories fragile, with no stability and, as previously stated, this was capitalized upon by ISIS. The chapter now considers the less obvious and more hidden ways in which states have facilitated terrorism. Although the book has largely explored the failures of the super macro-universal level to maintain human rights safeguards, such as those in IHRL and IHL, there has also been a failure at this level to reprimand those states which support terrorism. The term 'state sponsorship' includes the passive state support of terrorism and within the 'war on terror', examples of state sponsorship include the Saudi financial support of charities that finance Salafi madrassas in Pakistan, and in other countries (Levitt, 2002). When considering the existence and maintenance of ISIS, Cockburn (2015) explains how terrorism has continued because counter-terrorism measures have failed to stem the role of Saudi Arabia, the United Kingdom, the United States, Turkey and Pakistan in maintaining jihadism.

The 'war on terror' discourse, as this book argues, is based on constructed 'truths' and discourses whereby state practices are omitted from contributing to terrorism, thereby focusing exclusively on how non-state factors contribute to the existence of terrorist groups. Neglected factors include how states have promoted the political, economic, ideological and social climates that facilitate terrorism. Therefore, one can conceptualize the 'war on terror' as being a self-defeating war for two reasons. The first is the manipulation of universal concepts and, indeed, the destruction of these concepts via mechanisms which form part of the 'war on terror'. The second is through seeking to counter the manifestations and consequences of terrorism, rather than the root causes of terrorism. As Butt (2015) contends, eliminating the odd terrorist will not defeat terrorism, if thousands more are being trained in Saudi-funded Wahhabi madrassas, and therefore, if the west continues to support exporting radical Wahhabism.

The first way in which states are facilitating terrorism is via financial assistance and the weapons states provide groups to promote their own geo-political interest. The sale of arms contributes to the existence of state crime and terrorism. As UN Secretary-General Ban Ki-moon wrote in an opinion piece in August 2012,

> let us dramatically cut spending on nuclear weapons, and invest instead in social and economic development, which serves the interests of all by expanding markets, reducing motivations for armed conflicts, and in giving citizens a stake in their common futures. (...) Massive military spending and new investments in modernizing nuclear weapons have left the world over-armed and peace under-funded. (Ban Ki-moon, 2012)

All sales of arms should be conducted according to the Global Arms Trade agreement, which provides clear guidelines to ensure that arms are not diverted elsewhere and/or used for serious international human rights or humanitarian law violations (Amnesty International, 2017f). The treaty puts the onus on the state selling the arms and thus, according to Article 6.3 of the Arms Trade Treaty (ATT), a state cannot authorize a transfer if 'it has knowledge at the time of authorization that the arms or items would be used in the commission of genocide, crimes against humanity, grave breaches of the Geneva Conventions of 1949, attacks directed against civilian objects or civilians protected as such, or other war crimes as defined by international agreements to which it is a party'. (ATT monitor, 2016: 6). Under the Programme of Action to Prevent,

Combat and Eradicate the Illicit Trade in Small Arms and Light Weapons in All Its Aspects (SALW), which was introduced in 2001, governments agreed to improve national small arms laws, import/export controls, and stockpile management and to engage in cooperation and assistance. The programme recognizes that the illegal trade in SALW in all its aspects sustains conflicts and violence, contributes to the displacement of civilians, undermines respect for international humanitarian law, impedes the provision of humanitarian assistance to victims of armed conflict and fuels crime and terrorism (UNODA, 2005). These regulations have been adopted by the EU and the United Kingdom, leading to the creation of the Consolidated EU and National Arms Export Licensing Criteria—often referred to as the 'Consolidated Criteria'. This EU license outlines eight criteria that should govern the sales of arms, which include

- if there is an embargo or concern for the proliferation of weapons of mass destruction
- if there are human rights issues
- if there is ongoing armed conflict, or if regional stability is threatened by the exports (House of Commons, 2014).

Governments should also consider issues around any negative impact on UK national security, and terrorism, and the likely diversion of weapons to areas where exports would not be licensed directly (House of Commons, 2014). Although there are extensive safeguards to regulate the sale of weapons, especially given that they contribute to political instability and terrorism, within the 'war on terror' and more generally, weapons have been sold which have facilitated both state crime and terrorism.

The sale and purchase of weapons predominantly involve the United Kingdom, United States and Saudi Arabia, and this invariably contributes to the existence of an inter-state relationship which serves geopolitical interests and purposely neglects the state facilitation of state crime and terrorism. This then serves the continuation of macro-national-level inter-state crimes and intra-state crimes within the 'war on terror', with both facilitating terrorism. Therefore, other than oil, weapons also form an entity that binds the relationship between Saudi Arabia, the United Kingdom and the United States. As Green and Ward (2004) argue, the arms trade continues the proliferation of violence with both the United States and Britain being involved in contributing to torture and terrorism. When considering this symbiotic relationship, Stern and Shideler (2011) state, if we look at who armed whom in the past, we realize that the United States armed Saddam Hussein against Iran and Osama bin Laden against the Soviets. It is therefore worth considering the extent to which Osama bin Laden or Saddam Hussein would have been able to commit violence without acquiring arms. This reveals that although terrorist groups and regimes could well have the motivations to commit violence and terrorism, without possessing the necessary means, carrying out such large-scale acts of violence would have been more difficult and perhaps impossible.

In terms of assessing this symbiotic relationship, Saudi Arabia was the world's single largest recipient of weapons, and its share in world imports rose to a peak of approximately 24% in 1995, and then declined to 15% by 1999, with nearly half of Saudi Arabia's weapons coming from the United States, and another third coming from the United Kingdom (Khanna & Chapman, 2010). The United States has therefore been the main supplier of arms to Saudi Arabia, delivering arms worth $17.9 billion from 1998 to 2005 (Prados & Blanchard, 2007). In 2007, a $20 billion arms contract was signed between Washington and Riyadh, and in 2010 another $60 billion contract was signed (Adami & Pouresmaeili, 2013; Stern & Shideler, 2011). However, the US Army lost more than $1 billion worth of arms and other military equipment in Iraq and Kuwait between 2006 and 2016, with Amnesty International's Arms Control and Human Rights Researcher, Patrick Wilcken, arguing that this is worrying given the long history of leakage of US arms to multiple armed groups committing atrocities in Iraq, including the Islamic State (Amnesty International, 2017g). More than 20 countries have supplied Iraq with arms and ammunition over the last five years, with the United States and then Russia leading the supply of weapons, and according to the Stockholm International Peace Research Institute, arms exports to Iraq increased by 83% between the periods 2006–2010 and 2011–2015 (Amnesty International, 2017f). These figures demonstrate how the state sale of arms is directly linked to sectarian violence and political instability. As Amnesty International states, the vast array of weapons captured and illicitly acquired have enabled IS to carry out a horrific campaign of abuse, killings, rape and torture (Amnesty International, 2017f). One must therefore note the vital role of states in providing ISIS with arms and how this sustains groups such as ISIS within the 'war on terror'.

The United Kingdom has been equally complicit in selling weapons that have contributed to war crimes and terrorism. In 1985, then Prime Minister Margaret Thatcher closed the Al-Yamamah arms deal with Saudi Arabia, which was worth £42 billion ($55.3 billion) (Rebello, 2016). However, it was alleged that a slush fund worth millions of pounds was paid to members of the Saudi royal family, with Prime Minister Tony Blair stopping an investigation by the Serious Fraud Office into the funding of the Al-Yamamah arms deal in 2006 (Rebello, 2016). In 2010, BAE Systems reached a £286 million settlement over corruption claims with the Serious Fraud Office and the US Department of Justice (Rebello, 2016). In 2007, the United Kingdom agreed a $6.5 billion (£4.4 billion) deal with Saudi Arabia (ATT monitor, 2016) and 'between 1st January and 30th September 2015, the United Kingdom issued 152 licences for military exports to Saudi Arabia, totaling $4.16 billion' (£2.8 billion) (Oxfam, 2015). Available evidence demonstrates the vast disregard for arms treaties by the United Kingdom.

> In 2001, around 27.5% of the total value of Single Individual Export Licences (SIELs) granted by the government were for arms sales to 'Highly Sensitive' destinations, principally countries involved in conflict and those with a grave and consistent pattern of human rights abuses. A further 30.4% were for sales to 'Intermediate Sensitivity' destinations, including countries with serious human rights problems or high levels of tension with neighbours. (Dunne & Freeman, 2003: 3)

These sales indicate the relationship between arms sales, political instability and conflict, and human rights violations.

The legal firm Matrix Chambers prepared a legal opinion on the United Kingdom's supply of arms to Saudi Arabia in December 2015 and it concluded that the UK sale of arms to Saudi Arabia constitutes serious violations of IHL and IHRL (Amnesty International, 2015a). As Slijper (2013: 7) states, 'nothing has been learned from the uproar over arms sales to dictators in countries such as Bahrain, Egypt, Libya, Syria and Yemen'. As Milne (2015) states, the case of a Swedish man, Bherlin Gildo, further illustrates the relationship between arms and terrorism. Gildo was accused of terrorism in Syria and his case collapsed when it became clear that British intelligence had been arming the same rebel groups the defendant was charged with supporting. 'The defence argued that going ahead with the trial would have been an "affront to justice" when there was plenty of evidence the British state was itself providing "extensive support" to the armed Syrian opposition' (Milne, 2015: 1).

Although the Labour leader, Jeremy Corbyn has criticized the sale of British weapons to both Saudi Arabia and Bahrain, little change has occurred with the United Kingdom continuing to supply Saudi Arabia with weapons which are being used in Yemen (ATT Monitor, 2016; Corbyn, 2015). Arms have also been used by the Saudi regime to commit war crimes in Yemen. Since '2015, the Saudi conflict with Yemen has led to more than 35,000 people being killed and injured across Yemen' (O'Brien, 2016) and there is increasing evidence of serious violations of IHL and IHRL by all parties (Amnesty International, 2015b; Human Rights Watch, 2016; UNOCHA, 2016). Indirect actions, such as blockades, have been equally damaging with coalition naval forces imposing a blockade on Yemeni ports that is believed to have greatly exacerbated the humanitarian crisis, contributing to severe food and fuel shortages and possibly causing serious violations of IHL and IHRL (ATT monitor, 2016). Amnesty International's (2017h) own research in Yemen has demonstrated that these weapons have been used to commit serious violations, including war crimes against civilians in Yemen and that, given the clear risk, authorizing further transfers would be counter to the United Kingdom's obligations under international law. Therefore, Amnesty International, other NGOs and UN bodies have concluded that the Saudi Arabia-led coalition's pattern of attacks across Yemen raises serious concerns about an apparent disregard for civilian life, and a failure to take feasible precautions to spare civilians, as required by IHL.

The attacks have also led to civilian deaths, injuries caused by disproportionate and indiscriminate attacks, and the destruction of civilian homes and infrastructure, with coalition forces bombing hospitals, mosques, and markets (Amnesty International, 2017h). The sale of these weapons runs contrary to the legal obligation of countries to ensure that weapons are not contributing to IHRL and IHL violations, and has led ATT (2016: 6) to state, 'given the current situation in Yemen, State Parties to the ATT must adhere to their legal obligation not to authorise any potential export of lethal military equipment that could be used unlawfully in Yemen'. The UN Office for the Coordination of Humanitarian Affairs has reported that the conflict has left more than 2.5 million people internally displaced (UNOCHA, 2016). The UK government's cooperation with the Saudi regime has raised questions with Labour leader Jeremy Corbyn stating how the Saudi-led coalition bombing in Yemen, backed by the British government, has left thousands dead, 21 million people in need of humanitarian assistance and 3 million refugees uprooted from their homes (Whiteside, 2017).

The United States has spent at least $5 billion on training foreign armies in countering terrorism, with the most obvious example being the Taliban (Rashid, 2014). The violence between Shia Muslims and Sunni Muslims in Iraq and Syria has been predominantly funded through Saudi Arabia (Cockburn, 2015), and as Butt (2015) rightly contends, the 'war on terror' is a never-ending war if countries continue to supply the Saudis with arms because these arms end up being used by terrorist groups. The existence of arms in Iraq and Syria has contributed to the growth of instability and terrorism in these regions. A report by Amnesty International reveals that in the 1970s and 1980s at least 34 different countries supplied Iraq with weapons, and 28 of those same states were also simultaneously supplying arms to Iran (Amnesty International, 2017f). The Scott Inquiry revealed that 'despite the knowledge that Iraq had been engaging in chemical (and possibly biological) warfare against its own Kurds, Shi'ites and the Iranians, these deadly exports continued until late 1989' (Green & Ward, 2004: 205–206). As Green and Ward contend (2004: 206), the scandal demonstrated that Britain 'had breached its own rules, acted illegally and employed deception to conceal those breaches from the public' (Green & Ward, 2004: 206). These weapons formed part of the 'weapons of mass destruction' discourse that was used to legitimize the 2003 invasion of Iraq. After the invasion, the United States continued to supply the Iraqi government with weapons, supplying more than

US$500 million worth of small arms and ammunition to the Iraqi government by 2014 (Amnesty International, 2017i). The sales of weapons to these regions have therefore contributed to the existence of state crimes and terrorism in these regions.

The second entity which perpetuates the existence of terrorism is oil. In 1945, Franklin D. Roosevelt agreed to provide the Saudi regime with security in return for oil (Bronson, 2006; Pipes, 2011). The relationship between Saudi Arabia and the United States has been maintained through Saudi Arabia providing the United States with cheap oil, especially between 1991 and 2003 when Saudi Aramco sold to the United States heavily discounted oil (Peck, 2014). Security has also been vital in this relationship, with the total US aid to Saudi Arabia from 1946 to 1975 amounting to '$328.4 million, of which $295.8 million was military and $32.6 million was economic assistance' (Prados & Blanchard, 2007: 8). The US support for Saudi Arabia is therefore based on wider financial considerations (Green, 2002). Mandel (2002) points out how these financial transitions serve Saudi interests because without US support, the repressive Saudi government would fail to maintain power. This support also involves states facilitating one of the core entities of terrorism, Wahhabism and the jihadist ideology.

The third defining feature of how states have contributed to the existence of terrorism is through supporting the growth of Wahhabism. According to Elgot (2017), fifteen 9/11 survivors wrote to Prime Minister Theresa May asking her to release a report on terrorism financing in the United Kingdom, which places Saudi Arabia at its centre of culpability. According to Wintour (2017) in 2007 Saudi Arabia was estimated to be spending at least $2 billion (£1.5 billion) annually on promoting Wahhabism worldwide and by 2015 that figure was believed to have doubled. In 2007, estimates put the number of mosques in Britain adhering to Salafism and Wahhabism at 68 and seven years later, the number of British mosques identified with Wahhabism had risen to 110 (Wintour, 2017). This support was further evident during the Soviet invasion of Afghanistan, when the United States actively encouraged a form of Islam which legitimized destroying communism and the killing of non-Muslims. As previously stated, although the United States promoted the idea of Jihad, after the Soviet invasion, the jihad ideology continued to be spread across the globe (Abuza, 2011). It has also been argued that some Saudi elites applauded ISIS for fighting Iranian Shiite Muslims and establishing a new Sunni state (Crooke, 2015). It is therefore hardly surprising that ISIS has been perceived as a Saudi project to fight the Assad regime, especially given that they share the same hatred of Shia Islam (Saleh & Kerr, 2014). Therefore, although the United States turns a blind eye to the existence of Wahhabism in Saudi Arabia, it is this Wahhabism that leads to the more global anti-western and anti-American terrorism that exists within the 'war on terror'.

Milne (2015: 3) states

> American forces bomb one set of rebels while backing another in Syria, and mount what are effectively joint military operations with Iran against ISIS in Iraq while supporting Saudi Arabia's military campaign against Iranian backed Houthi forces in Yemen. However confused US policy may often be, a weak, partitioned Iraq and Syria fit such an approach perfectly.

It is impossible to assess the existence of both AQ and ISIS without including the vast number of state crimes which contributed to the emergence of both and have then sustained their existence. Therefore, with the 'war on terror' one ought to consider that if IHRLs and IHLs were maintained, and there were no human rights violations, training of groups, dispersal of discriminatory ideologies, sale of weapons and so on, then would terrorism still exist? And here it is important to remember that the 'war on terror' has facilitated the existence of the meso-societal-level conditions which promote terrorism, and it has also led to both super macro-universal-level and macro-national-level state crimes which have also positively impacted the micro-individual-emotional level.

This chapter has explored some of the factors which have and will continue to maintain the existence of terrorism within the 'war on terror'. In particular, ideology, weapons, oil and other vested state interests constitute to form powerful tools through which states influence terrorism. Within this interplay, the role of invasions and the neglect of states to secure political stability led to not only a humanitarian crisis but also the emergence of sectarian violence. The interaction between the super-macro level, macro-national level and micro-societal level also highlights how the 'war on terror' goes from an abstract level to a practical level. Of interest is how on an ideological super-macro level, state actions are stripped of their capacity to impact individuals. This purposeful construction is based on dehumanizing those who are impacted, and one can witness the very realization of this process at the macro-national level, whereby state crimes are not even acknowledged in terms of the harms they perpetrate against individuals. Within this transient flow from the super macro level to the internal level, which incorporates identity, beliefs, emotions and values, it is only when we reach the meso-societal level that the constructed 'war on terror' discourse recognizes variables which impact radicalization. Interestingly, it could be argued that radicalization and the variables which facilitate radicalization are only recognized at this level because these variables can be displaced as societal non-state-instigated variables. In this way, states avoid their role in promoting radicalization. However, such a construction of radicalization also promotes 'terrorists' as being solely responsible for their own radicalization. Space is not attributed to other factors, beyond the meso-societal level which might facilitate radicalization. The discourse is therefore restricted and within this, all the injustice, political grievances, oppression and so on which states instigate are -made invisible.

References

Aburish, S. K. (2005). *The Rise, Corruption and the Coming Fall of the House of Saud*. London: Bloomsbury.

Abuza, Z. (2011). Borderlands, Terrorism, and Insurgency in Southeast Asia. In J. Clad, S. M. McDonald, & B. Vaughn (Eds.), *The Borderlands of Southeast Asia: Geopolitics, Terrorism, and Globalization* (pp. 89–106). Washington, DC: NDU Press.

Adami, A., & Pouresmaeili, N. (2013). Saudi Arabia and Iran: The Islamic Awakening Case. *Iranian Review of Foreign Affairs, 3*(4), 153–178.

Admon, Y. (2007). *Saudis Criticize Their School Curricula—Again*. Middle East Media Research Institute: Inquiry and Analysis No. 325. Retrieved July 1, 2018, from http://memri.org/bin/articles.cgi?Page=archives& Area=ia&ID=IA32507

Ahmed, S. (2015). The Emotionalization of 'War on Terror': Counter-Terrorism, Fear, Risk, Insecurity and Helplessness. *Criminology and Criminal Justice, 15*(5), 545–560.

Al Arabiya. (2014). *Saudi Arabia Counterterrorism Law Goes into Effect*. Retrieved February 12, 2016, from http://english.alarabiya.net/en/News/middle-east/2014/02/02/Saudi-Arabia-counter-terrorism-law-goes-into-effect.html

Allam, A. (2010). Terrorism Funding Remains a Concern. *Financial Times*. Retrieved July 1, 2018, from https://www.ft.com/content/1c0ed36a-4bca-11df-a217-00144feab49a

Allen, P., Hall, J., Brown, L., Dolan, A., & Martin, D. (2014, November 17). ISIS' International Death Squad: Jihadist Executioners in Beheading Video Include Two Britons, Two Frenchmen and a German. Mail Online. *The Daily Mail*. Retrieved July 1, 2018, from http://www.dailymail.co.uk/news/article-2837742/Now-two-Frenchmen-German-jihadistidentified-ISIS-executioners-sick-beheading-video-Extremist-killers-came-Europe.html

Allhussein, E. M. (2018). Reforming the Religious Discourse in Saudi Arabia (2001–2010). In S. Akbarzadeh (Ed.), *Routledge Handbook of Political Islam* (pp. 179–190). Oxon: Routledge.

Amnesty International. (2015a). *UK Government Breaking the Law Supplying Arms to Saudi Arabia, Say Leading Lawyers*. Retrieved July 1, 2018, from https://www.amnesty.org/en/latest/news/2015/12/uk-government-breaking-the-law-supplying-arms-to-saudi-arabia/

Amnesty International. (2015b). *Nowhere Safe for Civilians: Airstrikes and Ground Attacks in Yemen*. Retrieved February 18, 2016, from https://www.amnesty.org/download/Documents/MDE3122912015ENGLISH.pdf

Amnesty International. (2017a). *Fourteen Men at Imminent Risk of Beheading as Saudi Arabia Continues Bloody Execution Spree*. Retrieved February 18, 2018, from https://www.amnesty.org/en/latest/news/2017/07/fourteen-men-at-imminent-risk-of-beheading-as-saudi-arabia-continues-bloody-execution-spree/

Amnesty International. (2017b). *Saudi Arabia: Death Penalty Used as Political Weapon Against Shi'a as Executions Spike Across Country*. Retrieved February 18, 2018, from https://www.amnesty.org/en/latest/news/2017/07/saudi-arabia-death-penalty-used-as-political-weapon-against-shia-as-executions-spike-across-country/

Amnesty International. (2017c). *Iraq at Any Cost: The Civilian Catastrophe in West Mosul, Iraq*. Retrieved February 18, 2018, from https://www.amnesty.org/en/documents/mde14/6610/2017/en/

Amnesty International. (2017d). *Iraq: Investigations, Not Denials Needed Over Appalling Civilian Death Toll in West Mosul*. Retrieved February 18, 2018, from https://www.amnesty.org/en/latest/news/2017/07/iraq-investigations-not-denials-needed-over-appalling-civilian-death-toll-in-west-mosul/

Amnesty International. (2017e). *Iraq: Battle Between US-Led Coalition, Iraqi Forces and Islamic State Creates Civilian Catastrophe in West Mosul*. Retrieved February 18, 2018, from https://www.amnesty.org/en/latest/news/2017/07/iraq-battle-between-us-led-coalition-iraqi-forces-and-islamic-state-creates-civilian-catastrophe-in-west-mosul/

Amnesty International. (2017f). *Iraq: 'Islamic State' Atrocities Fuelled by Decades of Reckless Arms Trading*. Retrieved February 18, 2018, from https://www.amnesty.org/en/latest/news/2015/12/islamic-state-atrocities-fuelled-by-decades-of-reckless-arms-trading/, 8 December 2015.

Amnesty International. (2017g, May 24). *Iraq: US Military Admits Failures to Monitor over $1 Billion Worth of Arms Transfers*. Retrieved February, 18, 2018, from https://www.amnesty.org/en/latest/news/2017/05/us-military-admits-failures-to-monitor-over-1-billion-worth-of-arms-transfers/

Amnesty International. (2017h). *Court Ruling over UK Arms Sales to Saudi Arabia a 'Deadly Blow' to Yemeni civilians*. Retrieved July 10, 2018, from https://www.amnesty.org/en/latest/news/2017/07/court-ruling-over-uk-arms-sales-to-saudi-arabia-a-deadly-blow-to-yemeni-civilians/

Amnesty International. (2017i). *Arming 'Islamic State'—Facts and figures*. Retrieved February 18, 2018, from https://www.amnesty.org/en/latest/news/2015/12/arming-islamic-state-facts-and-figures/

ATT Monitor. (2016). *Dealing in Double Standards: How Arms Sales to Saudi Arabia Are Causing Human Suffering in Yemen*. Retrieved May 1, 2019, from https://www.amnesty.org.uk/files/webfm/Documents/issues/att_monitor_case_study_2_-_saudi_arabia_-_final_version.pdf

Aziz, S. (2016). Rise of ISIS and Security Implications for Middle East. *CISS Insight: Quarterly News and Views*, pp. 49–59.

Bar, S. (2008). *Warrants for Terror: The Fatwas of Radical Islam and the Duty to Jihad*. Lanham, MD: Rowman & Littlefield.

Baran, Z. (2008). *The Roots of Violent Islamist Extremism and the Efforts to Counter it*. Senate Committee on Homeland Security and Governmental Affairs. Retrieved February 18, 2018, from https://www.investigativeproject.org/documents/testimony/354.pdf

Barnard, A., & Arango, T. (2015). Using Violence and Persuasion, ISIS Makes Political Gains. *New York Times*. https://www.nytimes.com/2015/06/04/world/isis-making-political-gains.html

Berger, J. M., & Morgan, J. (2015). *The ISIS Twitter Consensus: Defining and Describing the Population of ISIS Supporters on Twitter*. Brookings Institution. Retrieved February 18, 2018, from http://www.brookings.edu/research/papers/2015/03/isis-twitter-census-bergermorgan

Blaker, L. (2015). The Islamic State's Use of Online Social Media. *Military Cyber Affairs, 1*(*1*), 1–9.

Blanchard, C. M., & Humud, C. E. (2018). *The Islamic State and U.S. Policy*. Congressional Research Service. Retrieved February 18, 2018, from https://fas.org/sgp/crs/mideast/R43612.pdf

Bronson, R. (2006). *Thicker than Oil: America's Uneasy Partnership with Saudi Arabia*. Oxford: Oxford University Press.

Bunzel, C. (2015). *From Paper State to Caliphate: The Ideology of the Islamic State*. The Brookings Project on U.S. Relations with the Islamic World. Retrieved February 18, 2018, from https://www.brookings.edu/wp-content/uploads/2016/06/The-ideology-of-the-Islamic-State.pdf

Butt, Y. (2015). How Saudi Wahhabism Is the Fountainhead of Islamist Terrorism. *Huffpost*. Retrieved February 18, 2018, from http://www.huffingtonpost.com/dr-yousaf-butt-/saudi-wahhabism-islam-terrorism_b_6501916.html

Byman, D. (2005). Passive Sponsors of Terrorism. *Survival, 47*(4), 117–144.

Byman, D. (2016). ISIS Goes Global: Fight the Islamic State by Targeting Its Affiliates. *Foreign Affairs*. Retrieved February 18, 2018, from https://www.foreignaffairs.com/articles/middle-east/isis-goes-global

Centre for Religious Freedom. (2005). *Saudi Publications on Hate Ideology Invade American Mosques*. Washington, DC: Freedom House.

Cockburn, P. (2015). *The Rise of Islamic State: ISIS and the New Sunni Revolution*. London: Verso Books.

Corbyn, J. (2015). Jeremy Corbyn Raises Death Row Saudi's Case with PM. *BBC Online*. Retrieved February 18, 2018, from http://www.bbc.co.uk/news/uk-politics-34365856

Cordesman, A. H. (2006). Saudi Arabia: Friend or Foe in the War on Terror? *Middle East Policy, 13*(1), 28–41.

Cronin, A. K. (2015). ISIS Is Not a Terrorist Group: Why Counterterrorism Won't Stop the Latest Jihadist Threat. *Foreign Affairs, 94*(2), 87–98.

Crooke, A. (2015). You Can't Understand ISIS If You Don't Know the History of Wahhabism in Saudi Arabia. *New Perspectives Quarterly, 32*(1), 56–70.

Denoeux, G. (2011). The Forgotten Swamp: Navigating Political Islam. In F. Volpi (Ed.), *Political Islam: A Critical Reader* (pp. 55–80). London: Routledge.

Donaghy, R., & Atkinson, M. (2015). Crime and Punishment: The Islamic State vs Saudi Arabia. *Middle East*. Retrieved February, 18, 2018, from https://www.middleeasteye.net/news/crime-and-punishment-islamic-state-vs-saudi-arabia-0

Drennan, J. (2014). The Black-Market Battleground. *Foreign Policy*. Retrieved February 18, 2018, from https://foreignpolicy.com/2014/10/17/the-black-market-battleground/

Dunne, P., & Freeman, S. P. (2003) *The Impact of a Responsible Arms Control Policy on the UK Economy*. Oxfam. Retrieved February, 18, 2018, from http://carecon.org.uk/Users/paul/Oxfamreport7.pdf

Ehrenfeld, R. (2011). Their Oil Is Thicker Than Our Blood. In S. Stern (Ed.), *Saudi Arabia and the Global Islamic Terrorist Network: America and the West's Fatal Embrace* (pp. 123–152). Hampshire: Palgrave Macmillan.

Elgot, J. (2017). 9/11 Survivors Urge May to Publish UK Terror Funding Report. *The Guardian*. Retrieved June 16, 2018, from https://www.theguardian.com/uk-news/2017/jul/20/911-survivors-urge-may-to-publish-uk-terror-funding-report

Englund, S., & Stohl, M. (2015). *The World vs. Daesh: Constructing a Contemporary Terrorist Threat*. Trends Working Paper 02/2016. Retrieved October 21, 2016, from http://trendsinstitution.org/wp-content/uploads/2016/04/Constructions-Paper-Englund-Stohl-Final.pdf

Fernandez, A. M. (2015). *Here to Stay and Growing: Combating ISIS Propaganda Networks: The Brookings Project on U.S. Relations with the Islamic World*. Center for Middle East Policy. Retrieved February 18, 2018, from https://www.brookings.edu/wp-content/uploads/2016/06/IS-Propaganda_Web_English.pdf

Fishman, B. (2011). *Redefining the Islamic State: The Fall and Rise of Al-Qaeda in Iraq*. New America Foundation. Retrieved February 18, 2018, from https://static.newamerica.org/attachments/4343-redefining-the-islamic-state/Fishman_Al_Qaeda_In_Iraq.023ac20877a64488b2b791cd7e313955.pdf

Friis, S. M. (2015). 'Beyond Anything We Have Ever Seen': Beheading Videos and the Visibility of Violence in the War Against ISIS. *International Affairs, 91*(4), 725–746.

Gaffney, F. (2011). Sharia-Compliant Finance: Saudi Arabia's Trojan Horse. In S. Stern (Ed.), *Saudi Arabia and the Global Islamic Terrorist Network: America and the West's Fatal Embrace* (pp. 41–54). Hampshire: Palgrave Macmillan.

Green, P. (2002). A Question of State Crime. In P. Scraton (Ed.), *Beyond September 11th: An Anthology of Dissent* (pp. 71–76). London: Pluto Press.

Green, P., & Ward, T. (2004). *State Crime: Governments, Violence and Corruption.* Retrieved October, 15, 2015, from https://www.dawsonera.com/readonline/9781849641197

GTI. (2015). *Global Terrorism Index 2015: Measuring and Understanding the Impact of Terrorism*. Retrieved June 10, 2018, from https://reliefweb.int/report/world/global-terrorism-index-2015-measuring-and-understanding-impact-terrorism

GTI. (2016). *Global Terrorism Index 2016*. Retrieved June, 10 2018, from http://economicsandpeace.org/wp-content/uploads/2016/11/Global-Terrorism-Index-2016.2.pdf

GTI. (2018). *Global Terrorism Index 2016*. Retrieved March 10, 2019, from http://visionofhumanity.org/app/uploads/2018/12/Global-Terrorism-Index-2018.pdf

Gunaratna, R. (2016). Best Practices: Rehabilitating and Reintegrating Foreign Fighters. In H. Abadi (Ed.), *Countering Daesh Propaganda: Action-Oriented Research for Practical Policy Outcomes* (pp. 84–92). Atlanta: The Carter Center.

Gurule, J. (2016). *The Need to Refocus the U.S. Government's Post-9/11 Counter-Terrorist Financing Strategy Directed at al Qaeda to Target the Funding of ISIS*. Retrieved February, 18, 2018, from http://scholarship.law.nd.edu/cgi/viewcontent.cgi?article=2261&context=law_faculty_scholarship

Hafez, M. M. (2012). Tactics, *Takfir*, and Anti-Muslim Violence. In A. Moghadam & B. Fishman (Eds.), *Self-Inflicted Wounds: Debates and Divisions Within al-Qa'ida and its Periphery* (pp. 19–44). NY: Combatting Terrorism Center.

Hamid, A. F. A. (2016). *ISIS in Southeast Asia: Internalized Wahhabism Is a Major Factor*. Yusof Ishak Institute. Retrieved February 18, 2018, from https://www.iseas.edu.sg/images/pdf/ISEAS_Perspective_2016_24.pdf

Handley, P. (2010). US Cables: Saudi 'Critical' Finance Base for Qaeda, Taliban. *Middle East Online*. Retrieved February 18, 2018, from http://www.middle-east-online.com/english/?id=42881

Hasan, N. (2008). Saudi Expansion, the Salafi Campaign and Arabised Islam in Indonesia. In M. Al-Rasheed (Ed.), *Kingdom Without Borders. Saudi Arabia's Political, Religious and Media Frontiers* (pp. 263–281). London: Hurst Publishers Ltd.

Hashemi, N. (2016). *The ISIS Crisis and the Broken Politics of the Middle East*. Institute on Culture, Religion and World Affairs. Retrieved February, 18, 2018, from https://www.bu.edu/cura/files/2016/12/hashemi-paper1.pdf

Haykel, B. (2009). On the Nature of Salafi Thought and Action. In R. Meijer (Ed.), *Global Salafism: Islam's New Religious Movement* (pp. 33–57). London: Hurst.

Hegghammer, T. (2008). Islamist Violence and Regime Stability in Saudi Arabia. *International Affairs, 84*(4), 701–715.

House of Commons. (2014). *Consolidated EU and National Arms Export Licensing Criteria*. Hansard. Retrieved July 1, 2018, from https://hansard.parliament.uk/Commons/2014-03-25/debates/14032566000018/ConsolidatedEUAndNationalArmsExportLicensingCriteria

Hubbard, B., & Sheikh, M. (2015, July 16). Wikileaks Shows Saudi Obsession with Iran. *The New York Times*.

Human Rights Watch. (2016). *What Military Target Was in My Brother's House? Unlawful Coalition Airstrikes in Yemen*. Retrieved October 21, 2016, from https://www.hrw.org/report/2015/11/26/what-military-target-was-my-brothers-house/unlawful-coalition-airstrikes-yemen

Human Security Centre. (2005). *Human Security Report, 2005: War and Peace in the 21st Century*. New York: Oxford University Press.

Hussain, E. (2014). Saudis Must Stop Exporting Extremism. *The New York Times*. https://www.nytimes.com/2014/08/23/opinion/isis-atrocities-started-with-saudi-support-for-salafi-hate.html

ICRC. (2014). *International Humanitarian Law*. Retrieved June, 10, 2018, from https://www.icrc.org/en/doc/assets/files/other/icrc-002-0703.pdf

IEP. (2015). *Global Terrorism Index Report 2014*. Institute for Economics and Peace. Retrieved October 21, 2016, from http://economicsandpeace.org/research/iep-indices-data/global-terrorism-index

Jaffe, A. M., & Elass, J. (2007). *Saudi Aramco: National Flagship with Global Responsibilities*. Working Paper, Rice University, James A. Baker III Institute for Public Policy. Retrieved June, 21, 2017, from https://www.bakerinstitute.org/media/files/page/9f100176/noc_saudiaramco_jaffe_elass_revised.pdf

Jenkins, R. (2011). Moral Imperialism. In D. K. Chatterjee (Ed.), *Encyclopedia of Global Justice*. Cham: Springer. https://doi.org/10.1007/978-1-4020-9160-5_754

Johnson, K., & Trindle, J. (2014). Treasury's War on the Islamic State. *Foreign Policy*. Retrieved June 21, 2017, from http://foreignpolicy.com/2014/10/23/treasurys-war-on-the-islamic-state/

Jouannet, E. (2007). Universalism and Imperialism: The True-False Paradox of International Law? *European Journal of International Law, 18*(3), 379–407.

Kedar, M., & Yerushalmi, D. (2011). *Sharia* Adherence Mosque Survey: Correlations between Sharia Adherence and Violent Dogma in U.S. Mosques. *Perspectives on Terrorism, 5*(5-6), 81–138.

Khalaf, R., & Jones, S. (2014). Selling Terror: How ISIS Details Its Brutality. *Financial Times*. Retrieved 21 June 2017, from https://www.ft.com/content/69e70954-f639-11e3-a038-00144feabdc0

Khanna, N., & Chapman, D. (2010). Guns and Oil: An Analysis of Conventional Weapons Trade in the Post-Cold War Era. *Economic Inquiry, 48*(2), 434–459.

Ki-moon, B. (2012). *The World Is Over-Armed and Peace Is Under-Funded*. Retrieved February 18, 2018, from https://www.un.org/disarmament/update/20120830/

Ki-Moon, B. (2016). *Refugee Crisis About Solidarity, Not Just Numbers, Secretary-General Says at Event on Global Displacement Challenge*. Retrieved June 21, 2019, from https://www.un.org/press/en/2016/sgsm17670.doc.htm

Lemu, M. N. (2016). Notes on Religion and Countering Violent Extremism. In H. Abadi (Ed.), *Countering Daesh Propaganda: Action-Oriented Research for Practical Policy Outcomes* (pp. 43–50). Atlanta: The Carter Center.

Levey, S. (2005). *Terrorist Financing and Money Laundering in the Middle East*. Senate Committee on Banking, Housing, and Urban Affairs. Retrieved February 18, 2018, from https://www.investigativeproject.org/documents/testimony/298.pdf

Levitt, M. (2002). *Targeting Terror: U.S. Policy Toward Middle Eastern State Sponsors and Terrorist Organizations, Post-September 11*. Washington, DC: Washington Institute for Near East Policy. Retrieved June 21, 2017, from https://www.washingtoninstitute.org/policy-analysis/view/targeting-terror-u.s.-policy-toward-middle-eastern-state-sponsors-and-terro

Mahmood, M., O'Kane, M, Madlena, C, Smith, T, Ferguson, B, Farrelly, P, et al. (2013). From El Salvador to Iraq: Washington's man behind brutal police squads. *The Guardian*. Retrieved July, 10, 2018, from http://www.theguardian.com/world/2013/mar/06/el-salvador-iraq-police-squads-washington

Mandel, M. (2002). This War Is Illegal and Immoral and It Won't Prevent Terrorism. In P. Scraton (Ed.), *Beyond September 11th: An Anthology of Dissent* (pp. 77–83). London: Pluto Press.

Marshall, A. G. (2015). Why Paris Reveals the Horror—And the Hypocrisies—Of Global Terrorism. *Occupy*. Retrieved July 10, 2018, from http://www.occupy.com/article/why-paris-reveals-horror-%E2%80%93-and-hypocrisies-%E2%80%93-global-terrorism#sthash.wdgLcR18.dpbs

Middle East Monitor. (2014). *Saudis Most Likely to Join ISIS, 10% of Group's Fighters Are Women*. Retrieved February 12, 2016, from https://www.middleeastmonitor.com/20141020-saudis-most-likely-to-join-isis-10-of-groups-fighters-are-women/

Milne, S. (2015). Now the truth emerges: how the US fueled the rise of ISIS in Syria and Iraq. *The Guardian*. Retrieved February 12, 2016, from https://www.theguardian.com/commentisfree/2015/jun/03/us-isis-syria-iraq

Neumann, P. R. (2015). *Foreign Fighter Total in Syria/Iraq Now Exceeds 20,000; Surpasses Afghanistan Conflict in the 1980s*. International Centre for the Study of Radicalisation and Political Violence (ICSR). Retrieved February 27, 2017, from http://icsr.info/2015/01/foreign-fighter-total-syriairaq-now-exceeds-20000-surpasses-afghanistan-conflict-1980s/

O'Brien, S. (2016). *Statement to the Security Council on Yemen*. Retrieved February 27, 2017, from https://reliefweb.int/report/yemen/under-secretary-general-humanitarian-affairsemergency-relief-coordinator-stephen-o

OHCHR. (2015, May 1–October 31). *Report on the Protection of Civilians in the Armed Conflict in Iraq*. HUMAN RIGHTS Office of the United Nations High Commissioner for Human Rights. https://www.ohchr.org/Documents/Countries/IQ/UNAMIReport1May31October2015.pdf

Oxfam. (2015). *British Aid and British Arms: A Coherent Approach to Yemen?* Oxfam. Retrieved February 12, 2016, from http://policy-practice.oxfam.org.uk/publications/british-aid-and-british-arms-a-coherent-approach-to-yemen-577040

Parker, N. (2007). The Conflict in Iraq: Saudi Role in Insurgency. *Los Angeles Times*. Retrieved February 12, 2016, from http://articles.latimes.com/2007/jul/15/world/fg-saudi15

Peck, J. R. (2014). *Do Foreign Gifts Buy Corporate Political Action? Evidence from the Saudi Crude Discount Program*. Retrieved February 12, 2016, from http://economics.mit.edu/files/8300

Pipes, D. (2011). The Scandal of U.S. Saudi Relations. In S. Stern (Ed.), *Saudi Arabia and the Global Islamic Terrorist Network: America and the West's Fatal Embrace* (pp. 11–26). Hampshire: Palgrave Macmillan.

Prados, A. B., & Blanchard, C. M. (2007). *Saudi Arabia: Current Issues and U.S. Relations*. Washington, DC: CRS Report for Congress. Retrieved February 12, 2016, from https://apps.dtic.mil/dtic/tr/fulltext/u2/a468060.pdf

Ramsbotham, O., & Woodhouse, T. (2000). Introduction. In O. Ramsbotham & T. Woodhouse (Eds.), *Peacekeeping and Conflict Resolution* (pp. 1–7). London: Frank Class Publishers.

Rapoport, D. C. (2016). Why Has the Islamic State Changed its Strategy and Mounted the Paris-Brussels Attacks? *Perspectives on Terrorism, 10*(2), 24–32.

Rashid, A. (2014). ISIS: The New Taliban. *The New York Review*. Retrieved February 27, 2017, from http://www.nybooks.com/daily/2014/07/02/iraqs-new-taliban/

Rebello, L. (2016). Declassified files reveal Margaret Thatcher's role in controversial £42bn arms deal with Saudi Arabia. *International Business Times*. Retrieved February 12, 2016, from https://uk.news.yahoo.com/declassified-files-reveal-margaret-thatchers-070642164.html

Reid, J. (2005). The Biopolitics of the War on Terror: A Critique of the 'Return of Imperialism' Thesis in International Relations. *Third World Quarterly, 26*(2), 237–252.

Renard, T. (2016). *Fear Not: A Critical Perspective on the Terrorist Threat in Europe*. Security Policy Brief. Retrieved June 21, 2017, from http://aei.pitt.edu/86893/1/SPB77.pdf

Riedel, B., & Saab, B. (2008). Al Qaeda's Third Front: Saudi Arabia. *Washington Quarterly, 31*(2), 33–46.

Robinson, L. C. (2017). Just Terror: The Islamic State's Use of Strategic "Framing" to Recruit and Motivate. *ORBIS, 61*(2), 172–186.

Rohmaniyah, I., & Woodward, M. (2012). *Wahhabi Perspectives on Pluralism and Gender: A Saudi—Indonesian Contrast*. Arizona State University Centre for Strategic Communications Report. Retrieved June 1, 2019, from http://csc.asu.edu/wp-content/uploads/pdf/128.pdf

Sageman, M. (2004). *Understanding Terror Networks*. Pennsylvania: University of Pennsylvania Press.

Saleh, H., & Kerr, S. (2014). Saudi Arabia 'in Denial' Over ISIS Ideology. *Financial Times*. Retrieved February 12, 2016, from http://www.ft.com/intl/cms/s/0/ae16214c-47c311e4-be7b-00144feab7de.html#ixzz3I76k5m40

Sampson, A. (1975). *The Seven Sisters: The Great Oil Companies and the World They Made*. New York: Viking Press.

Scheuer, M. (2011). *Osama Bin Laden*. Oxford: Oxford University Press.

Shamieh, L., & Zoltán, S. (2015). The Rise of Islamic State of Iraq and Syria (ISIS). *AARMS Academic and Applied Research in Military and Public Management Science., 14*(4), 363–378.

Shea, N. (2006). *Saudi Arabia's Curriculum of Intolerance*. Washington, DC: Centre for Religious freedom of Hudson Institute.

Silverberg, M. (2003, February 27). *The Wahhabi Invasion of America*. Retrieved May 11, 2018, from http://www.marksilverberg.com/article/WahhabisminAmerica/68/1/print/

Slijper, F (2013). *GUNS, DEBT AND CORRUPTION: Military spending and the EU crisis*. Transnational Institute. Retrieved April 1, 2018, from https://www.tni.org/files/download/eu_milspending_crisis.pdf

Solomon, E., Chazan, G., & Jones, S. (2015). ISIS Inc: How Oil Fuels the Jihadi Terrorists. *Financial Times*. Retrieved February 12, 2016, from https://www.ft.com/content/b8234932-719b-11e5-ad6d-f4ed76f0900a

Speckhard, A., & Yayla, A. S. (2015). Eyewitness Accounts from Recent Defectors from Islamic State: Why They Joined, What They Saw, Why They Quit. *Perspectives on Terrorism, 9*(6), 95–118.

Stabile, C. A., & Kumar, D. (2005). Unveiling Imperialism: Media, Gender and the War on Afghanistan. *Media, Culture & Society, 27*(5), 765–782.

Starr, S. (2012). *Revolt in Syria, Eye-Witness to the Uprising*. London: C. Hurst & Co.

Stern, S. N., & Shideler, K. (2011). The Way Forward: Looking Backward and Looking Inward. In S. Stern (Ed.), *Saudi Arabia and the Global Islamic Terrorist Network: America and the West's Fatal Embrace* (pp. 235–248). Hampshire: Palgrave Macmillan.

Syria Network for Human Rights. (2015). *The Main Conflict Parties Who Are Killing Civilians in Syria: Civilian Death Toll up to End of October 2015*. Retrieved April 1, 2018, from http://sn4hr.org/wp-content/pdf/english/Who_Are_Killing_Civilians_in_Syria_en.pdf

The Guardian. (2015). Executions in Saudi Arabia at a 20-year high, says Amnesty International. Retrieved June 16, 2018, from https://www.theguardian.com/world/2015/nov/09/executions-saudi-arabia-20-year-high-amnesty-international

The Soufan Group. (2015). *Foreign Fighters: An Updated Assessment of the Flow of Foreign Fighters into Syria and Iraq*. Retrieved June 19, 2018, from http://soufangroup.com/wp-content/uploads/2015/12/TSG_ForeignFighters Update3.pdf

Tomé, L. (2015). The Islamic State: Trajectory and Reach a Year After Its Self Proclamation 49 as a Caliphate. *The Journal of International Relations, 6*(1), 116–139.

Tufft, B. (2015). Saudi Arabia publicly beheads woman in holy Mecca as blogger lashings are postponed. *The Independent*. Retrieved June 16, 2018, from http://www.independent.co.uk/news/world/middle-east/saudi-arabia-publicly-beheadswoman-in-holy-mecca-as-blogger-set-to-receive-second-lashing-9982134.html#

UN. (2005). *Resolution 1624 (2005)*. United Nations. Retrieved June 1, 2019, from https://www.un.org/en/ga/search/view_doc.asp?symbol=S/RES/1624%20%282005%29
UN. (2015). *Syria: Alienation and Violence: Impact of the Syrian Crisis*. United Nations Relief and Works Agency for Palestine Refugees. Retrieved June 1, 2019, from https://www.unrwa.org/sites/default/files/alienation_and_violence_impact_of_the_syria_crisis_in_2014_eng.pdf
UN. (2017). *Greater Cooperation Needed to Tackle Danger Posed by Returning Foreign Fighters, Head of Counter-Terrorism Office Tells Security Council*. Retrieved June 1, 2019, from https://www.un.org/press/en/2017/sc13097.doc.htm
UN. (2018). *UN Global Counter-Terrorism Strategy*. Retrieved June, 21, 2019, from https://www.un.org/counterterrorism/ctitf/en/un-global-counter-terrorism-strategy
UNHR. (1966). *International Covenant on Civil and Political Rights*. Retrieved June 21, 2017, from https://www.ohchr.org/Documents/ProfessionalInterest/ccpr.pdf
United States Department of State, Bureau of International Narcotics and Law Enforcement Affairs. (2009). *International Narcotics Control Strategy Report*. Retrieved June 21, 2019, from https://2009-2017.state.gov/j/inl/rls/rm/119890.htm
United States General Accounting Office. (2009). *Combating Terrorism—U.S. Agencies Report Progress Countering Terrorism and Its Financing in Saudi Arabia, but Continued Focus on Counter Terrorism Financing Efforts Needed*. Retrieved June 21, 2019, from http://www.gao.gov/new.items/d09883.pdf
UNOCHA. (2016). *Yemen: Humanitarian Needs Overview*. Retrieved June, 21, 2019, from https://reliefweb.int/sites/reliefweb.int/files/resources/2016_HNO_English_%20FINAL.pdf
UNODA. (2005). *Programme of Action on Small Arms and Its International Tracing Instrument*. United Nations Office for Disarmament Affairs. Retrieved July 1, 2018, from https://www.un.org/disarmament/convarms/salw/programme-of-action/
Vassiliev, A. (2000). *History of Saudi Arabia*. New York: NYU Press.
Vertigans, S. (2008). *Militant Islam: A Sociology of Characteristics, Causes and Consequences*. London: Routledge.
Volpi, F. (2011). Introduction: Critically studying political Islam. In F. Volpi (Ed.), *Political Islam: A Critical Reader* (pp. 1–8). London: Routledge.

Webb, T. (2007). Bribing for Britain—Government Collusion in Arms Sales Corruption. *Campaign Against Arms Trade*. Retrieved April, 1, 2018, from https://www.caat.org.uk/resources/publications/corruption/goodwin-5-web.pdf

Weissbrodt, D., & Hallendorff, M. (1999). Travaux Preparatoires of the Fair Trial Provisions—Articles 8 to 11—of the Universal Declaration of Human Rights. *Human Rights Quarterly, 21*, 1062–1096.

Whiteside, P. (2017). May Defends Relationship with Saudi Arabia. *Sky News*. Retrieved February 12, 2016, from http://news.sky.com/story/may-defends-relationship-with-saudi-arabia-10824258

Williams, P. R., Worboys, J., & Ulbrick, J. T. (2012). Preventing Mass Atrocity Crimes: The Responsibility to Protect and the Syria Crisis. *Case Western Reserve Journal of International Law, 45*(1), 473–503.

Wintour, P. (2017). Report Calls for Public Inquiry into Gulf Funding of British Extremism. *The Guardian*. Retrieved June 16, 2018, from https://www.theguardian.com/uk-news/2017/jul/05/report-calls-for-public-inquiry-into-gulf-funding-of-british-extremism

Wright, L. (2007). *The Looming Tower: Al Qaeda's Road to 9/11*. London: Penguin Books.

Yourish, K., Watkins, D., & Giratikanon, T. (2016). How Many People Have Been Killed in ISIS Attacks Around the World. *New York Times*. Retrieved June, 10, 2018, from https://www.nytimes.com/interactive/2016/03/25/world/map-isis-attacks-around-the-world.html

Zelin, A. Y. (2016). Filtering Meta-Narratives: From Global to Local. In H. Abadi (Ed.), *Countering Daesh Propaganda: Action-Oriented Research for Practical Policy Outcomes* (pp. 20–23). Atlanta: The Carter Center.

7

State Crime, Radicalization and the 'War on Terror'

This chapter explores the main themes of the book and the implications of these for the 'war on terror'. Within the 'war on terror', states have utilized their full capacity of power through not only introducing mechanisms of social control to counter terrorism, but also through introducing dangerous and divisive discourses. These discourses have obscured facilitators of the risk within the 'war on terror' and they have also contributed to populism. Many of the social control mechanisms introduced violated existing safeguards and impacted several of the variables associated with radicalization, thus positively facilitating radicalization in multiple ways. In terms of assessing this relationship from an individual lived experience perspective, multiple realities shape our lived experiences. Therefore, the violation of state crimes in the 'war on terror' is likely to impact an individual's perceptions of justice, human rights and the rule of law. On an interpersonal level, these individuals are also likely to experience discrimination, social exclusion and marginalization, and on a global level, they are likely to experience transitional experiences of injustice and suffering based on the Ummah. Therefore, the introduction of new counter-terrorism measures does not just impact one variable associated with radicalization, rather it feeds into the plethora of perceptions,

S. Ahmed, *The 'War on Terror', State Crime & Radicalization*, Palgrave Studies in Risk, Crime and Society, https://doi.org/10.1007/978-3-030-40138-2_7

experiences and lived realties which feed into the radicalization process in multiple ways.

Super Macro-Universal Level: Universalism, Geo-politics and Securitization

Within the 'war on terror' universalism and its associated principles of freedom, justice, democracy and human rights were found to have been used to justify the introduction of new counter-terrorism measures. However, as this book has demonstrated, far from defending and maintaining universalism, the 'war on terror' is undermining these very values. The super macro-universal level directly influenced the erosion of these values via resolution 1373 and resolution 1624, which encouraged and accelerated the existence of state practices which could constitute state crimes. As stated previously, although UN General Assembly resolution 60/158, the Protection of Human Rights and Fundamental Freedoms While Countering Terrorism, 2005 (General Assembly, 2006), maintains that states should protect human rights, there was little oversight of the measures that were introduced. As Trapp (2011) contends, these obligations conceptualized states as a mechanism to control terrorism and the terrorist, thereby dismissing the state as a facilitator of terrorism. Many of the counter-terrorism measures introduced failed the test of legality, necessity and proportionality and therefore legality. In assessing the cumulative impact of these resolutions, an interesting interaction between the super macro-universal level and the macro-national level becomes apparent, and one can note how within the 'war on terror', the super macro-universal level exists as a facilitator of IHRL violations. One can also note the conflicting roles of the UN. On the one hand, it places a duty on states to create laws and legislation to counter terrorism, but it also reveals the very entities that give rise to terrorism and when states facilitate these factors, there is a lack of action. States have introduced the very mechanisms which impact the micro-individual-emotional level. For example, invasions and domestic counter-terrorism measures have impacted perceptions of inequality, human rights, a lack of belonging and so on, and these collectively induce the very conditions identified by the UN as being conducive to terrorism. It could therefore be argued that within the 'war on terror', state terror is prevalent because states are directly engaged in terrorist activities (Grabosky & Stohl, 2010).

However, the ability to engage in state terror, whilst also claiming to be maintaining and preserving universalism, was linked to geo-political power. Although equality is a core principle of universalism, geo-politics was found to influence the breakdown of universalism in favour of states and their vested interests. The book revealed how states were able to manipulate safeguards. For example, the United States has argued that IHL is the only legal system applicable and therefore the only system governing the use of force against military targets within the 'war on terror'. This construction and use of power has contributed to the presence of macro-national level inter-state crimes and intra-state crimes in the 'war on terror'. The discourses created in the 'war on terror' have legitimized acts of state crime and have constructed the context within which IHRL and IHL have been breached. It could therefore be argued that there is a need to widen the scope of state crime to incorporate the state manufacture of discourses because any treatment, documentation and analysis of state harm must include their power to manipulate knowledge and construct self-serving truths. It could therefore be argued that the super macro-universal level operates according to geo-political power, and this bias and manipulation of super macro-universal power is used by states to progress and disperse their social control. However, the inequality that is the result of geo-political power not only undermines international laws designed to protect all of humanity equally, it also leads to powerlessness, injustice, grievances and inequality, all factors which positively impact radicalization (Hamm & Spaaij, 2015; Post, Sprinzak, & Denny, 2003; Speckhard & Akhmedova, 2005). The UN resolutions and actions of states within the 'war on terror' have collectively shifted the super macro-universal level towards securitization. This shift has led to policies which cause harm and perpetuate suffering because the simultaneous existence of geo-politics and securitization of the super macro-universal level means that as Tactaquin (2001) elucidates, national leaders condemn genocide and war crimes in poorer nations while deploying strategies that result in deaths, injuries and the dehumanization of millions. Not only do extreme policies emerge, but their harm is denied. The whole construction of the 'war on terror' sets the boundaries of necessity. There is the active mechanism of construction to contour the boundaries of the discourse to legitimize its use. This move towards securitization leads to enormous changes in policies, such as refugees being responded to through securitization, rather than humanity, and the protection that their status deserves.

The manipulation of universal values and the existence of geo-politics and securitization in the 'war on terror' were found to have severe consequences in changing the super macro-universal level. The 9/11 and the Paris terrorist attacks were catalysts for spurring a series of international and national measures which increased the power of states to violate and deviate from established safeguards. This represents a worrying trend because it demonstrates that acts of terrorism not only lead to the death of innocent civilians, but they also lead to measures that are permanently changing the exercise of state power and the capacity of safeguards to protect human rights. It could therefore be argued that the 'war on terror' is setting a dangerous precedent for the violation of international human rights, and the most disturbing part of this development is how this process has been normalized. As mentioned in the introduction, the event-focused 'war on terror' conceptualizes states as a mechanism to control terrorism, and such a perspective fails to acknowledge or even create a space where one can discuss how states facilitate terrorism. This focus conceals the harm prevalent in state responses to acts of terrorism and all state practices which promote terrorism. Therefore, the 'war on terror' discourse continues to mask over and make invisible war crimes, state crimes and the plethora of suffering that also exists as part of the terrorism—the 'war on terror' cycle. Within this context, humanity is not prioritized for all; instead nationalism and security are elevated at the expense of universality. The 'war on terror' discourse has therefore become one of the primary avenues through which states are promoting exclusionary nationalist ideologies, increasing mechanisms of social control to facilitate the marginalization and criminalization of those labelled as a threat to the nation-state and, through these practices, permanently altering the power and capacity of the super macro-universal level to protect human rights.

Self-defeating 'War on Terror'

These processes lead to wider and equally dangerous ramifications, namely the 'war on terror' being a self-defeating war. There are various entities which feed into this process, whereby the very actions introduced to reduce radicalization and terrorism within the 'war on terror' feed into the existence of radicalization and terrorism within the 'war on terror'. The first entity that feeds into this process is the violation of safeguards. The 'war on terror' is a war that states portray as being needed to preserve and maintain universal values of human rights, freedom, democracy and yet, states introduce measures which violate these very values. And perhaps more importantly, the destruction of these universal values undermines the moral basis of the 'war on terror' through fuelling a perspective in which the self-defeating nature of the 'war on terror' can be evidenced, legitimized and exploited by terrorists. Therefore, the violation of safeguards directly feeds into the existence of terrorism.

The second entity which feeds into the self-defeating nature of the 'war on terror' is discriminatory policies. The 'war on terror' encourages the separation of humanity into those that are constructed as deserving human rights and those that are constructed as less deserving of human rights. The concern of the 'war on terror' is the protection of western countries and this leads to an inherent separation of humanity. In this way the 'war on terror' can be likened to colonialist and imperialist projects.

This invariably leads to the third entity which feeds into the self-defeating nature of the 'war on terror', the ethnocentricism of the 'war on terror'. As already noted, the 'war on terror' is ethnocentric, with the invasions being perceived solely through their impact on western countries and what these countries believed would be the impact on the territories invaded. Although the choice to describe these actions as ethnocentric may not be obvious, when one considers the number of civilians that died, or indeed the imposition of pro-coalition governments following invasions, it really does demonstrate the power of these countries to define what they believe is freedom from their perspective. As the book demonstrates, such an imposition, as in Afghanistan and Iraq, led to anything but freedom, with the conditions created in these countries directly contributing to the existence of AQ and ISIS. Research demonstrates how the suffering, trauma and political repression associated with wars facilitates radicalization (Lemu, 2016; Speckhard & Akhmedova, 2005). Thus, one can note how the 'war on terror' is a self-defeating war because the very suffering and fear it aims to counter and eliminate, it breeds itself. It renders invisible the very principles of freedom, liberty and respect for human rights it claims it is trying to preserve through creating mechanisms of power, and more importantly, institutional practices which abandon these very principles.

The fourth entity is the failure of states to tackle the causes of terrorism. Through seeking to counter the manifestations of and consequences of terrorism, rather than the causes of terrorism, the 'war on terror' is a self-defeating war. State-instigated causes of terrorism include financial assistance and the weapons states provide groups to promote their own geo-political interest. Within the 'war on terror' state sponsorship of terrorism also includes the Saudi financial support of charities that finance Salafi madrassas in Pakistan and in other countries (Levitt, 2002). The final entity which makes the 'war on terror' a self-defeating war is the creation of meso-societal level conditions conducive to terrorism.

In UK legislation, terrorism is defined as the use or threat of action where the use or threat is designed to influence the government or to intimidate the public or a section of the public, and the use or threat is made for the purpose of advancing a political, religious, racial or ideological cause (Statutory Instruments, 2011). The 'war on terror' was created to eliminate the suffering and fear that is endured due to terrorism, but in doing so, it has led to wars, prisons and other mechanisms of social control which cause suffering. Therefore, does the 'war on terror' cause far more suffering and damage than the very acts it is meant to counter? Further, given the self-defeating nature of the 'war on terror', and how it positively impacts the micro-individual-emotional level, could it not be argued that it incites terrorism? When considering radicalization, the role of the state must be taken into consideration. States have a far more destructive and corrosive impact on individuals. When states claim that terrorism threatens to violate universal values, this construction is the exploitation of fear to gain power.

It appears that within the 'war on terror' states are not only damaging universal values, but the very construction of terrorism, as an entity that can damage universal values, is equally as corrosive. It falsely manipulates individuals into believing that the very actions and mechanisms that are introduced to counter terrorism are required to protect those very values, when they in fact erode these values. It falsely portrays terrorists as being able to damage such values, as is evident in phrases such as, 'they will not alter our way of life' or the construction of terrorists as wanting to take individuals' freedom. One must ask, is it terrorist groups that can alter freedom and the way of life or do states have that capacity? The construction of terrorists as having the ability to violate these values and the use of fear by states to influence political action, then leads one to think, do state actions within the 'war on terror' fall into the definition of terrorism and therefore constitute terrorism? It could be argued that states use actions and threats to intimidate the public into advancing their own political cause. In this way, the 'war on terror' has managed to intimidate whole populations into surrendering their values and freedoms.

Belief in Humanity

Taking the above factors into consideration, one must ask, what are the consequences of the permanent alteration of universal values, and the self-defeating and discriminatory nature of the 'war on terror' on individuals? And, what about the impact of the false manipulations of fear to intimidate populations? Within this context, and as the radicalization chapter revealed, the socio-political context drives some individuals with their lived experiences of oppression, injustice and grievances towards radicalization. But within this process, what happens to make individuals believe that committing an act of violence is their only option? And prior to this decision, what impact do all the contradictions, manipulations and self-serving legitimacy and vested geo-political interests have on individuals and their beliefs? Human beings are accepted as possessing free will, with our autonomy and free will dictating the emergence and construction of modern legal systems and subsequent procedural laws. The socialization of humanity is based on concepts of freedom, justice, equality and fairness, and within cosmopolitanism these concepts are conceptualized as constituting the binding forces of humanity (Ahmed, 2019). However, within the 'war on terror' this free will and autonomy is denied because even though states have introduced measures which violate these very principles, there is no space afforded to and recognition of how such actions impact individual's free will and autonomy, and by extension, their perceptions and beliefs. It cannot be the case that individuals are afforded the autonomy to believe in these concepts and then not be expected to exercise such autonomy when these very concepts are violated.

The impact of a breakdown and deviation from these concepts and values is recognized in relation to secondary victimization, with research on secondary victimization demonstrating how the violation of these values constitutes yet another form of victimization (Elliott, Thomas, & Ogloff, 2012; Wemmers, 2013). Institutions can and do impact our beliefs in a just world (Correia, Vala, & Aguiar, 2001) and our experience with them is a pivotal one that can, in some cases, be much more damaging than primary experiences of victimization (Orth, 2002; Skinner & Taylor, 2009). Only in the last few decades has the 'institutional' component of institutional sexual abuse been acknowledged as further impacting trust and involving institutional betrayal which accelerates experiences of victimization, trauma and PTSD (Mcalinden, 2006; Smith & Freyd, 2013). Research by Ahmed (2015, 2016) found that British Muslims believed that certain fundamental rights, such as the right to be presumed innocent until proven guilty, and the right to a fair trial would always exist because they constituted birth rights, and the erosion of these rights in the 'war on terror' negatively impacted their faith in universal human rights. Furthermore, as this book has explored, the 'war on terror' has disintegrated many of the principles and concepts which are held as being the binding values of humanity, and without them our very commonality and meaning is damaged.

> The shattering of these values does nothing less than shatter one's belief in humanity and when this has been damaged, then what is left?

It follows that the process of having fundamental beliefs, trust and values broken constitutes victimization and trauma, and therefore it is possible to comprehend how the 'war on terror', with all its implications for universal values and damage to what individuals perceive as their birth rights, can make individuals vulnerable to radicalization. Especially where individuals are led to believe that their actions, even if these are acts of violence, can remedy the damage to such values and therefore maintain 'justice'. And, surely the 'war on terror', with its vast implications for justice, human rights, equality and so on also constitutes secondary victimization.

It might also seem plausible to suggest that because IHRL and IHL (and the human rights, liberalism and humanity they convey) are not maintained, their existence damages humanity. Here one can ask the question, if these values did not exist and individuals were socialized to know and believe inequality is prevalent, would they still experience grievances, injustice, powerlessness and so on? One must also ask the question: Would it be better to have rights at the super macro-universal level which are being violated or not have rights at all? As the next section demonstrates, when discussing the macro-national level inter-state crimes and intra-state crimes, the 'war on terror' has violated a substantial number of IHLs and IHRLs and in doing so, it has had vast implications for the variables which facilitate radicalization.

Macro-national Level: Invasions, Counter-terrorism Legislation and Statelessness

The book demonstrated the existence of many macro-national level intra-state crimes and inter-state crimes. These were found to facilitate terrorism through leading to divisive state-constructed discourses and discriminatory state policies. The 'war on terror' has included the invasions of Afghanistan, Syria and Iraq. These invasions have had devastating immediate and long-term consequences which have positively impacted the variables associated with radicalization. The post-invasion conditions have included the following factors which have been recognized by the UN (2018) as being conducive to the spread of terrorism—unresolved conflicts, a lack of rule of law, violations of human rights, ethnic, national and religious discrimination, political exclusion, socio-economic marginalization, and lack of good governance. As already stated, the invasions created a three-tier system of facilitating radicalization. First, the immediate consequences of witnessing murder, suffering and injustice had the potential to facilitate radicalization. Second, the unlawful nature of the invasions, and finally, the long-term consequences stated above also facilitate radicalization. Wider inter-state crimes included torture—which, as previously stated, is one of the most legislated forms of war crime—the sale and purchase of arms, and state funding and training of extremists and rebels.

On a UK national level, various pieces of counter-terrorism legislation were introduced and collectively these contravened various safeguards, including the right to life: as present in Article 3 UDHR, the right to a public and fair hearing: as present in Article 10 UDHR, the Protection of Human Rights and Fundamental Freedoms While Countering Terrorism, 2005 UN resolution 60/158 (General Assembly, 2006) and Article 4 (1) ICCPR which specifically states that counter-terrorism measures should not involve discrimination. The legislation introduced included quashing long-standing procedural rights, such as the right to a fair trial and those pertaining to citizenship.

Perpetuation of Discrimination and Legislation that Pre-disposes Religious and Ethnic Discrimination

The state-dispersed 'war on terror' discourse perpetuates and predisposes religious and ethnic discrimination. The counter-terrorism measures introduced increase the likelihood of religious discrimination and ethnic discrimination, leading to possible perceptions of injustice, marginalization and powerlessness (Boyns & Ballard, 2004; Henderson-King, Henderson-King, Bolea, Koches, & Kauffman, 2004; Speckhard &

Akhmedova, 2005). Terrorist attacks, such as the Paris attacks, led to the introduction of emergency powers which constituted macro-national level intra-state crime and impacted the micro-individual-emotional level. The refugee crisis was also securitized and racialized, which led to the abandonment of conventions and safeguards designed to protect refugees. One can question if refugees from non-Islamic countries would have also been constructed as terrorists and therefore not afforded the protection this status requires under international law? On a national level, the Channel programme increased institutions' ability to profile and criminalize those suspected of being radicalized (Bonino, 2013; Ragazzi, 2017; Thomas, 2016).

The Ideological Battle of the 'War on Terror'

However, ideologies such as universalism, jihad and Wahhabism have been equally dangerous in perpetuating harm within the 'war on terror'. Two opposing state-led discourses, universalism and Wahhabism have been manipulated to justify the violation of safeguards within the 'war on terror'. The discourse of universalism, as stated above, leads to injustice, marginalization and discrimination whereas Wahhabism directly encourages terrorism.

These discourses became infused with the need to self-preserve, and this then leads to beliefs regarding the need to marginalize and otherize in order to survive. Again, one can note the existence and manipulation of fear. The 'war on terror' is therefore immersed with ideologies that incite terrorism, through encouraging some of the dominant concepts within extremist ideologies. Although there is evidence of states dispersing extremist discourses which encourage terrorism, the ideological construction of states doesn't even allow these ideas to emerge in public discourse. The room and space for such truths to be even heard is absent and this represents the vast power of the super-macro level and macro-national level to construct, shape, and manipulate reality. Therefore, the 'war on terror', both at the level of discourse and practice involves actions which facilitate terrorism.

These discourses facilitate radicalization through creating and perpetuating the dualism 'us' and 'them' which, as previously stated, is present in the 'war on terror' discourse. The 'us' and 'them' dualism exists around several classifications. The first is within universalism where it portrays humanity as 'us' and terrorist suspects and marginalized groups, such as refugees, as 'them'. The second is where those within the nation-state are classified as 'us' and those outside the nation-state as 'them'. And the third is those that follow Wahhabism are viewed as 'us' and those that are labelled as not doing so, are labelled as 'them'. These classifications influence terrorism through predisposing marginalization and the ideology of 'us' and 'them'. And one must also remember that it is illegal for states to engage in discriminatory practices.

These macro-national level state crimes and their associated discourses have enormous consequences for the 'war on terror' as is now discussed. The first relates to the restriction of alternative, more moderate discourses. Both universalism and Wahhabism restrict more moderate voices. For example, the radicalization chapter revealed how the government conceptualization of the AQ narrative problematizes accurate perceptions of the 'war on terror'. Within this context, because the 'us' and the insider group has been constructed as those tied to the national territory, only actions which secure the rights of these populations are constructed as acceptable. Therefore, voices which speak of a more humane approach to terrorists and the 'war on terror' are labelled as being sympathetic to terrorists, unpatriotic and can be criminalized. The second restriction is in relation to more moderate Islamic interpretations. Therefore, within the 'war on terror' two very opposing discourses are created, and the existence of both discriminatory policies and discriminatory discourses positively facilitate the micro-individual-emotional level.

New Spaces of Exploitation

Through conducting an analysis on the 'war on terror', the book has revealed how the 'war on terror' has carved open new spaces within which exceptional measures take place. The 'war on terror' has exploited the space above nations, on the super macro-universal level and between nations to extend its power and engage in violations of safeguards. The creation of these spaces within the 'war on terror' represents the complete abandonment of universal values and safeguards. One must ask, how are individuals, who could be subjected to these measures and know that they are at risk of these measures because of their identity, going to be impacted? Research by Ahmed (2015, 2016) demonstrated that the inequality prevalent in counter-terrorism measures was perceived as injustice, which led British Muslims to experience negative emotions including vulnerability, helplessness, anger and fear (Ahmed, 2015, 2016). Within this context it is possible to conceive how the eradication of the most basic standard of human rights, such as that of nationality, can be no less devastating than impacting and shattering one's belief in justice, humanity and equality. And as already stated, these are such powerful and meaningful concepts that a betrayal in them and a breakdown in trust in the existence of them can lead to victimization and trauma (Mcalinden, 2006; Smith & Freyd, 2013).

Meso-Societal Level: Giving Terrorism Roots

As the book explored, the meso-societal level of state-facilitated terrorism is dangerous. It included various failures, such as the failure of the super macro-universal level to maintain the safeguards prevalent at this level, and the failure of invading and occupying states to ensure public safety and political stability. Here the three levels interact because if the safeguards which exist at the super macro-universal level—such as the duty of states to ensure the safety of individuals in occupied territories, the duty to ensure political stability, to maintain human rights and so on—were all maintained, then there would be no macro-national level state crimes as states would have met their legal duties. There would also cease to be the creation of the social, political, ideological and economic conditions which facilitate terrorism. And in such a context, extremists would not be able to manipulate political grievances, injustices, political oppression, suffering and so on because these very things would not exist, and therefore they would be asking individuals to reflect on a reality that simply does not exist. As previously stated, the 'war on terror' is a vicious cycle because it gives a sense of legitimacy to extremist narratives, which in turn gives a sense of legitimacy to the 'war on terror' narrative.

The final condition which fuels terrorism is the institutionalization of radicalization-facilitating ideologies. As stated above, the manipulation of universalism to legitimize the introduction of counter-terrorism measures leads to real methods of social control that harm individuals. States can and have in the 'war on terror' institutionalized the 'war on terror' ideology, most notably within the criminal justice system. Within this changing reality, each method introduced then forms an avenue through which this discourse is reaffirmed. For example, when individuals watch raids on the media, they are watching a phenomenon that conveys the discourse it represents and thus, the threat of terrorism and the need for extraordinary human rights deviating methods. Within this context, such methods and discourses are normalized and, as previously stated, there is a permanent alteration of human rights and the universalism level. The second discourse that has become institutionalized is that of Wahhabism, which has become institutionalized in global religious educational institutions. However, the institutionalization does not stop here because, as younger generations shift towards Wahhabism, they will want to transform societies and countries so that the strict rules of Wahhabism govern every sphere of life including education, law and the economy. The power of the two ideologies mentioned is that they are prevalent globally and they are transforming a global landscape where universal human rights are permanently being altered and eradicated, and one of the largest religions in the world is shifting towards extremism. Within this political landscape and given the findings of the book, is it clear that the power and need to diminish and change this dangerous landscape resides with states.

The Future of the 'War on Terror'

The book has proposed a theory for understanding radicalization in the 'war on terror', and where permissible it has grounded this framework in the events that form the 'war on terror' and the safeguards that should guide state practice. In locating state practices and state crimes in the 'war on terror', the book has sought to understand if state crimes promote the radicalization process. And, how state crimes impact established factors which induce radicalization? This concluding section considers the future of the 'war on terror'. It explores the need to combat harmful state practices that both facilitate the existence of terrorism and those that are implemented as a reaction to terrorist attacks. And through doing so, it challenges the terrorist attack—state practices hyphen and demonstrates the nuanced fluidity between state crime and terrorism in the 'war on terror'. States facilitate terrorism through financial assistance, weapons and ideology, and through introducing mechanisms to counter terrorism, all of which positively impact the micro-individual-emotional level. There needs to be an active attempt to disrupt the role of states in maintaining terrorism. Weapons, foreign policy, exporting religion, oil, and state crime are all implicitly tied to terrorism and they all have an active role to play in maintaining terrorism. In the quest to counter terrorism, states need to stop participating in terrorism and giving life to the micro-individual-emotional level.

A New Policy Agenda

Demonstrating the vast role of states in facilitating radicalization through these levels and their associated variables has revealed the dialectic reality of radicalization, and through doing so, it challenges the role of the state within the 'war on terror'. By demonstrating how many of the factors which induce radicalization and have elsewhere been labelled as cognitive radicalization are natural emotional reactions to the other levels, it is then possible to work with these emotions and divert individuals away from violent radicalization. Current state approaches are reductionist; they fail to acknowledge their own role in facilitating terrorism. However, preventing terrorism must be about including, acknowledging and giving space to all the factors which induce radicalization. This chapter proposes a holistic approach and outlines the main factors which should be part of such an approach.

Cognitive and Violent Radicalization

Counter-terrorism interventions homogenize feelings, perceptions, emotions and violence, thereby failing to acknowledge the space between cognitive radicalization and violent radicalization. It is the pre-crime orientation of counter-terrorism interventions that criminalizes a variety of emotions and perceptions. However, this space between cognitive radicalization and violent radicalization is where counter terrorism needs to be placed.

The neglect of this space has hampered efforts to counter terrorism because there has been a failure in recognizing that what has been defined by the state as 'radicalization' is in fact a process that also includes safe and legitimate perceptions. For example, what has been conceptualized as cognitive radicalization includes perception of injustice, and emotions of insecurity, helplessness and anger. The lack of space afforded to these sentiments means that individuals are not afforded a space where these feelings can be worked through, and in the absence of acknowledgment and recognition and therefore a space where non-violent means can be explored, the possibility of violence increases. Therefore, cognitive radicalization is safe, and it is the over criminalization of this perspective that pushes individuals towards violent radicalization. This process does not allow individuals their humanity to perceive injustice, marginalization etc. Counter terrorism measures act to criminalize thoughts, emotions and perceptions and through doing so they further marginalize and perpetuate feelings of injustice, thereby increasing individual's capacity for violence. State centric approaches negate that some of the feelings, perceptions and emotions associated with cognitive radicalization are reactions to counter-terrorism measures and their destruction of values such as justice and liberalism.

In proposing and grounding the constitutive theory of radicalization outlined, this book has attempted to demonstrate how the levels and their associated variables impact identity, thoughts, emotions and perceptions, and just how rationale and natural this process is. This process is as much about autonomy and the values which bind humanity, as it is about equality, justice and fairness. However, within the 'war on terror' those that are marginalized, otherized and dehumanized are not afforded the right to pursue equality, justice and fairness. If these principles and entities were recognized in terms of the damage they do to the internal order, then they would not be damaged in the multi-faceted ways they are. There would be a space within the 'war on terror' discourse which states just how powerful and destructive inequality, injustice and unfairness can be to identity, thoughts, emotions and perceptions. This book does not seek to take the responsibility of acts of violence away from those that commit these acts, but it does contend that the boundaries between good and bad, perpetrator and victim are not clear. It also highlights a vast number of variables and asks, what are the implications of these on our sense of humanity? Is it possible to contend that those that have their values destroyed see violence as the only solution? Is there indeed a connection between the greater the belief in these values, the greater the sense of pain and betrayal when these values are eroded? Any interventions to prevent terrorism must treat the individual with humanity and the suggestions below are based on such an approach. It cannot be the case that individuals are asked to respect humanity when their own is denied, and this necessitates procedures and methods which maintain integrity. The lack of integrity makes it impossible to attribute blame and to have a system which can prevent radicalization without facilitating radicalization.

Acknowledging Grievances

The very first principle of a holistic approach needs to be the acknowledgment of grievances and the 'specific aims of violent extremism—such as liberation from discrimination, restoration of Muslim/human dignity, greater self-determination, a more just world order' (Lemu, 2016: 47). These aims need to be understood, empathized with and acknowledged as drivers of radicalization and as structural conditions which threaten social cohesion. It is also important to recognize how the progression of justice, equality, human rights, and the curtailment of oppression and suffering are consistent with liberalism. The 'war on terror' is shrouded in binaries; it promotes universalism and liberalism and then leads to measures which undermine these values. Until all factors which influence radicalization are recognized, it will not be possible to deter individuals away from this process. An imposed perspective creates a false reality of the factors which influence radicalization and through doing so, it neglects some of the key factors which should be the focus of counter-terrorism strategies.

At present, state approaches fail to adequately recognize the role of structural conditions which facilitate radicalization and the overlap between motivations and actions to remedy these conditions and liberalism. Such a conceptualization of radicalization has vast implications for understanding the causes of radicalization and the aims of counter-terrorism interventions. It does not label minority suspect populations as instigators or creators of the unequal and unjust structural conditions which shape their lived experiences. Similarly, it does not label them as enemies for pursuing actions based on promoting justice and equality. It acknowledges the humanity present in their grievances, and through doing so, it provides a space where it becomes possible to reduce the very conditions which exacerbate the processes of radicalization. This conceptualization also recognizes the humanity of these individuals, and that although they may commit acts of violence, in many cases these are based on promoting universalistic concepts.

Tackling Terrorism Through Co-produced Approaches and Accepting Responsibility

The creation of this space allows for the second principle which should be part of a holistic approach, the co-production of counter-terrorism interventions. Traditional approaches treat those that are radicalized as subjects; they strip them of autonomy and follow the premise that being subjected to counter-terrorism measures will 'cure them'. These approaches fail to convey the need and power to counter radicalization onto individuals. Current interventions are based on encouraging individuals to abandon their moral responsibility to the Ummah and their need to fight injustice, not to perceive injustice etc. are not realistic. As previously stated, these sentiments constitute an individual's humanity and therefore, these very motivations could be interpreted as humanistic.

Individuals must be guided towards their own responsibility to counter radicalization; they must be empowered to believe that their aims, such as fighting oppression, promoting equality, fulfilling their Islamic obligation, can be achieved through other non-harmful, non-violent means. Such an approach allows individuals their humanity. It does not negate all the factors, beliefs and aspirations associated with radicalized individuals, it does not regard them as valid or invalid factors, instead it starts with the premise that these are real factors, real enough to motivate individuals to sacrifice their life. Starting from such a premise reduces the risk of placing oppressive, restrictive and possibly ethnocentric objective discourses onto individuals. Such discourses, as this book demonstrates, construct radicalization according to pre-existing understandings and feed into the self-defeating nature of the 'war on terror'.

Show Alternatives

The third necessity is the need for individuals to be shown alternatives to violence. The main weakness of counter-terrorism approaches is the lack of alternatives. Words such as empower are of vital importance because extremists give young people power through giving them a solution to their grievances, and this solution is violence. Therefore, any counter-terrorism strategy needs to combine ideology with practice and thus offer young people a solution. However, as already stated, such a perspective and standpoint can only be used when individuals' emotions, beliefs and experiences are taken as they are. The restriction of this voice and judgement of this voice have become part of traditional counter-terrorism approaches which further alienate individuals and promote the belief that their duty to humanity and Islam can only be fulfilled through using violence.

There is a lack of institutions which provide individuals with an environment where they can react freely and safely to the 'war on terror'. It is essential that while conflict is characterized by violence, death and destruction, there is also the existence of another way which reacts to conflict through peace, compassion and humanistic values. Research by Ahmed (2015) revealed that the 'war on terror' has impacted emotions, and emotions are crucial to understanding the radicalization process. It could therefore be argued that interventions are failings because they fail to provide an environment where emotions can be dealt with and acknowledged. This perspective also allows for a greater number of counter-terrorism strategies to emerge. For example, through recognizing this process, as Vidino and Brandon (2012) explains, a softer approach could not only return citizens to their lives and reduces ISIS numbers, but also provides potential assets for counter messaging and debunking ISIS propaganda.

In the first instance, these alternative actions must be placed in the context of Islam and Islamic obligation and an individual's duty to humanity. As Lemu (2016: 47) contends, individuals need to be shown

> how alternative nonviolent approaches are closer to the prophetic method (*sunnah*) even if such alternative approaches might require more self-sacrifice and discipline, collaboration and unity, study of Islam and the world, respect for scholarship, compassion and forgiveness of human weaknesses, sincerity of purpose and humility, greater commitment to the *sunnah* and trust in Allah's *qadr* (decree), and patient perseverance and effort. (other nonviolent forms of jihad)

Secondly, they must also be placed in the context of state harm. A perspective which considers the existence of state harms, as this book does, would then open the possibility of how these state harms could be decreased and how individuals could be guided towards responding to state harms in non-violent ways. Thirdly, 'show the effect of the strategies adopted by violent extremism groups—whether they have actually helped in furthering the claimed aims of the group or whether they have, in fact, been counterproductive' (Lemu, 2016: 47). Interestingly, the approach advocated can be likened to a 'truth and reconciliation' approach whereby all constructed sides of the binary are interrogated for their claims, their ideological truth and the reality to which they contribute.

Contributing as Part of Self-development

Fourthly, empowering individuals through addressing emotions, perceptions and religious interpretation should be part of a wider programme of personal development. As Gunaratna (2016: 84) indicates, such an approach should include 'a range of government and civil society partners for religious and spiritual counseling, educational instruction, vocational instruction, social and family services, psychological counseling, creative arts therapy, and recreational rehabilitation'. Such an approach places the core facilitators of radicalization at the centre of the approach. It makes 'young people aware of their civic duty' and demonstrates how 'they can participate and cooperate in the shaping of social life' (Arshad, 2016: 80).

Humanist Standpoint

The fifth aspect, which relates to all the previous principles identified, is the promotion of a humanist standpoint. As previously stated, current approaches are based on trying to banish feelings and emotions through constructing such sentiments as suspect. A humanist standpoint would recognize that although there is evidence to demonstrate that some returnees from Syria are highly disillusioned by their experience, others feel sympathy for the struggle in Syria (Frenett & Silverman, 2016). State centric approaches have neglected the role of foreign policy and state-created suffering as a radicalizing element. This denial has done tremendous damage through closing the door to the possibility of a dialogue. This neglect also fails to recognize the existence of humanism and how this can be used to facilitate commonality and cohesion. Such a perspective also needs to involve states acknowledging how their actions are diminishing the universal level and the destructive impact of these actions on humanity.

Tackling Terrorism Through Challenging Extremist Attitudes

Such an approach should also demonstrate the commonalities between cosmopolitan and Islamic perspectives. The sixth aspect is the inclusion of religious interpretations. State centric approaches cannot and must not work on the assumption of secularizing individuals through constructing religiosity as dangerous. Attempting to reduce religious affinity demonizes religiosity leading to marginalization. It also fuels the dualism of Muslim–non-Muslim, which is so vital to Islamist constructions of non-Muslims as enemies, and thus constitutes another avenue through which Muslims are reduced to perceiving themselves and the world through binaries. Therefore, it is a must that not only should Islamic interpretation be addressed, but it should form an area of exploration thereby facilitating individuals' understanding of how they can fulfil their religious duties without using violence.

Role of Scholars

The process of deradicalization must involve 'theological refutation and ideological debate between religious scholars and their beneficiaries' (Gunaratna, 2016: 88). Religious scholars must attempt to 'provide a strong moral conscience, disavow all violence committed in the name of religion, and work together to increase understanding and tolerance' (Jain, 2016: 36). If other interpretations of Islam were banned in the United Kingdom, then it would not have been possible for 130 imams and Muslim religious leaders, all from different schools of Islam to unite and refuse to say funeral prayers for the perpetrators of Westminster terrorist attacks (Sherwood, 2017).

However, this does not mean resisting Salafism because it has been argued the community is far more able to counter extremism interpretations of Islam because they are familiar with texts and the sources which are manipulated to legitimize extremism (Lambert, 2008). Lambert (2008) argues that the lack of differentiation between different forms of

Salafism has contributed to the marginalization of the whole Salafi community. This does suggest that an approach which differentiates between cognitive radicalization and violent radicalization is far more likely to be able to engage with individuals in ways which allow them to maintain their beliefs, without using state actions to further perpetuate injustices, discrimination and other factors which Islamist use to gain support and indeed push individuals further into the path of violent radicalization.

Criminological Approaches to Terrorism and the 'War on Terror'

This book has attempted to push the boundaries of criminological work on terrorism and the 'war on terror'. Within this context, criminology must abandon power relations. One must recognize the interplay between Islamist extremist ideologies, the radicalization process and state practices because together they sustain terrorism and the 'war on terror'. The lack of focus on the past and the actual factors which induce terrorism further constructs terrorism and terrorists as being outside humanity and dismisses how state crimes contribute to terrorism. Thus, they perpetuate the fallacy of terrorism being the sole product of radical Islam. Therefore, it is important that criminology also adopts a perspective that explores the intersection of state crime and terrorism.

References

Ahmed, S. (2015). The Emotionalization of 'War on Terror': Counter-Terrorism, Fear, Risk, Insecurity and Helplessness. *Criminology and Criminal Justice, 15*(5), 545–560.

Ahmed, S. (2016). Citizenship, Belonging and Attachment in the 'War on Terror'. *Critical Criminology, 24*(1), 111–125.

Ahmed, S. (2019). A Cosmopolitan Response to the 'War on Terror'. *Journal of Theoretical and Philosophical Criminology, 11*, 64–78.

Arshad, M. (2016). Kompass–Muslim Youth Education: Empowerment and Prevention Through Education. In H. Abadi (Ed.), *Countering Daesh*

Propaganda: Action-Oriented Research for Practical Policy Outcomes (pp. 77–80). Atlanta: The Carter Center.
Bonino, S. (2013). Prevent-ing Muslimness in Britain: The Normalisation of Exceptional Measures to Combat Terrorism. *Journal of Muslim Minority Affairs, 33*(3), 385–400.
Boyns, D., & Ballard, J. D. (2004). Developing a Sociological Theory for the Empirical Understanding of Terrorism. *The American Sociologist, 35*(2), 5–25.
Correia, I., Vala, J., & Aguiar, P. (2001). The Effects of Belief in a Just World and Victim's Innocence on Secondary Victimization, Judgements of Justice and Deservingness. *Social Justice Research, 14*(3), 327–342.
Elliott, I., Thomas, S. D. M., & Ogloff, J. R. P. (2012). Procedural Justice in Contacts with the Police: The Perspective of Victims of Crime. *Police Practice and Research, 13*(5), 437–449.
Frenett, R., & Silverman, T. (2016). Foreign Fighters: Motivations for Travel to Foreign Conflicts. In A. de Guttry, F. Capone, & C. Paulussen (Eds.), *Foreign Fighters Under International Law and Beyond* (pp. 63–76). The Hague: T.M.C. Asser Press.
General Assembly. (2006). *Protection of Human Rights and Fundamental Freedoms While Countering Terrorism*. Retrieved May 10, 2019, from https://www.un.org/en/ga/search/view_doc.asp?symbol=A/RES/65/221
Grabosky, P., & Stohl, M. (2010). *Crime and Terrorism*. London: Sage.
Gunaratna, R. (2016). Best Practices: Rehabilitating and Reintegrating Foreign Fighters. In H. Abadi (Ed.), *Countering Daesh Propaganda: Action-Oriented Research for Practical Policy Outcomes* (pp. 84–92). Atlanta: The Carter Center.
Hamm, M., & Spaaij, R. (2015). *Lone Wolf Terrorism in America: Using Knowledge of Radicalization Pathways to Forge Prevention Strategies*. Washington, DC: National Institute of Justice.
Henderson-King, D., Henderson-King, E., Bolea, B., Koches, K., & Kauffman, A. (2004). Seeking Understanding or Sending Bombs: Beliefs as Predictors of Responses to Terrorism. *Peace and Conflict: Journal of Peace Psychology, 10*(1), 67–84.
Jain, B. (2016). In H. Abadi (Ed.), *Countering Daesh Propaganda: Action-Oriented Research for Practical Policy Outcomes* (pp. 34–37). Atlanta: The Carter Center.
Lambert, R. (2008). Salafi and Islamist Londoners: Stigmatised Minority Faith Communities Countering Al-Qaida. *Crime Law Social Change, 50*, 73–89.

Lemu, M. N. (2016). Notes on Religion and Countering Violent Extremism. In H. Abadi (Ed.), *Countering Daesh Propaganda: Action-Oriented Research for Practical Policy Outcomes* (pp. 43–50). Atlanta: The Carter Center.

Levitt, M. (2002). *Targeting Terror: U.S. Policy Toward Middle Eastern State Sponsors and Terrorist Organizations, Post-September 11*. Washington, DC: Washington Institute for Near East Policy. Retrieved June 21, 2019, from https://www.washingtoninstitute.org/uploads/Documents/pubs/TargetingTerror.pdf

Mcalinden, A. M. (2006). "Setting 'Em Up": Personal, Familial and Institutional Grooming in the Sexual Abuse of Children. *Social and Legal Studies, 15*(3), 339–362.

Orth, U. (2002). Secondary Victimization of Crime Victims by Criminal Proceedings. *Social Justice Research, 15*(4), 313–325.

Post, J. M., Sprinzak, E., & Denny, L. (2003). The Terrorists in Their Own Words: Interviews with 35 Incarcerated Middle Eastern Terrorists. *Terrorism and Political Violence, 15*(1), 171–184.

Ragazzi, F. (2017). Countering Terrorism and Radicalisation: Securitising Social Policy? *Critical Social Policy, 37*(2), 163–179.

Sherwood, H. (2017). Imams Refuse Funeral Prayers for 'Indefensible' London Bridge Attackers. *The Guardian*. Accessed June 21, 2019, from https://www.theguardian.com/uk-news/2017/jun/05/imams-refuse-funeral-prayers-to-indefensible-london-bridge-attackers

Skinner, T., & Taylor, H. (2009). "Being Shut Out in the Dark": Young Survivors' Experiences of Reporting a Sexual Offence. *Feminist Criminology, 4*(2), 130–150.

Smith, C. P., & Freyd, J. J. (2013). Dangerous Safe Havens: Institutional Betrayal Exacerbates Sexual Trauma. *Journal of Traumatic Stress, 26*, 119–124.

Speckhard, A., & Akhmedova, K. (2005). Talking to Terrorists. *The Journal of Psychohistory, 33*(2), 125–156.

Statutory Instruments. (2011). Prevention and Suppression of Terrorism. *The Terrorism Act 2000*. Retrieved May 10, 2019, from https://assets.publishing.service.gov.uk/government/uploads/system/uploads/attachment_data/file/97940/terrorism-act-remedial-order.pdf

Tactaquin, C. (2001). Immigration and Globalisation: The UN Conference Against Racism Takes on Migrant Issues. *Corp Watch*. Retrieved February 18, 2018, from https://corpwatch.org/article/immigration-and-globalization-un-conference-against-racism-takes-migrant-issues

Thomas, P. (2016). Youth, Terrorism and Education: Britain's Prevent programme. *International Journal of Lifelong Education, 35*(2), 171–187.
Trapp, K. N. (2011). *State Responsibility for International Terrorism*. Published to Oxford Scholarship Online. Retrieved June 10, 2018, from https://doi.org/10.1093/acprof:oso/9780199592999.001.0001
UN. (2018). *UN Global Counter-Terrorism Strategy*. Retrieved June 21, 2019, from https://www.un.org/counterterrorism/ctitf/en/un-global-counter-terrorism-strategy
Vidino, L., & Brandon, J. (2012). *Countering Radicalization in Europe*. London: The International Centre for the Study of Radicalization and Political Violence (ICSR). Retrieved May 1, 2018, from http://icsr.info/wp-content/uploads/2012/12/ICSR-Report-Countering-Radicalization-in-Europe.pdf
Wemmers, J.-A. (2013). Victims' Experiences in the Criminal Justice System and Their Recovery from Crime. *International Review of Victimology, 19*(3), 221–233.

Index[1]

[1] Note: Page numbers followed by 'n' refer to notes.

S. Ahmed, *The 'War on Terror', State Crime & Radicalization*, Palgrave Studies in Risk, Crime and Society, https://doi.org/10.1007/978-3-030-40138-2

The manufacturer's authorised representative in the EU is Springer Nature Customer Service Centre GmbH, Europaplatz 3, 69115 Heidelberg, Germany. If you have any concerns regarding our products, please contact ProductSafety@springernature.com

Printed and bound by CPI Group (UK) Ltd, Croydon, CR0 4YY
30/09/2026
02225644-0004